"This is a fascinating and timely study of the medieval origins of today's Europe. It is extraordinary how many of the themes and ideas in this book reverberate through the arguments of the twenty-first century."

Rt Hon Christopher Patten, CH, Member of the European Commission

"The Middle Ages was a fulcrum epoch that compared with the Renaissance and the trading, industrial, and technological revolutions as eras of systemic change in Europe. But whilst the significance of the historic surges since the late fifteenth century is widely known, the formative relevance of the age before that is less recognized. Professor Le Goff addresses that and brilliantly provides an intriguing and convincing explanation of the vital importance of the early centuries of the second millennium for the shaping of Europe and its identity and diversities."

Neil Kinnock, Vice-President, European Commission

"Jacques Le Goff has capped off a lifetime of contemplating the Middle Ages with this work of great insight and learning. A fascinating rumination on the structure of medieval culture and society."

Norman F. Cantor, Late Professor Emeritus, New York University

"This book distils the life's work of one of the great historians of our time. It is remarkable equally for the breadth of its learning, the clarity of its exposition, and the depth of its humanity and wisdom. Anyone who asks why Europe needs its history, or why history needs Europe, should read it."

R. I. Moore, Professor Emeritus, University of Newcastle

The Making of Europe

Series Editor: Jacques Le Goff

The Making of Europe series is the result of a unique collaboration between five European publishers – Beck in Germany, Blackwell in Great Britain and the United States, Critica in Spain, Laterza in Italy and le Seuil in France. Each book will be published in all five languages. The scope of the series is broad, encompassing the history of ideas as well as of societies, nations, and states to produce informative, readable, and provocative treatments of central themes in the history of the European peoples and their cultures.

Also published in this series

* Title out of print

The Birth of Europe

Jacques Le Goff

Translated by Janet Lloyd

Blackwell
Publishing

BLACKWELL PUBLISHING
350 Main Street, Malden, MA 02148-5020, USA
108 Cowley Road, Oxford OX4 1JF, UK
550 Swanston Street, Carlton, Victoria 3053, Australia

First published 2005 by Blackwell Publishing Ltd

Library of Congress Cataloging-in-Publication Data

Le Goff, Jacques, 1924–
  [Europe est-elle née au moyen âge. English]
  The Birth of Europe / by Jacques Le Goff; translated by Janet Lloyd.
    p. cm.—(The making of Europe)
  Includes bibliographical references and index.
  ISBN 0-631-22888-8 (hardcover: alk. paper)
  1. Middle Ages—History. 2. Civilization, Medieval. 3. Europe—History—476–1492.
I. Title. II. Series.

D117I42 2005
940.1—dc22

2004011509

A catalogue record for this title is available from the British Library.

Set in 10 on 12.5pt Sabon
by Kolam Information Services Pvt. Ltd, Pondicherry, India
Printed and bound in the United Kingdom
by MPG Books Ltd, Bodmin, Cornwall

The publisher's policy is to use permanent paper from mills that operate a sustainable forestry policy, and which has been manufactured from pulp processed using acid-free and elementary chlorine-free practices. Furthermore, the publisher ensures that the text paper and cover board used have met acceptable environmental accreditation standards.

For further information on
Blackwell Publishing, visit our website:
www.blackwellpublishing.com

Contents

Conclusion   194

For Bronislaw Geremek

Series Editor's Preface

Europe is in the process of constructing itself. The hope that it holds out is great. This will only be realized if Europe is mindful of its history, for a Europe without its history would be a sorry orphan. Today comes from yesterday and tomorrow emerges out of the past. It is a past that should not paralyze the present but help it to be faithful to its inheritance yet different and innovative as it progresses. Our Europe, flanked by the Atlantic, Asia and Africa, has existed for a very long time, marked out by its geography and modeled by its history ever since the Greeks gave it the name that it has retained to the present day. The future must rest upon the legacies which, ever since antiquity or even prehistory, have made Europe a world of exceptional richness and extraordinary creativity, in both its unity and its diversity.

   The Making of Europe series was generated by the initiative of five publishers, all with different nationalities and languages: Beck in Munich, Blackwell in Oxford, Crítica in Barcelona, Laterza in Rome, and le Seuil in Paris. The aim of the series is to illuminate the construction of Europe, together with all the unforgettable trump cards that Europe holds, but without concealing its inherited problems. In its pursuit of unity, the continent of Europe has survived bouts of internal dissension, conflict, division, and contradiction. *The Making of Europe* series does not seek to hide them. Commitment to the European endeavor must accommodate a knowledge of the entire past as well as a vision of the future. Hence the proactive title of the series. It does not yet seem the moment to write a synthetic history of Europe. The essays that this series presents are works by the best historians of the present day, some European, some not, some already well known, some not. They will be tackling themes that are essential to the history of Europe right across the board, in domains economic, political, social, religious, and cultural; and they will be based not only on the long historiographical tradition inherited from Herodotus but also on new ideas elaborated in Europe that have deeply reinvigorated twentieth-century historical studies, particularly in the last few decades. These essays should be accessible to a wide readership, for one of their prime objectives is clarity.

Our ambition is to provide at least partial replies to the major questions posed to those engaged in the making of Europe both now and in the future: "Who are we? Where did we come from? Where are we going?"

Jacques Le Goff

Acknowledgments

First I should like to thank the Éditions du Seuil team who have worked with great competence, intelligence, commitment, and flexibility in the production of this book: Nicole Grégoire, with whom collaboration has been an exceptional pleasure, also Grégoire Monteil and Catherine Rambaud.

Special thanks go to the friends who read my book in manuscript so attentively: Richard Figuier and my colleague and dear friend Jean-Claude Schmitt, whose enlightened comments and advice were of the greatest value; and Jacques Berlioz , for his unfailing friendly support. I am also extremely grateful to Patrick Gauthier-Dalché for his help with matters of space and cartography, and to Pierre Mounet for all his valuable assistance with the medieval Germanic area.

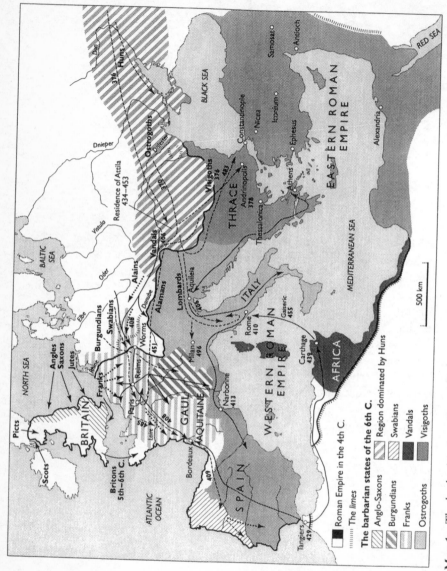

Map 1 The barbarian invasions, fifth to sixth centuries, which led to the medieval mixing of races
Source: Georges Duby, *Grand Atlas historique* (Paris: Larousse, 1995), p. 30.

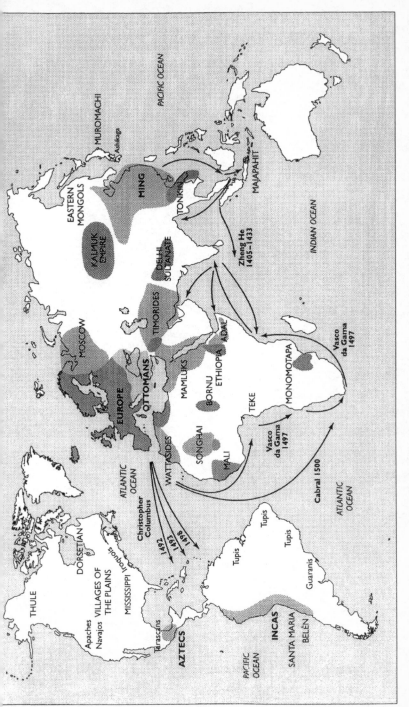

Note Lying between, on the one hand, the America of Indian tribal settlements and the Inca and Aztec empires, and, on the other, the Far East of the Chinese Ming dynasty, little Europe discovered Africa and America, while Zheng He's ambassadorial missions to the Near East and Africa were never followed up. The Ottoman Empire and the Muscovite state constituted a barrier to Europe in the east.

Map 2 Europe's position in the world between the Middle Ages and Modern Times (1400 to 1500: Zheng He, Columbus, Gutenberg, the Renaissance)

Source: Jacques Bertin, *Atlas historique universel* (Geneva: Minerva, 1997), p. 116.

Introduction

Every historical work, even those concerned with periods in the far distant past, relates to the present. This book is directly relevant to the present European situation. I wrote it in 2002–3, between the moment when a number of European states adopted a common currency and the point at which the European Union expanded to admit several of the states of central and eastern Europe. Furthermore, this book is published in the *Making of Europe* series, in which five publishers in different languages are collaborating in an effort to create a common cultural domain. The title of the series is in itself a clear enough indication of the determination of publishers and authors alike to make the most of their respect for historical truth and the impartiality of historians with a view to illuminating the circumstances in which the European community is being constructed.

The present essay lays no claim to erudition, nor is it intended to present either a continuous history of the Middle Ages in Europe or a comprehensive, let alone a detailed, account of the principal aspects of this history.

Instead, it sets out to illustrate the thesis that it was in the Middle Ages that Europe first appeared and took shape both as a reality and as a representation. This was the decisive time of the birth, infancy, and youth of Europe, even though the people living in those medieval centuries never dreamed of constructing a united Europe nor desired to do so. Only Pope Pius II (Aeneas Silvius Piccolomini, pope from 1458 to 1464) possessed a clear idea of Europe. In 1458 he produced a text entitled *Europa*, which he followed up, in 1461, with another on *Asia*, thereby indicating the importance, even then, of the comparison and contrasts between Europe and Asia.

On the eve of World War I and in its aftermath, the Middle Ages was widely hailed as the time of Europe's birth. These were years of lively thinking about Europe, when many economic, cultural, and political projects were elaborated within a European framework. The most stimulating essays on the "idea" of Europe at this time were produced by two specialists in the sixteenth century, Denis Hay in Britain (*Europe: The Emergence of an Idea*, 1957) and Federico Chabod in Italy (*Storia dell'idea dell'Europa* (A history of the idea of Europe), 1961), a work based on his university lectures of 1943–4 and 1947–8. However, the idea of the medieval birth of Europe had already been suggested on the eve of World War II by the two great French historians who founded the *Annales* review, which revived historiography. It was Marc Bloch who declared, "Europe arose when the Roman Empire crumbled," while Lucien Febvre echoed his words, adding, "Or rather, Europe became a possibility once the Empire disintegrated." In the first of his course of lectures delivered to the Collège de France in 1944–5 (*L'Europe. Genèse d'une civilisation* (Europe: the genesis of a civilization), p. 44), Lucien Febvre stated, "Throughout the Middle Ages (which must be recognized to extend well into modern times), Christian civilization, now detached from its roots, projected continuous waves of influence across the uncertain frontiers of a kaleidoscope of kingdoms. It thereby helped to bestow upon Westerners a common consciousness which transcended the frontiers that separated them and which, as it gradually became secularized, turned into a specifically European awareness."

But it was above all Marc Bloch who elaborated the theme of a Europe with its roots in the Middle Ages. As early as the International Congress of Historical Sciences in Oslo in 1928, he produced a paper entitled "Toward a Comparative History of the Societies of Europe," which was published in the *Revue de Synthèse historique* in December of that year. He returned to this "plan for the teaching of the comparative history of European societies" in the collection of papers that he submitted in support of his candidature to the Collège de France in 1934. Here he memorably declared: "The European world, inasmuch as it is European, is a medieval creation which, virtually at a single stroke, shattered the at least relative unity of the Mediterranean civilization and indiscriminately tossed into the melting pot peoples that had been Romanized alongside others never conquered by Rome. This was the birth of Europe from the point of view of its population... And this European world, defined as such, has been swept by common currents ever since" (M. Bloch, *Histoire et historiens* (History and historians), ed. Étienne Bloch (Paris: Armand Colin, 1995), p. 126).

These rough adumbrations of Europe and the structures that anticipated what Europe was to become from the eighteenth century onward by no means constitute a linear process, nor do they justify the idea of an entity necessarily determined both geographically and historically. (The adjective *européen* first appeared in French in 1721, the expression *à l'européenne* in 1816.) The Europe of today was still to be created or even to be fully thought through. The past suggests but does not determine the future; in the creation of the present, there is as much of a role for chance and free will as there is for continuity.

The present work sets out to reveal the nature of those medieval adumbrations of a future Europe and the factors that contributed more or less to impede their development, although there was never any question of a continuous process moving sometimes forward, sometimes backward. But it will also try to show that those medieval centuries (the fourth to the fifteenth) did play an essential role and that, of all the legacies at work in the Europe of today and tomorrow, that of the Middle Ages is the most important.

The Middle Ages manifested, and frequently embodied, the major real or supposed features of Europe: these include the combination of a potential unity and a fundamental diversity, the mixing of populations, West–East and North–South oppositions, the indefinite nature of its eastern frontier, and above all, the unifying role of culture. The present work will draw upon both what are called historical facts and also the imaginary representations that constitute phenomena produced by human mentalities or attitudes. The formation of those attitudes and those particularly vivid medieval representations constitute an essential feature in the genesis of Europe both as a reality and as a concept. Right from the start, we must recognize that, in any case, in the Middle Ages the frontier between reality and representation remained indeterminate. Strict, linear frontiers, such as the Roman *limes* had traced over long distances, had disappeared, reflecting the permeability between this earthly world and the Beyond: Jacob's ladder, up and down which the paths of angels and human beings crossed, was an everyday image for the men and women of the Middle Ages. Frontiers of the modern, linear kind, indicated by a line of posts or boundary markers, were to be found only here and there, appearing late on, associated with the constitution of states. The introduction of customs posts, as the general economy revived and economies of a more or less national nature developed, did not take place until the turn of the thirteenth/fourteenth century. The establishment of real frontiers in the Middle Ages was the eventual outcome of a fumbling process and a series of clashes. This is illustrated by the annexation of the Roussillon region of the French Languedoc at the end of the thirteenth century, and the conflicts that took place between the Catalan merchants, the king of Aragon and the king of Majorca over the levying of taxes on

Catalan merchandise in Collioure, then the last port before the starting point of the French Mediterranean coastline. Medieval historians have rightly rejected the American notion of frontiers elaborated by Turner, a historian of the Far West, for it is not applicable to European history. They have also stressed that what served as frontiers in the Middle Ages up until the eventual creation of states were zones that constituted meeting places, where plenty of clashes occurred, but also many trading deals and much intermingling. At the beginning of the ninth century, Charlemagne turned these areas into *marches*, whose importance in medieval Europe cannot be too strongly emphasized. As Jean-François Lemarignier has shown, marches were a highly valued feudal institution, for it was there that vassals would express their march-homage to their lords; and it is reasonable to suggest that the indeterminacy or permeability of these pseudo-frontiers favored the development of a racially mixed Europe. As for major rivers, which often serve as frontiers, these were regarded not so much as watery barriers but rather as neutral meeting places for powerful personages (the emperor and the king of France, for example). The kingdom of first western France, then France as a whole was thus bounded on the east by the Four Rivers, the Escaut, the Meuse, the Sâone, and the Rhône. As David Nordman has pointed out, in Froissart, the most "European" of the fourteenth-century chroniclers, the term most often used to designate what we would call a frontier is *marche*, *frontière* being reserved for a "front" in warfare.

Before pursuing our quest for Europe in the Middle Ages, we should note that rival notions have been used both in the Middle Ages and by modern historians. As we have seen and shall see again, the notion of Europe was set in opposition to that of Asia and, more generally, the East. The "West" may thus sometimes designate a territory that essentially constitutes that of Europe. The West was not a term much used in this way in the Middle Ages, but in the domain of imaginary representations it was strengthened by Christendom being split between the Byzantine Empire and Latin Christendom, the two corresponding, respectively, to an Eastern empire and a Western one. This was the major division bequeathed by the Middle Ages. Since the demise of the Roman Empire, it had been magnified by the split, at once linguistic, religious, and political, between an eastern and a western Europe. The "western" nature of Latin Christian Europe, which lies at the origin of present-day Europe, was further accentuated by a theory that certain Christian intellectuals developed in the twelfth and the thirteenth centuries. This was the idea that power and civilization had shifted from the east to the west. It was a *translatio imperii* and a *translatio studii* that underlined the fact that power had transferred from the Byzantine Empire to the Germanic one, just as learning had shifted from Athens and Rome to

Paris. That westward march of civilization certainly encouraged a belief in the superiority of western European culture among many Europeans in subsequent centuries.

Contrary to what is often believed, that notion did not date from the earliest centuries of Christianity. It is true that in Charlemagne's time, people did speak of a Christian empire. However, it was only with the aggressive Christianity of the eleventh century, what is known as the Gregorian reform, introduced by the great religious order of Cluny, and with the ideology of the crusades that the term Christendom came to designate the territory that was to become the core of Europe. This term "Christendom" itself may give rise to confusion. There can be no denying the capital importance of Christianity in the constitution of Europe and in the Europeans' own ideas of their identity. Even when the spirit of the Enlightenment and secularization became dominant in Europe, that Christian basis, whether acknowledged or implied, remained crucial. However, Christendom was but one long and very important episode in a history that began before Christianity and still continued after it began to wane. Finally, it is worth noting the imprecision of the names that we use. Thus, at the time of the crusades, the Muslims called all Christians Franks, just as the Christians spoke of Saracens (a term that originally designated one particular Arab tribe but that first the Byzantines, then Westerners subsequently applied to Muslims in general) or Moors, a word derived from "moriscos," the Spanish name for Muslims.

Since this book will be concerned with the history of Europe, it is important, first, to cast some light on the history of that very term, for I myself, a modern historian, reckon, as did the medieval scholars, that, as God demonstrated in Genesis, existence is linked to naming. At the same time, however, it has to be said that even the seemingly most reliable of names have been tossed this way and that by history and their changing fortunes no doubt indicate a similar element of indeterminacy about the people or entities that bear them.

Preludes: Before the Middle Ages

A study of the history of Europe requires historians and their readers to adopt a long-term perspective. They cannot confine themselves to the period of ten centuries stretching from the fourth to the fifteenth, tradition-ally known as the Middle Ages. While we speak of the adumbrations of the Europe of that period, it is important to remember the legacies left by earlier civilizations, which the Middle Ages then invested in what was potentially a European consciousness. In part, the medieval impact on the construction of Europe stems from the fact that the Middle Ages was not a period that was content to absorb earlier legacies in a passive fashion. Rather, its concept of the past prompted it, consciously and deliberately, albeit with a measure of discrimination, to take over a large part of that past with a view to nurturing the future that it was building. Important progress has recently been made in the field of prehistory. However, a description of all that the Middle Ages passed on from its prehistoric legacy would require a study that is beyond both my own competence and the scope of the present work. I should nevertheless note that a number of the great events of prehistory in Europe certainly did leave their mark on the medieval centuries. The medieval period passed on many elements of antiquity, in particular by virtue of its notion of a renaissance, but also in more diffuse ways. I am thinking, for example, of the impact made by the agriculture of the ancient world, even if its essential aspects were borrowed from Mesopotamian prehistory; for instance the spread of herding, particularly in the Mediterranean region; and also the presence of metals, which gave rise to the metallurgical techniques that barbarians brought into medieval Europe. Initially those techniques were devoted to the production of weapons, in particular the two-edged sword, the instrument that brought victory to so many invaders. But subsequently they assured the medieval civilization of successes in the domain of tools as well as that of weaponry.

Geography

We should not forget that the first of the legacies from the ancient world was geographical in nature. The men and women of the Middle Ages were inevitably affected by certain geographical factors, and they turned most of these to the advantage of Europe. Europe constitutes one end of the Euro-Asiatic landmass. The widely differing nature of its soils and relief patterns ensured that geography occasioned the diversity that is one of Europe's most characteristic features. At the same time, though, certain geographical factors contributed to unification. One of these was the large expanse of plains, which favored the cultivation of cereals that was developed in the Middle Ages and even today remains one of the stronger (albeit controversial) points of the European Common Market. Another is the vast area covered by forests which, once penetrated, exploited and partially cleared, turned into a world with two faces, one of which was constituted by its wildness, the other by its riches such as the abundance of wood, game, honey, and pigs bred from its wild boars. This duality still constitutes a feature of the Europe of today. Other obviously unifying geographical elements of the Europe of the Middle Ages were the presence of the sea and the length of its coastlines. Despite people's fear of the ocean, these eventually led them to overcome it by introducing important technological innovations such as the stern-post rudder and the compass, a Chinese invention. The people of the Middle Ages also appreciated and exploited the advantages of their temperate climate. Above all, they sang the praises of the intermediate seasons of the year, the spring and the autumn, which have always held such a special place in European literature and sensibility. The Middle Ages was not affected by the ecological preoccupations that have arisen only over the past century. However, the quest for solitude on the part of monks, and demographic expansion from the eleventh century on began to cause damage. From the fourth century on, this led towns, particularly in northern Italy, to introduce measures designed to save woodland threatened by incipient deforestation.

Ancient Legacies

The fact that the medieval period passed on such legacies in Europe provides the most convincing testimony of its importance as a transmitter of values and achievements of the past. In the first place, it passed on Europe's name. Europe began as a myth and a geographical concept, for, according to myth, Europe was born in the East. It was in Greek mythology, that most ancient strand of civilization within the territory that was to become Europe, that both the word and the myth appeared. Nevertheless, Europe was borrowed from the East. The word is derived from the Semitic term that was taken over in the eighth century BC and that was used by Phoenician sailors to designate the setting sun. Europe made its appearance as the daughter of Agenor, the king of Phoenicia (now Lebanon). She was said to have been abducted by the king of the Greek gods, Zeus, who had fallen in love with her. Taking the form of a bull, he carried her off to Crete, where their union produced Minos, a civilizing king and lawgiver who, after his death, became one of the triad of judges in Hades. The Greeks thus bestowed the name Europeans upon the inhabitants of the extreme western tip of the continent of Asia.

For the Greeks, the contrast between the East and the West, with which Europe was identified, reflected a fundamental clash of civilizations. Hippocrates, the famous Greek doctor of the late fifth and early fourth centuries BC, saw the opposition between Europeans and Asiatics in the light of the conflicts that had set the Greek cities against the Persian Empire and were probably the earliest manifestation of the antagonism between West and East. Those Persian Wars saw a Greek David overcome the Asiatic Goliath, at Marathon. According to Hippocrates, the Europeans were courageous but aggressive and bellicose, while the Asiatics were wise and cultivated but peace-loving to the point of lacking initiative. Europeans were committed to liberty, for which they were prepared to fight and even die. Their favorite political regime was democracy. Asiatics, on the other hand, were content to accept servitude in exchange for prosperity and tranquility.

That image of Orientals persisted down the centuries. In the eighteenth century, the European *philosophes* of the Enlightenment put forward the theory that enlightened despotism was the political regime best suited to Asia; and later, adopting a similar line, nineteenth-century Marxism defined an Asiatic mode of production upon which the authoritarian regimes were held to be based. Medieval society, which incorporated warriors alongside peasants, did not give the lie to Hippocrates' view, and its *chansons de geste* duly transmitted to Europe the image of the Christianized hero-warrior.

Ancient Greece's legacy to Europe was thus twofold: its opposition to the East, that is to say Asia; and the democratic model. The Middle Ages itself paid no attention to the latter, which only reappeared, in improved forms, in Europe at the time of the French Revolution. However, the sense of a contrast with the East became ever stronger in the medieval West. To be more precise, the Middle Ages promoted two images of the East. The first, which was closer to home, was that of the Greek Byzantine world, and had grown out of the opposition between Greek and Latin bequeathed by the Roman Empire. The medieval period intensified this by emphasizing the growing disparity between the Roman Catholic and the Greek Orthodox varieties of Christianity, thereby destroying any real sense of Christian solidarity. That hostility found its most extreme expression in 1204, when the Latin warriors of the Crusade, on their way to the Holy Land, changed course to conquer and sack Constantinople.

However, for the Westerners of the medieval period, there meanwhile lurked a more distant East beyond this Greek one. For centuries its image remained ambiguous. On the one hand it was the source of misfortunes and menaces, for from the East came epidemics and heresies; and the eastern extremities of Asia teemed with the destructive hordes of Gog and Magog, whom the Antichrist would unleash at the end of time. At the same time, however, the East was seen as a distant dreamworld and a repository of many marvels. It was the land of John the Priest, a priest-king with many treasures, who became a seductive political model for twelfth-century Christendom. All in all, the Greek geographers of antiquity bequeathed to the people of the Middle Ages a considerable fund of geographical knowledge, laden with problems, some of which subsist today. To the north, the west and the south, the sea constituted a natural frontier for Europe, since the seafaring skills and boats of the Westerners of the Middle Ages were so inadequate. But where did its eastern frontier lie? Even taking into account my earlier remarks about the uncertain nature of medieval frontiers over many centuries, the eastern boundary of medieval Europe posed a most serious problem. In general medieval scholars subscribed to the views of the ancient Greek geographers. For them, the frontier between Europe and Asia was the River Tanais or Don, which flowed into the Sea of Azov. Thus defined, the territory of Europe incorporated present-day Belorussia and Ukraine, but hardly any of Russia. Medieval Europe most certainly did not stretch from the Atlantic to the Urals! Then, in the course of the Middle Ages, there appeared beyond the Byzantine Empire yet another East, one more real and more threatening than ever: namely, the Muslim East which, in the fifteenth century, overwhelmed the Byzantines and replaced them by the Turks, who were destined to embody Europe's worst nightmare for centuries to come.

Four main ancient legacies may be distinguished among those transmitted, and in some cases revived, by the people of the Middle Ages.

(1) *The Greek heritage* The bequests from the Greeks to the Middle Ages included the following: the figure of the hero, who, as we shall see, once Christianized, became either a martyr or a saint; humanism, likewise modified by Christianity, to such a degree indeed that in the twelfth century many people would speak of Christian Socratism; religious edifices, temples, some of which were destroyed then reconstructed as churches, while others were simply put to a new use; wine, which was passed on by way of the Romans to become both the beverage of the aristocracy and also the sacred liquid of the Christian liturgy. To these should be added the distant ancestor of the medieval town, namely the city, *polis*; the word democracy, which found no concrete embodiment until long after the medieval period; and, of course, the name Europe.

(2) *The Roman heritage* This was richer by far, for medieval Europe emerged directly from the Roman Empire. The latter's first legacy of capital importance was its language, the vehicle of civilization. Medieval Europe spoke and wrote Latin and when Latin retreated in the face of vernacular languages in the tenth century, the so-called Romance tongues (French, Italian, Spanish, and Portuguese) perpetuated that linguistic heritage. The other parts of Europe also benefited from the Latin culture, albeit to a lesser degree, particularly in the domains of universities, the Church, theology, and scientific and philosophical terminology. The Romans also bequeathed their military skills to the men of the Middle Ages, warriors who belonged to the same European tradition. Here Vegetius, the relatively late author of a treatise on the military art (ca. AD 400), was largely instrumental, for this work inspired many of the military theories and practices of the men of the Middle Ages. More important still was the architectural legacy of the Romans to these people, who discovered and proceeded to develop it from about AD 1000 onward. It included stone masonry, the arch, and the extremely influential handbook composed by the Roman architectural theorist Vitruvius. There were, however, some major Roman techniques that the people of the Middle Ages appropriated only partially. Marc Bloch has noted how very different Roman roads were from medieval ones. The former were mostly constructed for military purposes, drawing on the Romans' superior technical skills. They were straight and paved. In contrast, the men and women of the Middle Ages walked along winding

earthen roads, pushing their carts or using mules or horses, to make their way from one church to another or from one temporary market to the next. The stretches of Roman roads that survived did nevertheless remain symbolic landmarks. Also bequeathed by Roman antiquity, though in a modified form, were the opposition and complementarity that obtained between town and countryside. The *urbs–rus* opposition, with its cultural contrast between urbanity and rusticity, survived in new forms. Once it had been ruralized, medieval Europe proceeded to become urbanized. Except in Italy, the aristocracy for the most part lived in fortified castles located in the countryside. The attitude of warriors and peasants alike toward soft town-dwellers was one of hostility tinged with an element of envy. Those town-dwellers, for their part, meanwhile despised the uncouth peasants, the more so because Christianization had begun in the towns, and the countryside remained pagan for considerably longer. "Pagan" and "peasant" are both terms derived from the Latin *paganus*.

As we shall see, the Middle Ages was a period in which intense energy was devoted to the creation of a legal system, in the elaboration of which the legacy and revival of Roman law clearly played a major role. Bologna, the very first university, established in the twelfth century, was essentially devoted to legal studies and, thanks to its reputation, was recognized to be the European center of law.

Medieval Christianity made a number of crucial cultural choices. Most notably these included scientific classification and particular methods of instruction. Martianus Capella, a Christian Latin rhetorician of the fifth century AD, was largely responsible for establishing the dominance of classification and the practice of the liberal arts in medieval education. Those recommended by Saint Augustine fell into two groups, the *trivium* or arts of speech (grammar, rhetoric, and dialectic) and the *quadrivium* or numerical arts (arithmetic, geometry, music, and astronomy), and in the twelfth and thirteenth centuries it was these that formed the basis of university teaching in the propaedeutic studies in the so-called faculty of arts.

The aim of this book is to assess the words, ideas, and imaginary representations which, just as much as material structures, constituted the basis of the sense of what it was to be European. Remaining within that framework, let me briefly note that the name still generally applied to an emperor or whoever symbolizes supreme power is the one that the Romans adopted for their emperors: Caesar. Even in the vernacular languages this legacy produced first *Kaiser* among the Germanic peoples, then *tsar* among the Slavs, Russians, Serbs, and Bulgarians. The Greeks and Romans likewise bequeathed to Europe the term *tyrant*, used to designate bad kings. The symbolic political tradition goes on.

(3) Another legacy that was diffused in a more discreet or even subconscious fashion in the Middle Ages also rates a mention. This is the trifunctional Indo-European ideology to whose wide diffusion ever since the earliest times Georges Dumézil has rightly drawn attention. Between the ninth and the eleventh centuries a number of Christian authors who took over this concept defined all societies, in particular those in which they themselves lived, as associations of men who specialized in the three functions that were essential for the society to operate satisfactorily. The clearest expression of this idea and the one that has enjoyed the most success among historiographers is to be found in a poem that Bishop Adalberon of Laon addressed to King Robert the Pious in 1027. According to Adalberon, a well-organized society incorporates priests (*oratores*, those who pray), warriors (*bellatores*, those who fight), and workers (*laboratores*, those who work). This classification, which was adopted by many medieval scholars to describe and understand their societies, runs into problems above all over the definition of the *laboratores*. A number of conflicting interpretations of this term have been suggested. For some, the *laboratores* are not positioned on the same level as the first two categories, but are subservient to them: essentially, they constitute the peasant masses. For others, including myself, the overall schema designates three elite groups, all placed on an equal footing. The *laboratores* comprise the upper, innovative and productive strand in the stratum of peasants and craftsmen. I would be in favor of calling them "producers," a term that somehow promotes the concept of work in the ideology and mentality of the medieval period *circa* AD 1000.

(4) Finally, the fourth heritage of capital importance is that of the Bible. This was transmitted to the people of the Middle Ages not by the Jews, from whom the Christians were soon increasingly distancing themselves, but by the Christians of the first centuries AD. Despite growing anti-Jewish feeling, right down to the end of the Middles Ages the legacy of the Old Testament remained one of the strongest and richest elements of not just religion but the whole of medieval culture. Plenty of books have been written on the Middle Ages and the Bible, so I will limit myself here to pointing out that the Old Testament constitutes first and foremost a proclamation of monotheism. It is fair to say that it was through the intermediary of Christianity that God became a part of the thought and history of Europe. In the Middle Ages, the Bible was regarded and used as an encyclopedia that contained all the knowledge that God had passed to humankind. It was also a basic historical handbook which, after telling of the patriarchs and prophets, proceeded to unfold the meaning of history ever since the advent of royalty in the persons of Saul and David. The readoption of sacred unction by the

Pepin dynasty and the Carolingians indicated that the normal course of history desired by God had been resumed. We should never forget that the historical memory that has become an essential element in European consciousness stemmed from a twofold source: on the one hand, Herodotus, the Greek father of history; on the other, the Bible.

A Schema of the Medieval Genesis of Europe

Let me now sketch in the various strata that the Middle Ages produced over successive periods, for these one by one formed the bases of Europe.

The first was set in place between the fourth and the eighth centuries, during the periods of barbarian invasions and the establishment of those barbarians within the Roman Empire of antiquity. This was the stage at which Europe was conceived.

Next, in the eighth to tenth centuries, came the Carolingian stratum, which produced an abortive Europe that nevertheless left behind a legacy.

In about AD 1000, the dream of a potential Europe made its appearance.

This was succeeded, in the eleventh to thirteenth centuries, by a feudal Europe.

The thirteenth century saw the establishment of an expanding Europe characterized by towns, universities and scholasticism, cathedrals, and the Gothic style.

Finally, the trials of the fourteenth and fifteenth centuries shook but did not destroy those pre-European structures.

As I see it, the structure of this book conforms with the movement of history. It is built up by a succession of chronological phases and strata. This involves a number of rapid sweeps through segments of history by which the reader will not, I trust, be bored, for they will take him or her to the very heart of the new faces and new uncertainties of this space that is Europe.

1

The Conception of Europe (Fourth to Eighth Centuries)

The transition from antiquity to the Middle Ages is a historiographical convention. But for anyone seeking to understand the historical development of Europe, it seems an unquestionable reality, provided we reject the simplistic ideas expressed from the eighteenth century down to the mid-twentieth, according to which that transition constituted a cataclysmic event. One well-known historian went so far as to declare: "The Roman Empire did not die a natural death; it was assassinated," the implication being that the birth of the Middle Ages stemmed from that assassination. Today, historians believe that the transition from antiquity to the Middle Ages resulted from a long and positive evolution, albeit one marked by certain violent and spectacular events. To underline this change of view, we are nowadays more inclined to use the expression "late antiquity" to refer to the period stretching from the fourth to the eighth century. This seems to me better suited to the general evolution of history in which revolutions are few and far between and in some cases illusory. All the same, even if the birth of the Middle Ages was not speedy, it nevertheless did shake the history of the western regions of the Euro-Asiatic landmass to its very foundations. The American historian Patrick Geary has convincingly shown that the Merovingian period was, strictly speaking, not yet part of the Middle Ages, but belonged, precisely, to late antiquity, the period of a long drawn-out transition in which Europe began to emerge. This happened in the course of the Christianization of the Roman Empire, which, as is well known, came about between the so-called Edict of Milan of 313, in which Emperor Constantine recognized the Christian religion, and the adoption of Christianity as the official state religion by Theodosius I, who died in 395. The link between that decision of Theodosius and the subsequent history of Europe is clearly marked by the fact that, at his death, Theodosius divided the Roman Empire into two, giving each part to one of his sons as emperor: Honorius took the West, Arcadius the East. The Europe with which we are concerned evolved from the western empire.

Christianization, Saint Augustine

The emergence of this Europe was conditioned by two essential phenomena of the fourth and fifth centuries, which we now need to consider. The first was the elaboration of a core of Christian doctrine based on the Bible and the New Testament, which the Church Fathers bequeathed to the Middle Ages. This is not the place to describe the personalities and achievements of all of these cofounders of Christianity. I shall mention only two, whose influence on the development of European culture was particularly strong: Saint Jerome and Saint Augustine. Saint Jerome (ca. 347–420) lived at the intersection of the West and the East, where for many years he was a hermit, so his life was not solely linked with the future of Europe. However, he deserves a mention here because he produced an important Latin translation of the Hebrew text of the Bible, which superseded the earlier Greek translation known as the Septuagint, which was considered to be defective. This Latin Bible was then used throughout the Middle Ages in various revised forms. The most interesting revision was that produced in the early thirteenth century by the University of Paris. It was based on a ninth-century version by Charlemagne's Anglo-Saxon councilor, Alcuin, and is known as the Vulgate.

The other Church Father of major importance is Saint Augustine (354–430). After Saint Paul, he was the figure who played the most important role in the establishment and development of Christianity. Let me cite just two of the works of this great medieval professor, for they are fundamental for European history. The first, *The Confessions*, presents a record of his conversion. Not only was it one of the most widely read works of the Middle Ages, but in the long term it must be recognized as the first in the long line of introspective autobiographies that have succeeded each other right down to the present day.

Augustine's other great work is as objective as his *Confessions* are subjective. *The City of God* was written following the sack of Rome by Alaric and his Goths, in 410. This episode terrified ancient Roman groups and new Christian ones alike, fueling a belief that the end of the world was imminent. Augustine rejected such millenarian fears. Having suggested that the end of time would come at some probably distant future date known only to God, he went on to set out a program for relations between the City of God and the City of men. This work remained one of the greatest texts of European thought for centuries.

Augustinianism has been described in the following reductive terms: "A doctrine of unconditional predestination combined with free will giving access to salvation, as developed by Saint Augustine at the end of his life." But Augustine's thought throughout his life was far too rich to be limited to the theme of predestination. A fairer, yet still oversimplistic description of it might be that it constituted a quest for a balance between free will and grace. All medieval theologians without exception were to some extent followers of Augustine. There has also been talk of political Augustinianism, suggesting that Augustine exerted great influence over medieval rulers, attributing to them "a tendency to absorb the natural law of the state into supernatural justice and ecclesiastical law." However, that theocratic interpretation was severely criticized by Cardinal de Lubac. If there really was any such thing as political Augustinianism in medieval Europe, it would be better described as a desire to introduce moral and religious values into a government that observed a separation between God and Caesar. Augustinianism should thus be regarded as an ancient layer of European political ideology which the totally opposed layer of Machiavellianism, at the end of the Middle Ages, never quite managed to bury. Another of Augustine's legacies to the Middle Ages was a monastic rule, the only one that survived in the face of the Benedictine rule. It was mainly followed by urban clergy, in particular canons.

There survive 258 manuscripts of the *Confessions*, 376 of the *City of God*, and 317 of Augustine's *Rule*, but many others have been lost.

The Cultural Founders of the Middle Ages

The impact of this legacy of intermingled ancient and Christian culture left to the Middle Ages and to Europe by the Church Fathers continued to be felt from the fifth to the eighth centuries, within the framework of a fusion between ancient Roman culture and developments characterized by the needs of the peoples that had come under barbarian sway. A number of great names stand out from this period, and Karl Rand has dubbed these figures the founders of the Middle Ages. It would also be fair to call them the cultural fathers of Europe.

The first is Boethius (484–520). He came from an old, aristocratic Roman family and entered the service of the barbarian king of the Ostrogoths, Theodoric. But he then became involved in a conspiracy favoring the Byzantine emperor, and subsequently died in prison. Up until the mid-twelfth century, the Middle Ages was indebted to him for all it knew of Aristotle. This knowledge was purveyed by Boethius' *Logica vetus* (The old logic). It contained, "in easily assimilable doses, the earliest basis for scholasticism." One typical example is its definition of a person: *naturae rationabilis individua susbstantia*, "an individualized substance of rational nature." Abelard was to say of Boethius, "He constructed our faith and his own in an enduring fashion." The work that Boethius wrote while in prison, *The Consolation of Philosophy*, was widely read in the Middle Ages. He was one of the creators of medieval humanism and was also instrumental in getting music to be recognized as a superior cultural tool, in accordance with the ancient ideal.

Cassiodorus (ca. 490–580) was just as important for medieval European culture. He came from a great family of southern Italy and initially played a political role of the first importance in Ostrogothic Italy, acting as a mediator between the Romano-Byzantine world and barbarian society. Justinian's short-lived reconquest of Italy (539) brought his brilliant career to an end. He retired to the monastery of Vivarium in Calabria, where he set about providing for the intellectual education of the new peoples by translating a number of Greek works and making copies of Latin ones. He was the first to promote a Europe of books and libraries, the first to stress the sanctifying value of intellectual work and to suggest a new field of activity for monks: namely, study, the means of perfecting oneself and influencing others. The second part of his chief work, *Institutiones divinarum et saecularium litterarum*, constitutes a veritable encyclopedia of the profane sciences, intended for the use of monks.

Throughout the Middle Ages, the encyclopedia was to be a favorite literary genre for clerical and lay scholars alike, for it provided a distillation of past culture and made it possible to press on further. For Europe, the encyclopedia, yet another legacy from the Greeks, was a key inheritance from the Middle Ages for, as is well known, it has been an essential instrument of instruction and culture from the eighteenth century down to the present day.

The third cultural founder was a Spaniard, Isidore of Seville, the greatest encyclopedist of the Middle Ages (ca. 570–636). Isidore, who came from a great Catholic Hispano-Roman family, became archbishop in about 600, at the time when the Visigoths abjured the Aryan heresy and converted to orthodox Catholicism. His contemporaries called him "the most learned man of modern times." His *Book of Etymologies* rests upon the conviction that names are the key to the nature of things and that profane culture is necessary for a sound understanding of the Scriptures. It constitutes the basis of Isidore's attempt to summarize the whole of human knowledge; and for the people of the Middle Ages and their European descendants it became a kind of second Bible in the field of profane knowledge.

Finally, the fourth cultural founder was an Anglo-Saxon, Bede (673–736). He took over from the monks who had converted England, bringing with them the legacy of ancient culture from Italy. Bede's work is also of an encylopedic nature and was so widely read and used in the Middle Ages that he was given the title "Venerable" and was regarded as the last of the Church Fathers. His ecclesiastical history of the English people was the first attempt at a national history and, in the late ninth century, King Alfred translated it into the vernacular. Bede's scientific work, which was inspired by the ecclesiastical need to compute and determine the liturgical calendar, was remarkable for its day. His *De temporibus* tries to establish a scientific way of measuring time. His *De temporum ratione* contains not only an account of how the mechanism of the tides is linked to the phases of the moon, but also a description of "the fundamental elements of the natural sciences." Above all, perhaps, Bede, although nurtured by classical culture, as were most educated Anglo-Saxons of the Early Middle Ages, was prepared to turn his back on it and steer the Middle Ages toward the independent path along which Europe was to proceed.

Gregory the Great

This group of founding scholars should also include Pope Gregory the Great. A number of important figures of the Middle Ages have recently been hailed as fathers of Europe (Saint Benedict and Charlemagne, for instance), and we shall in due course be considering whether that title is merited in their cases. But it has seldom been granted to Gregory the Great, who is probably more deserving of it than many others.

Gregory the Great, who was born in about 540 and died in 604, belonged to a patrician Roman family. In 573, as a prefect, he proved his worth as an organizer of the town's food supplies. In his patrimonial estates, in Sicily, he created six monasteries and then himself retired to a seventh, in Rome, on the Caelius. Pope Pelagius II ordained him Deacon and sent him to Constantinople as a resident ambassador. When he reluctantly became pope in 590, at a time of serious flooding by the River Tiber and a Black Death epidemic in Rome ("there is also a Europe of natural catastrophes"), he organized resistance, both material and spiritual, to these scourges. Fearing that the end of the world was nigh, he strove to ensure that as many Christians as possible were in a fit state to face the Last Judgment. To that end, he took action in many distant outposts of Christendom and produced several general works on piety. He defended Rome and the Church's possessions in Italy against the Lombards. He sent the monk Augustine with a group of missionaries to reconvert England. And he set up two great models for Christians, one biblical, the other modern. The former was Job, a model of submission to God and of abiding faith in the face of many trials, to whom he devoted his *Moralia in Job*, a moral commentary on the Book of Job. The latter, modern, model was Saint Benedict, whose historical fame he ensured by devoting to him the entire second book of his *Dialogues*. He also composed a pastoral handbook for clerics entitled *Liber regulae pastoralis*; and he reformed the liturgical chant, thenceforth known as the Gregorian Chant.

Alongside all this religious and cultural activity, below the surface, in churches and schools (although only a minority had access to these), in the territories of the great estates a fusion and intermingling of barbarians (essentially Celts and Germans) and Latino-Europeans was taking place. Christianity was the vehicle for this intermingling. Following upon the legacies of antiquity, the next decisive cultural layer was that produced by Christianization.

The acculturation between barbarians and Romans had begun long before. The *limes* (boundary), though militarily effective until the third century AD, had not proved an impermeable cultural frontier. Bartering and present-giving, and contacts and exchanges had paved the way for the great cultural intermingling that occurred despite all the clashes and violence of what are known as the barbarian invasions. It is important to recognize that this ethnic and cultural intermingling was not limited to meetings between the peoples of the ancient Roman Empire and the invading barbarians. For within the barbarian peoples, too, regroupings of previously scattered tribes and peoples were being formed. On both sides of the ancient *limes* there was a far-flung and profound redisposition of peoples. It resulted in not only new, mixed peoples, but also, among the barbarians themselves, movements that involved ethnic regroupings or even produced larger groups known as *nations* in the Latin of those times. In this great intermingling at the time of Europe's birth, a salient feature, right from the start, was the dialectic between unity and diversity, Christendom and nations, which even today is still one of the fundamental characteristics of Europe.

The amalgamation between barbarians and Romans either side of the *limes* began in the Roman Empire of the second and third centuries. It was followed by the arrival of waves of new so-called barbarian peoples.

Invasions and Acculturation

The first great wave of new arrivals took place at the end of the third century, but it was above all the widespread invasion of Germans in Italy, in Gaul, and in Spain, in 406–7, at the time of Alaric's capture of Rome, that marked the major establishment of Germans within the Roman Empire. As Peter Brown has noted, in the fifth century, throughout Europe, the military frontier of the Roman Empire disappeared. To understand the great upheavals of that century in Europe, it is helpful to read an exceptional document recording the life of a holy man who witnessed those events on the frontier formed by the middle reaches of the Danube in Norica, in what later became Austria. That holy man was Saint Severinus whom Peter Brown calls the saint of open frontiers. He also tells us that, as a result of the implosion of Romans and barbarians, new cultural and social entities took shape here.

The German influx continued throughout the fifth and sixth centuries, following the entry of eastern Germans, Visigoths and Ostrogoths, and the great wave of Swabians, Vandals, and Alans, who had crossed the Rhine at the beginning of the fifth century. Gradually Burgundians, Franks, and Alamans pushed in toward western and southern Gaul. Meanwhile Jutes, Angles, and Saxons crossed the North Sea, forcing the Britons of Great Britain to retreat to the western tip of Gaul. The last Germanic conquest on the former territory of the empire was that of the Lombards, who pushed into Italy in the second half of the sixth century. To the east of the Rhine, the place of those invaders was taken by Saxons, Frisians, Thuringians, and Bavarians. The seventh century saw the beginning of a massive advance by Slavs, who proceeded, up until the ninth century, to settle down, mostly in the East, in the region of the Baltic Sea and the River Elbe, but also further west, centrally around the mountains of Bohemia, and eventually, moving toward the southwest, in the northern Balkans.

These invasions might well have led to major divisions between the new peoples. Most had been converted to Aryanism, which Latin Christians considered to be a heresy. We should therefore recognize that the waning of Aryanism and the conversion of Aryan barbarians to orthodox Catholicism spared what was to become Europe further confrontations. This period of the birth of Europe was nevertheless marked by many dramatic events.

Huns, invaders who were particularly feared, managed to advance right into Gaul, where their leader, Attila, a terrifying bogeyman to all Europeans except the Hungarians, was defeated by the Roman Aetius in the battle of the Catalaunian Fields, close to Troyes, and was then forced to withdraw. An event of particular importance was the conversion of the Franks, mediated by their leader Clovis, between 497 and 507. Despite the Frankish custom of inheritance which divided kingdoms between all the sons of the king, Clovis and his successors came to control a vast area. After the expulsion of the Visigoths, who were pushed into Spain, and the absorption of the kingdom of the Burgundians, this territory encompassed the whole of Gaul. The Ostrogoth Theodoric (496–526) set up a short-lived but brilliant kingdom in northeastern Italy, in the region of Ravenna, where Boethius became his councilor. The Visigoths, after their ejection from Gaul, founded an equally prestigious kingdom centered on Toledo. It has sometimes been claimed that Europe was the heir to Visigothic Spain, but in truth that inheritance was mainly constituted by the works of Isidore of Seville. It has also been said that the Visigoths were responsible for a more calamitous legacy: the measures that their kings and councils took against the Jews may have been the source of European anti-Semitism.

A single example suffices to show that it is not an exaggeration to describe the new network of relations as European. In 658, the Abbess Gertrude of Nivelles, close to present-day Brussels, died on Saint Patrick's Day. (Patrick had already become one of the North's major saints and was the future patron of the Irish.) *The Life of Gertrude* states that the abbess was "well known to all the inhabitants of Europe." So, at the level of the clergy at least, the new Christianized societies did feel that they belonged to a world that could be designated by the name Europe. The same text also testifies to an important development that even today deeply affects the main problems of European union. The political and cultural center of gravity of the western part of the Roman Empire had slipped from the Mediterranean to north of the Alps. The exemplary Gregory the Great had looked to Canterbury for leadership. The most powerful newly Christianized barbarian leader, Clovis, had made Paris, in northern Gaul, his capital. The Anglo-Saxon and, even more, the Irish monasteries were outstanding centers for the training of missionaries, who went forth to preach on the continent, like Saint Columban (543–615), who founded the Abbey of Luxeuil in eastern Gaul and that of Bobbio in northern Italy, while his disciple, Saint Gall, founded the monastery that bears his name in what is now Switzerland.

This shift northward of the center of gravity in the extreme west was also deeply linked with two events that had a most profound effect on the history of Europe. The first was the loss of prestige suffered by the bishop of Rome and the threat to Rome represented by barbarians ranging from Goths to Lombards. Byzantium no longer acknowledged the superiority of the bishop of Rome. Rome was no longer the center of Europe either geographically or politically. The second event was the Muslim conquest. After Muhammad's death in 632, the Arabs and other converts to Islam, the Muslims, with lightning speed conquered the Arabian peninsula, the Near and the Middle East, and northern Africa, from Egypt to Morocco. From there, whether intent on raiding or on conquest, they launched themselves on to the opposite shore of the Mediterranean. Between 711 and 719, the Berbers of North Africa, who had converted to Islam, conquered most of the Iberian peninsula. By the beginning of the ninth century, they had occupied the ancient Roman islands of Corsica, Sardinia, Sicily, and Crete. This geographical rearrangement, besides setting up an opposition between northern Europe and southern, Mediterranean Europe, revealed the new importance of the outer edges of the new Christian Europe. The Celtic periphery was now joined by the Anglo-Saxon periphery and subsequently by the Norman, Scandinavian, and Slavic ones. The Mediterranean now represented an essential front for the Christian reconquest and other dealings with the Muslims.

Finally, a development that dealt a sad blow to Christianity was nevertheless perhaps beneficial to Europe. Northern Africa which, thanks to Tertullian and, above all, Saint Augustine, was one of the most important centers of Christianity within the Roman Empire, was ravaged, initially by the Vandals. In 430, Augustine himself died in Hippo, which the Vandals were then besieging. But it was above all the Muslim conquest in the seventh century that destroyed and eradicated the Christian civilization in North Africa. Europe no longer had cause to fear competition from an Africa that had played an essential part in the elaboration of Christian theology and a pioneering role in the struggle against heresies, in particular Donatism.

Government by Bishops and Monks

Certain developments took place in the nations founded on the ancient demarcations of the Roman world and also in the new ethnic groups. But it was Christianization that, above all, brought uniformity to the West in the Early Middle Ages. In the first place, this whole area was governed by bishops whose power was increasing, in particular in the administration of towns. From the seventh century on, a higher ranking group emerged among the bishops: these figures were called archbishops. Under the bishops, the Christian West was divided into territories in the main based on the ancient Roman administrative divisions. They were known as dioceses. Alongside the bishops and priests, new religious figures who had originated in the East appeared: the monks. In the West, most monks, despite their name, which means "solitary," were not hermits but lived together in groups. They were cenobites, and they dwelt in monasteries which, however, were usually situated away from the towns, in more or less isolated valleys or forests. From the fourth century to the eighth, monks played an essential role in the Christianization of the pagan peasants. Many monks were itinerant. Outstanding among these were the Irish monks mentioned above, who exercised their apostolic mission across the board from eastern Gaul to northern Italy. But in effect the territory that they covered incorporated the whole of the Christianized West.

Religious women were also to be found within this new Christian space. Even before they came together in groups, likewise in monasteries (or rather, convents), they were characterized by their state of virginity. They thus embodied the new ideal of chastity, which was a feature of Christianity in general. However, although chastity and virginity were observed by monks and these virgins generally, bishops and priests did not yet practice celibacy

New Heroes: Saints

At the head of these new religious institutions, new heroes emerged: the saints. In the earliest centuries of Christianization, the heroism of saints consisted in laying down their lives for the God of the Christians. They were martyrs. But as Christianity became increasingly widely accepted, the number of martyrs diminished and the most remarkable Christians came to be confessors, more and more of whom were likewise hailed as saints. The Church assured saints of a special destiny. The reward of paradise awaited them and, while still on earth, they became the objects of veneration or even of cults that promised salvation. According to Christian orthodoxy, only God performed miracles; but popular belief also attributed miracles to saints. Such miracles took place in special places, in particular wherever saints had been buried. Christians were cured or saved through contact with the bodies of saints, "these exceptional corpses," as Peter Brown calls them. Like bishops, many saints belonged to the upper Romano-barbarian strata of society. The leaders of the new Christian society came from aristocratic families. The aristocracy was educated and it ensured that government fell to the new, Christian, elite.

A New Way of Measuring Time

Monastic life deeply influenced European *mores*. It taught Christian society to organize its use of time. By both day and night, the monks themselves would gather together at regular intervals and at special times (the eight monastic or canonical hours) to recite prayers. From the monks, Christians also learned to pay attention to their regimen. The fasts observed by monks and pious laymen constituted not only a religious penitential rite but also a pattern of health-conscious behavior, comparable to blood-letting. The effects of epidemics could not be controlled; but the struggle against *gula*, gluttony, was at least a way of combating dietary excesses. Finally, the monks introduced a new rhythm of existence that affected life even outside their monastic societies: it involved a combination and alternation of work and leisure, prayer and *otium*.

The influence of Christianity was particularly marked in the field of time measurement. Although the Christian Middle Ages continued to use the Roman Julian calendar, important innovations were introduced: first and foremost, the weekly rhythm. The reference to divine creation in Genesis singled out Creation's seven-day time span: six working days, plus one of rest. Soon it became obligatory for all Christians to keep Sunday as a day of rest. Charlemagne even found it necessary to get the Church to agree to make exceptions in the cases of peasants for whom it was essential not to waste good weather in the completion of their rural tasks, in particular their harvesting. In the European world, right down to very recent times, this organization of human activity according to a weekly rota has probably provided the best means of alternating work and rest.

Christianity also introduced profound changes to the calendar. It gave the Christian era a new starting point when, in 532, the monk Dionysius the Little made the birth of Christ the new beginning of history. In point of fact, however, Dionysius made a mistake in his calculations, so the birth of Christ, which marks the beginning of the Christian era, was probably in 4 BC. On the other hand, for a long time the Church did not select a single date to mark the beginning of the year throughout Christendom. The dates most commonly chosen for the beginning of the year were 25 December (the Incarnation), 25 March (the Annunciation), and Easter, which was a movable feast. Hence the importance, throughout Christendom, of complex, accurate calculations, based on observations of the moon, to define and compute the date of Easter each year. The Christian calendar is a solar one, except for the insertion of a lunar portion at Easter. For the whole of the future Europe, except the Orthodox eastern region, the Christian calendar ensured the promotion of the two great days that became the major yearly festivals: Christmas Day, marking the birth of Christ, which in the fourth century was fixed to 25 December; and Easter Day, the anniversary of the Resurrection of Christ, a movable feast. Apart from the great festivals devoted to Christ or to the Virgin Mary, the different days of the year were called after saints and marked the anniversaries of their deaths. The reorganization of the measurement of time also affected ordinary daily life. In the West, the seventh century witnessed an innovation the impact of which was widely felt, namely the introduction of church bells and the construction of bell-towers or campaniles. In the hands of the monks, the passing of the hours remained imprecise, but now bells announcing each hour could be heard both in the towns and in the countryside. This audible measuring of time was an innovation of capital importance.

The Remodeling of Space

Christianity's remodeling of space was no less important than its remodeling of the measurement of time; and in both cases, the changes affected the whole of western Europe. Their organization led to new diocese divisions, although it took some time to define the territories of the various dioceses precisely. Networks linking particular points and particular regions were also set in place. The cult of holy relics led to the promotion of places that contained particularly famous ones. One such place was Tours, which harbored the relics of Saint Martin; another, even more prestigious, was Rome, with its relics of Saint Peter and Saint Paul. The cult of holy relics led to pilgrimages that forged links between the peoples of the extreme European west and, most importantly, the routes of these pilgrimages were soon organized into definite stages and networks. Relations were also established between the various monastic orders. In the seventh century, for example, the abbot of Saint-Aignan, in Orléans, founded the monastery of Fleury-sur-Loire, which became a great center of pilgrimages once it acquired the relics of Saint Benedict, which, following the invasion of the Lombards, had been abandoned on Mount Cassino in southern Italy. The role of such networks as these became even more important in the later Middle Ages.

Two Hostile Poles, Byzantium and Islam: The Choice of Images

We need to return to two negative events that played an essential part in the genesis of Europe between the seventh and the fourteenth centuries. They led to or at least consolidated the construction of a religious or national identity in the context of conflict and opposition. The notion of an "other," particularly an opponent or an enemy, creates identity.

In the case of western Christendom, the hostile "other" was twofold. At first it was Byzantium. Several factors increased the distance that separated Latin and Byzantine Christians: Byzantine claims to dominate the whole of Christendom, Latin as well as Greek, along with Byzantium's refusal to acknowledge the bishop of Rome, together with the difference of its liturgical language (Greek, not Latin) and various theological divergences. An extremely important decision taken by the Latin Church aggravated matters. The Byzantine world was rocked by the quarrel over images, which began with a bout of iconoclasm (a rejection of images) between 730 and 787. Following the second Council of Nicaea (787), Charlemagne, in his *Libri carolini*, firmly established the attitude of western, Latin Christianity. It was a moderate attitude that condemned both the destruction and rejection of images, or iconoclasm, and also image worship. In contrast to Judaism and Islam, both of which rejected images, and Byzantium, which was swept by bouts of iconoclasm, western Christendom sanctioned and revered images, as a form of homage to God, the Virgin, and the saints, although since those images were anthropomorphic it did not make them the objects of any cult. Apart from the Holy Ghost, the personae of the Godhead were portrayed with a human face. This constituted an important stage along the way that led to European humanism; it was a path that was to prove richly rewarding for European art.

The conflict with Islam from the seventh century onward was of a more virulent nature. Just as eastern Europe remained a part of the Byzantine world, Islam and Latin Christendom established their respective territories on either side of a border that served as a front, along which military conflicts often took place. After overrunning North Africa, Islam, in the shape of Arabized Berbers, launched an assault on Christian Europe. Between 711 and 719, they rapidly conquered the Iberian peninsula. The Christians retained a hold only along a northern fringe, particularly to the west, in the Asturias region. From northern Spain, the Muslims, whether intent on simply raiding or on extending their conquest, swept on northward across the Pyrenees. However, whatever their intentions, their advance was halted, in 732, by what is known as the Battle of Poitiers. This was the last Muslim invasion to penetrate to the north of the Pyrenees, although in the ninth century there were further Muslim conquests in the Mediterranean islands, in Italy, and in Provence.

European historiography has produced a number of divergent interpretations of the Battle of Poitiers. At one extreme are certain historians who regard the battle as a mere skirmish of scant significance, since the Muslim conquest had already run out of steam. For others, in contrast, the Battle of Poitiers was a hugely important event, representing a triumph over Islam for Christianity, both in reality and in myth. For a highly aggressive anti-Muslim minority, Poitiers became a symbol. The truth lies somewhere between those two extremes. However, certain Christian chroniclers represented the Battle of Poitiers as a *European* event. One anonymous work, the *Continuatio hispana* (The continuation of the chronicle of Isidore of Seville), describes the Battle of Poitiers as a *victory for the Europeans*, who forced the people known in the West as the Saracens to retreat.

Three other changes or innovations also played a part in making the new extreme west of Europe homogeneous.

The Ruralization of Europe

The first, which was of an economic nature, was the above-mentioned ruralization of a world that had been strongly urbanized under the Romans. Roads fell into disrepair, along with workshops, warehouses and irrigation systems, and agriculture declined. It was a technological regression in which the use of stone as a major building material diminished and wood made a comeback. The flow of town-dwellers returning to the countryside did not fill the gap left by demographic decline. In the place of the town, *urbs*, the *villa*, or large estate, now became the basic economic and social entity, with small manors as the units where people lived and farmed. The area at the disposal of these manors varied, but in most cases was quite small and capable of providing sustenance for no more than a single family.

The monetary economy shrank and bartering took its place. Long-distance trading almost disappeared, except for indispensable commodities such as salt. Recently, historians have tended somewhat to discount the decline of the towns. But in truth the only ones that continued to flourish to any degree were centers where bishops and the occasional barbarian chieftain resided, such as Tours, Reims, Lyon, Toulouse, Seville, Mainz, Milan, and Ravenna.

Kingship and Barbarian Laws

Two other factors, one of a political, the other of a legal nature, contributed to the developing uniformity of the world under barbarian sway.

First, kings (much detested by the Roman world) now appeared at the head of the new political formations. They were kings of limited stature, really no more than tribal chieftains. The Anglo-Saxon kings, the Frankish kings from Clovis on, and the Burgundian, Gothic, Visigothic and Lombard kings wielded little power, even if they assumed the trappings of the Roman Empire. (In this respect, the prestige of a leader such as Theodoric, in Ravenna, was exceptional.) But kingship was nevertheless to enjoy a fine future in Europe.

Secondly, the laws promulgated by these kings were markedly barbarian in character. They consisted of lists of the tariffs, fines, and monetary or physical forms of compensation that applied to offenses and crimes. These varied according to the ethnic status and the social rank of the guilty parties.

We should not be misled by the presence of these laws, for they were of an extremely rudimentary nature even in the case of the edict produced by the last true heir to the Roman tradition in the West, the Ostrogoth Theodoric the Great. The Salic law of the Franks, written in Latin under Clovis, was particularly basic. Gondebaud, the king of the Burgundians, promulgated his Gombette law right at the beginning of the sixth century. The customs of the Visigoths were first codified by Euric (466–485), followed by Leovigild (568–586), and were then revised by Receswinth (649–672) for the use of both Visigoths and Romans, replacing the Breviary of Alaric (506), which had simplified the Theodosian code of 438 for the Romans, as did the *Lex Romana Burgundiorum*, among the Burgundians. The edict that Rotharis produced for the Lombards (643) was later expanded by several of his successors. At the beginning of the eighth century, the Franks inspired a *Lex Alamanorum*, followed in the mid-eighth century by a *Lex Baiavariorum*. Saint Martin, Archbishop of Braga from 579 on, composed a handbook entitled *De correctione rusticorum*, based on the legislation passed by various councils and synods. It laid down a program for the correction of the violent behavior of the peasants living in what is now northern Portugal.

Rudimentary though it was, this barbarian legislation resting upon the ruins of Roman law did ensure that the Europe of the Early Middle Ages continued to be based on law.

2

An Aborted Europe: The Carolingian World (Eighth to Tenth Centuries)

The next period produced an episode that has often been called the first great attempt at the construction of Europe. It is associated with Charlemagne, whose short-lived empire is claimed to be the first true blueprint of Europe.

Even supposing that view to be correct, it should be stressed that it was also the first example of a perverted Europe. Charlemagne's vision was a "nationalist" one. The empire that he founded was first and foremost Frankish and was inspired by a truly patriotic spirit. Charlemagne even envisaged giving Frankish names to the calendar months. This is an aspect that historians seldom dwell upon. However, it is important to draw attention to it, because Charlemagne's was the first of a string of failed attempts to construct a Europe dominated by one people or one empire. The Europes of Charles V, Napoleon, and Hitler were, in truth, anti-Europes, and Charlemagne's attempt already smacked of a project that was contrary to any true idea of Europe.

The Rise of the Carolingians

The rise of the Franks took place in two phases. At the end of the fifth century and in the sixth, Clovis and his sons divided Clovis's kingdom between them, reuniting it briefly from time to time. The second phase came in the eighth century. In the course of the seventh century the power of the Merovingians had gradually waned as their kings, known at the time as "the useless kings" and nowadays as "the good-for-nothing kings," were dispossessed of their power, which they abandoned to their chief administrator, the mayor of the palace. The situation was similar to that of modern Japan, where the emperors abandoned their power to the shogun. In the eighth century, the palace mayors were selected from the Pepin family, which hailed from the Liège region, and their function became hereditary.

Charles Martel, who succeeded his father, Pepin of Herstal, in 714, was considered to be the true king and his prestige was further increased thanks to the victories that he won, one of which was the battle fought near Poitiers against the Muslims in 732. At his death, his son Pepin the Short seized all his power, dethroned the last of the Merovingians, and in 751 arranged for the crown to be conferred upon himself by an assembly of leading laymen and clerics, in Soissons.

The most significant and lasting consequence was that in 754 Pepin had himself consecrated in Saint-Denis, together with his two sons Carloman and Charles. This return to the ritual of biblical kingship consecrated the person of the king as a Christian leader. It strengthened the prestige of monarchy which, here and there in Europe, has survived right down to the present day. Consecration was initially practiced in Visigothic Europe but then lapsed and was not restored by the Spanish Christian monarchy of the *Reconquista*. Only the kings of England, who inherited Anglo-Saxon rituals which, in the eighth century, also established consecration as an institution, likewise brought about a consecrated monarchy. This resulted in a symbolic rivalry between the kings of France and England throughout the Middle Ages. The king of France claimed primacy on the grounds of having transferred Clovis's baptismal ritual to the consecration of the king. Consequently, as the only ruler crowned by the Holy Ghost, the king of France then took the title *christianissimus* and, as the prestige of the emperor had declined, he proclaimed himself the foremost of the kings of Christendom. The history of Europe was to be full of such jealousies, rivalries, and claims that tended to institute a hierarchical order within the political space of Europe.

Pepin the Short left his kingdom and his power to his two sons, who divided these between them, in accordance with Frankish custom. However, in 771 Carloman died, leaving his younger brother Charles the sole king of the Franks. Charles was the future Charlemagne, and it was he who set the new dynasty of the Carolingians firmly upon the throne.

Was Charlemagne the First European?

Charlemagne was first and foremost a great warrior, as was traditional among Franks and other Barbarians. The wars that he waged were simultaneously Christianization campaigns, but they were chiefly characterized by brute force, violence, and cruelty. Charlemagne's conquests extended to the east, the southeast, and the south. In the east, in southern Germany, Charles defeated the Avars and, in 788, annexed Bavaria. In northern Germany, from 772 to 803, he was forced to engage in a series of hard campaigns against the pagan Saxons.

Pepin's great ally against the Germans had been Boniface, the Anglo-Saxon Wynfrith, Archbishop of Mainz. He had created numerous bishoprics, among them Salzburg, Ratisbonne, and Passau. Above all, at his instigation, in 744 his disciple Sturmi had founded the abbey of Fulda, in Hesse. Here, in 755, Boniface was buried, having been massacred by pagan Frisians while he was on a mission among them.

Charlemagne's most significant victory was won in the southeast. He was fighting against the king of the Lombards, who was a convert to Christianity. But as the latter persisted in harassing the pope's possessions in Italy, including those in Rome, the pope himself had invited Charlemagne to take action against the Lombards. Thanks to his iron-clad cavalry, Charlemagne won a dazzling victory against Didier, the Lombard king, then had himself crowned in Didier's place, in Pavia, where he received the traditional Lombard crown of iron. The Lombards nevertheless retained two independent duchies in central Italy, at Spoleto and Benevento.

Charlemagne was less successful on Gaul's southern front, where he confronted the Muslims. He was not well briefed on the situation in Spain and was defeated outside Saragossa. He then retreated to north of the Pyrenees. In a skirmish here, the Basques massacred a rearguard unit led by Charlemagne's nephew Roland. In the *Chanson de Roland*, this minor episode was later transformed by legend into a tragic defeat at the hands of the Saracens. With great difficulty, Charlemagne retained control of one of the Spanish marches, in what was later to become Catalonia, and also of Septimania, in Languedoc. To the north of the Pyrenees, in the west, he also managed to reconquer Gascony, but then presented it, as a kingdom, to his son Louis.

The Alliance between the Franks and the Papacy: Emperor Charlemagne

The most important factor in this situation was the alliance between the Franks and the papacy. In the Frankish sovereigns the popes sought and found a strong secular arm to protect them against their enemies, in particular the Lombards. The Frankish sovereigns' reward for their partnership in this alliance was the consecration of Pepin and his sons.

In the second stage of the alliance, the papacy seems to have had in mind an undertaking of a "European" nature: it wanted to restore the extreme Christian West as an empire centered on the Franks. On Christmas Day, AD 800, while Charlemagne was on a visit to Rome, Pope Leo III crowned the Frankish sovereign as emperor.

This was to strengthen western, Latin, Christendom's nascent independence from the Greek Orthodox Byzantine Empire. In my view, however, to present Charlemagne as the father of Europe is, in all other respects, a distortion of history. It is true that in his lifetime a number of texts referred to him as "the head of Europe," but that was more by way of paying him homage at an imaginary level, and did not really reflect the concrete historical situation. From a territorial point of view, Charlemagne's Europe was very restricted. It included neither the British Isles, which, in the hands of the Anglo-Saxons and the Irish, remained independent, the Iberian peninsula, which was mostly under Muslim control, southern Italy and Sicily, likewise in the hands of the Saracens, nor, finally, Scandinavia, which was still pagan and from which the Norman Vikings launched themselves either intent on pillage, or else in order to impose trading deals that were much to their advantage. Furthermore, the Carolingian Empire hardly impinged at all on territory to the east of the Rhine. Most of Germany lay beyond its grasp. Above all, the Slavs remained beyond its reach and were still pagan. Prague had evolved hardly at all since the seventh century, when the Frankish merchant Samo, who dominated the slave market, had had himself elected king by the Slavs and had then proceeded to advance into the heart of Bohemia.

For both the papacy, whose idea Charlemagne's imperial coronation was, and for Charlemagne himself, who accepted it more or less passively, this formality essentially represented a return to the past. It was an attempt to resurrect the Roman Empire rather than a project that looked ahead to the future destiny of Europe. When he founded his new capital, Aix-la-Chapelle, in the ancient territory of the Franks, Charlemagne was no doubt dreaming of making it "the Rome of the future," essentially in defiance of

"New Rome," namely Constantinople. But the main point is that he was looking back, toward a Rome that was not a seat of a Carolingian European empire, but simply the capital of a pope with little power. After Charlemagne, Aix-la-Chapelle went into decline. Shortly after its creation, it ceased to be the capital of the West, even if its myth did endure throughout the Middle Ages. All that were left in Aix were a few prestigious monuments that continued to testify to Charlemagne's dream. Today, the demonstrations of European solidarity that are set in Aix-la-Chapelle are no more than nostalgic ceremonies celebrating the past. Seen in the long term, and particularly in a European perspective, the Carolingian Empire was a failure.

The European Legacy of Charlemagne

Nevertheless, the modern Carolingian myth does include certain basic elements that are relevant to the future Europe. The first is Charlemagne's rough blueprint for *legal unification*. Charlemagne decreed rules affecting the major fields of government, rules that applied to the entire territory of the empire. They affected everywhere and everybody: the large rural estates, teaching, legislation, the various divisions of the kingdom, and the emperor's own envoys, the *missi dominici*. These rules were known as the *capitularies*. In similar fashion, Charlemagne strove to unify the currency of his empire by establishing a monetary system based on a silver coin, the denier. But the reestablishment of long-distance trading, in particular with the Muslim world, remained very limited. Another of Charlemagne's important reforms likewise remained incomplete. It concerned the basis of law and legislation. As we have noted above, barbarian legislation was founded on personal rights and was markedly ethnic in character. Franks, Burgundians, Lombards, and Goths all had their own laws. Charlemagne sought to replace this legal diversity with a single law of the land that applied to every man and woman resident within the empire's territory. Although never completed, this plan must be classed among Charlemagne's most revolutionary efforts and was one of those that afforded at least a glimpse of the possibility of *European legal unity*.

Thanks to the efforts of Charlemagne and his successors, *monastic unification* was more successful and, given the number, prestige, and activity of the monks, it played an important role in the organization of early medieval Europe. The beginning of the Early Middle Ages had witnessed the establishment of a number of different monastic rules. Charlemagne, as always, was keen on order and unity, so he supported the efforts to promote unification by a Catalan monk who founded a monastery close to Montpellier, at Aniane, and who, in particular, revived and revised the sixth-century rule of Saint Benedict of Nursia. The adoption of the revised rule of Saint Benedict by all the monasteries in the Frankish kingdom of the empire headed the agendas of five councils simultaneously set up in 813. In 816, at the council of Aix-la-Chapelle, Charlemagne's son and successor, Louis the Pious, decreed this Benedictine rule to be compulsory. Saint Benedict had ruled that the monks' time should be divided in such a way as to allow them to fulfill a number of different functions. There was a time for liturgical prayer and meditation, a time for manual labor, and a time for intellectual work; and to these functions Saint Benedict of Aniane added the mission of preaching to pagans and converting them. The monastic world was thus to play an essential social and cultural role throughout Christendom from the ninth to the twelfth century, even if, as Ludo Milis claims, that role has been somewhat exaggerated.

A Europe of Warriors...

Under the government of bishops and the secular clergy, and as the monks pursued their activities, the ninth century witnessed the unification of *a Europe of warriors and a Europe of peasants*. In accordance with the Frankish model, all the subjects of Charlemagne's empire depended directly upon the sovereign and were warriors. They were all in duty bound to do military service. Every free man was a potential warrior who, either directly or serving in a contingent of men provided by his overlord, had to take part annually in the sovereign's military campaigns from the spring to the autumn, the period when the horses could be sure of finding pasture.

Out of the 46 years of Charlemagne's reign, only two, 790 and 807, were free of military campaigns. The heavy cavalry was the strongest force in the army. When called up, every free man was expected, either personally or through the intermediary of his lord, to provide his own horse, shield, and weapon. The weapon would be either a light spear, a single-edged short sword for fighting on foot, or, for fighting on horseback, usually a long, two-edged sword. If the campaign was victorious, as was frequently the case under Charlemagne's leadership, it would be rounded off by an amassing of more or less rich booty. The Carolingian Empire lived partly off its conquests and booty, as have all great empires, from Alexander down to Muhammad.

In total, the number of soldiers at their sovereign's disposition was probably around 50,000 men, of whom 2,000 to 3,000 would be on horseback. However, they were seldom all summoned for action at the same time. Medieval society and culture did not involve huge numbers of individuals, particularly in the domain of warfare, for which it is best known. Its army leaders were men whose wealth stemmed essentially from the income produced by their large estates. The land itself was the other basis of the fortune and power of future Europeans. It has been suggested that the birth of the Middle Ages came about when taxes up till then paid to the government were converted into dues paid to the great landlords, the future seigneurial lords. About 90 percent of the lay population lived and worked on the land owned by these powerful figures.

...and Also a World of Peasants

The domination of a minority of militaristic landlords made Europe a world of warriors. But it was also a world in which the majority of inhabitants were peasants. The social statuses of these peasants varied. There were still slaves, for Christianity had done nothing to improve their lot. But new links were established between a lord, his estates, and the peasants. A growing number of men and plots of land became directly subject to the local lord. Taking the place of slaves, serfs now appeared, living on plots of land that they could neither exchange nor sell. Despite an early wave of land clearance in the sixth and seventh centuries, the West had remained a land of forests. The great seigneurial estates were generally divided into two sections. One was the *court* or *preserve* that the lord exploited directly, aided by his peasants, who did forced labor for him several times a week. The rest of the estate was farmed by the peasants for themselves. As well as providing for their families, they would try to produce a small surplus to sell, so that they could buy whatever necessary goods were not provided on the estate. A higher proportion of the peasants than is usually claimed owned what was called an *allodium*, or freehold land.

In Charlemagne's time there were already the beginnings of a development that was to be of major importance to the Middle Ages and would lead to one of the most characteristic features of Europe. The peasants forced their lords to emancipate them, and thereby formed a free category, exempted from forced labor. The lords were now obliged either to accept a reduction in the size of their estates or to reimpose servitude on the peasants. The latter solution was mainly adopted in eastern Europe and became a further cause of the differences and distancing between western and eastern Europe. The importance of rural life and society, which has remained a feature of Europe right down to the present day, was recognized by Charlemagne, who turned his attention to it and produced the capitulary entitled *De villis* (800). This consisted of a complete set of rules for agricultural life, which was applicable even outside the royal estates. It plotted out the rural landscape of the Early Middle Ages from which Europe would emerge. Many of its effects are still detectable today.

Carolingian Civilization, a Cultural Layer in the Formation of Europe

In its most successful aspects, Carolingian Europe was a civilizing influence. Charlemagne himself cannot be described as a cultured man: he could barely recognize the letters of the alphabet, was unable to write, and his knowledge of Latin was minimal. Nevertheless, in government he held firmly to the principle that knowledge and instruction respectively constituted a manifestation and an instrument of the necessary power of a sovereign. One of his primary duties was to promote and protect knowledge. He was well aware that in this task a monarch must rely on the clergy, who were the best trained in this domain, and above all he must turn to the sons of the powerful laymen who operated as his auxiliaries in the government of the empire. In implementing such a program, it was not enough to appeal solely to Franks. He needed to draw on the empire's full cultural potential. He even summoned representatives of countries that were not part of his empire – Irishmen, Anglo-Saxons, and Spaniards, for example. It is an exaggeration to portray Charlemagne as a forerunner of Jules Ferry, sallying forth to encourage pupils in the classroom. (Jules Ferry was Minister of Public Education and later, from 1879 to 1885, Prime Minister of France. He championed secular education.) The schools that Charlemagne created or developed were intended above all for the sons of the aristocracy. From 781, Charlemagne surrounded himself with educated and scholarly men. Jean Favier has gone so far as to describe them as "palace intellectuals." They included, for example, the Lombard Paul the Deacon, whose real name was Warnefried; the Italian Paulinus of Aquileia; the Spaniard Theodulf, who became bishop of Orléans and abbot of Fleury-sur-Loire (or Saint-Benôit-sur-Loire) in 797; and, above all, the Anglo-Saxon Alcuin, who was born in about 739 and died in 804. Alcuin became Charlemagne's principal councilor, but he always remained a simple deacon, even when he was made the abbot of Saint-Martin, in Tours, and proceeded to turn it into one of the most lively centers of what is sometimes called the Carolingian renaissance.

This world of learning was essentially masculine, but a few feminine figures did emerge in it. For example, Alcuin was also councilor to Gisèle,

Charlemagne's sister and the abbess of Chelles, and he encouraged her to favor intellectual life in her convent, along with intense activity devoted to the copying of manuscripts. Meanwhile, far from the court, Dhuoda, a great aristocrat of Aquitaine, acquired learning that she then determined, at the beginning of the ninth century, to pass on to her son, Bernard, the duke of Septimania, for whom she herself proceeded to write an educational handbook.

The Carolingian renaissance that developed around Charlemagne was somewhat more limited than is suggested by the triumphal and brilliant image that is sometimes purveyed of it. In Charlemagne's court, this cultural movement was not exclusively serious, but also had a playful side. Charles and the principal members of his entourage formed a Palatine Academy, a literary amusement whose members took nicknames reminiscent of antiquity. It is interesting to note that these included both Greek and Latin names, and also biblical ones. Alcuin was Albinus or Flaccus (in other words, Horace); Engilbert was Homer; Theodulf was Pindar; a young poet, Maudoin, was Naso (Ovid); Pepin of Italy was Julius (Caesar). But others were Aaron or Samuel; Adalard was Augustine; and, most importantly, Charlemagne was David, "the king of peace." The program of this academy was well in line with Alcuin's aims: namely, to make Charlemagne's court "an Athens even more beautiful than the ancient one, since it was ennobled by the teaching of Christ."

After Charlemagne, under Louis the Pious and Charles the Bald, a second wave of scholars continued and even developed this "renaissance." It was promoted not only in the palace but also in new abbeys. For instance, Eginhard studied at the new abbey of Fulda, in Germany where, from 822 on, the great Raban Maur was abbot.

Without exaggeration, it is fair to say that the intellectual activity of the Carolingians produced a layer of European culture of its own. In his capitulary entitled *De litteris colendis*, Charlemagne himself stressed the importance of learning for the government and prestige of a state.

Some of the reforms effected by Charlemagne and his councilors were important. One was the reform of writing. The new *Carolingian minuscule* was clear, consistent, elegant, and easier to read and write. It has been claimed that this was the first European writing. Amid the intense activity of copying manuscripts in the monastic, royal, and episcopal *scriptoria*, Alcuin encouraged a new concern for clarity and the use of punctuation. Charlemagne also encouraged the emendation of the texts of the Scriptures. The pursuit of correction that inspired the widespread activity of biblical exegesis in the medieval West constituted an important preoccupation. It combined a healthy respect for the original sacred text with a recognition of the legitimacy of amendments justified by the progress of knowledge and learning.

We still find some products of the Carolingian renaissance impressive today, above all the richness of its illustrated illuminated manuscripts. Outstanding Carolingian masterpieces include a number of gospels and psalm books. The delight in the text of the Psalms that swept the Middle Ages was at the root of an attraction toward biblical poetry, still evident in today's Europe.

We should also note the appearance of a fashion not particularly influenced by the Carolingians but that made its appearance in the same period, and then developed and persisted throughout the Middle Ages, and even survives today. After the sixth century, the so-called Apocalypse of Saint John, frequently excluded from the canonical texts of the New Testament, was ignored by clergy and the faithful alike. But a work produced in the late eighth century renewed its fortunes in startling fashion. This was a *Commentary* composed in about 780 by the monk Beatus, in the monastery of Liebana, close to Santander. In the ninth and tenth centuries, illustrated copies of this commentary abounded. Many of the illustrations testified to the artistic genius of western miniature painters when it came to expressing anxiety and terror. Beatus gave Europe its first great thriller.

The ninth century was also crucial to the future of religious architecture in the West. Two of its innovations constituted a legacy of the first importance to European architecture. One was the introduction of the symbolism of the transept, which integrated the cross into the linear design of the ancient Roman basilica. The earliest transepts appeared around 800 in Saint Maurice of Agaune, the cathedral of Cologne, and in the cathedral of Besançon. During this same period, the abbey of Saint-Riquier produced another innovation that was to enjoy great success: the west front with flanking towers that made the doorways of Romanesque and Gothic buildings so dramatic. A number of splendid examples of this type were erected. They include the monastery of Saint-Denis and that of Fulda, and the imperial palace and church of Aix-la-Chapelle. Both those seeking to hire skilled workers, and representatives of workshops would travel widely. Thanks to their collaboration, master craftsmen, later to be hailed as artists, presented the Europe of the future with works of beauty that many later monuments reproduced in the same style from one region to another.

France, Germany, Italy: Where did the Heart of Europe Lie?

A number of medieval texts referred to the united empire as Europe. The *Carmen de Carolo Magno* calls Charlemagne "the venerable head of Europe" and "the father of Europe." As early as 781, Charlemagne had entrusted the kingdom of Aquitaine to his son Louis, to whom he bequeathed his entire empire when he died in 814. Unable to cope with the pressure from his sons, or to resolve the problems of government for such a vast area, Louis the Pious reverted to the practice of dividing the empire between his sons. Following his death, that division was confirmed by an agreement between Lothar and Louis the German. It was then given concrete form, first by the oaths that were sworn in Strasburg in 842 and recorded in the first official text written in two vernacular versions, one Frankish, the other German, and later by the treaties of Verdun (843) and Minden (844), which ratified the division of the empire. Following these dramatic events, the extreme west was reorganized into two regions, western and eastern Francia, held respectively by two peoples, the one destined to become the French, the other the Germans. Between these two ran a third area extending from north to south and incorporating the two capitals, Aix-la-Chapelle and Rome. Part of this region was known as Lotharingia, the rest as Italy. Soon Lotharingia proved to be an artificial entity that was hard to maintain. The territorial and political reality of the situation found expression in the emergence of three predominant regions. In a ninth-century document, these regions are called the *prestantiores Europae species*, the three dominant parts of Europe: Italy, Gaul, and Germany. Although these entities possessed no precise identifiable frontiers nor any clearly defined institutional structures, they prefigured the three nations of the distant future in modern, contemporary Europe: France, Germany, and Italy. That concrete development provides considerable food for thought on the slow, historical emergence of Europe. Very early on, certain powers established themselves as greater than others. The present construction of Europe must face up to the pretensions of the France/Germany axis. It is no doubt a factor necessary for the stability of Europe, but at the same time creates inequalities and jealousies within the European community.

3

A Dream of Europe and the Potential Europe of the Year 1000

Imperial Ottonian Europe

In the mid-tenth century, Charlemagne's dream of imperial unity was taken up by Otto I, the king of Germany, who was the son of Henry I and Saint Matilda. He had been crowned in 936, in Aix-la-Chapelle, and had then annexed various territories in Germany and won a number of victories over invaders, including a famous one at Lechfeld, over the Hungarians, in 955. In 962, he was crowned emperor in Rome, by Pope John XII. To establish his position as an equal and to improve relations with the Byzantine Empire, he obtained the hand in marriage of the Byzantine princess Theophano for his son. To foster relations with the Slavs, in 968 he established an archbishopric in Magdeburg, where he was buried when he died in 973. Although Otto's creation lost real power in the course of the Middle Ages, it nevertheless provided the basis for an institution and authority which, unlike Charlemagne's empire, was relatively long-lived, according to European standards. The name given to this empire of his was the Germanic Holy Roman Empire. This conveyed first the sacred nature of the empire and secondly that it was the Roman Empire's successor, with Rome as its capital. Thirdly, it underlined the preeminent role that the Germans played in this institution. The vision that Louis the Pious had nurtured was thus to a certain extent resurrected and prolonged. The backbone of a potential Europe, running from north to south, all the way from the North Sea to the

Mediterranean, was constituted by Germany and Italy. The Alps, which had never proved a real barrier between Italy and northern Europe, now, more than ever, became an essential passageway connecting the north and the south of medieval "European" Christendom, in which the emperors' descents to Italy took on the character of a kind of political ritual. As Alpine passes were made negotiable, hospices sprang up to house pilgrims, and commercial and human relations intensified, the importance of the Alps, at the heart of medieval "European" Christendom, was increasingly affirmed. The three cantons of Uri, Schwyz, and Unterwalden protected and policed the Alpine passes, especially after the construction of the Saint-Gothard pass, in the second half of the thirteenth century. In 1291, those three cantons united to form the Swiss Confederation, the modest and unexpected seed from which European democracy was to grow in the distant future.

The "New Europe" of the Year 1000

Otto I's son, Otto II, consolidated the structures of the empire and his son Otto III, who was crowned in Rome immediately after his father's death in 983, was hailed as the bringer of a brilliant future for the whole of Christendom. The gifts and brilliance of this 13-year-old emperor, who died at the age of 21, in 1002, earned him the description of a *mirabilia mundi*, one of the world's wonders. In Rome, he received a particularly prestigious education at the hands of Saint Adalbert of Prague, then living there, and Gerbert of Aurillac, the archbishop of Reims, who had been ejected from his see. Gerbert was a remarkable scholar for his time. In Catalonia, where he made contact with the Arabs, he had studied arithmetic, geometry, music, and astronomy. With the support of the emperor, in 999, Gerbert became pope, taking the name Sylvester II. Together with his imperial pupil, he devised an ambitious plan to promote European Christendom. Alexander Gieysztor has described clearly how the Slavs and Hungarians of newly Christianized Europe came to hold an essential position in this program elaborated by Otto III and Sylvester II. Miniatures of the time depict the emperor in all his majesty, escorted by Rome, "Gallia," "Germania," and also "Sclavinia," the land of the Slavs. Clearly, in AD 1000, the dream of Europe that the pope and the emperor shared was one of a Europe extending further eastward. History was more or less to realize that dream. The entry of the Slavic world into a united Christendom that prefigured Europe still represents even today one of the major events of European unification: this problem, too, has roots that lie in the Middle Ages.

Today a question much discussed is whether or not the year 1000 marked the beginning of a major surge in the growth of medieval Christendom. There certainly seems to have been a spurt of economic activity in Christendom between 950 and 1050. That economic growth constituted the background to the religious and political dreams of the year 1000. It affected more or less the whole of Christendom. The testimony of the Cluny monk Raoul Glaber is particularly telling:

> As the third year of the new millennium approached, almost everywhere, but above all in Italy and Gaul, churches were being rebuilt. Although many of them, of extremely solid construction, had no need of rebuilding, in a positive surge of rivalry, every Christian community felt compelled to possess a more sumptuous church than its neighbors. You would have thought that the world itself was trying to shake off its ancient fustiness and everywhere be covered by a white mantle of churches. Virtually all the churches in the bishoprics, those of monasteries consecrated to all kinds of saints, and even little village chapels were rebuilt by the faithful, so as to be more beautiful.

This surge of activity provided a great boost for all the crafts and trades involved in the wave of construction: it promoted the provision of raw materials, transport for them, the fabrication of tools, the recruitment of labor, and the financing of work projects. This was a time when building sites multiplied, testifying to the dynamism of the Christendom from which Europe would inherit wave after wave of Romanesque and Gothic edifices. The saying, "If building is booming, all is well" was certainly borne out in the year 1000 in Europe. This great spate of material activity was accompanied by intense collective fervor, at once religious and psychological. Georges Duby has brilliantly described the many prodigies of the millennium, beginning with signs visible in the heavens. The millennium produced a vast movement of penitence and purification, an efflorescence of cults centered on relics and miracles, and a vast mixture of hopes, fears, and dreams. When the heart of Europe beat, it beat more or less strongly throughout, from west to east and from north to south. The Europe of sensibility brooked no internal boundaries.

The "Newcomers": Scandinavians, Hungarians, and Slavs

At this point we need to return to the last wave of invasions and Christianization, which I touched upon in connection with Otto III. The Slavs had already made their way into Christendom, thereby contributing to the creation of a racially mixed Europe. In the seventh and eighth centuries, Croats infiltrated the territory lying between the Adriatic and the Danube and between Rome and Byzantium. The peace treaty of Aix-la-Chapelle (812) placed them under the authority of the Franks. Positioned between the Latins and the Byzantines, they managed to preserve their identity. However, they inclined more toward the Latins, and in 925 Pope John X made a king of the Croat Tomislav. At the Councils of Split that met in 925 and 928, the pope placed the Slavs under the jurisdiction of Rome and established a metropolitan archbishopric in Split.

The "newcomers" fell into three groups. The slow process of their Christianization was speeded up by the atmosphere around the year 1000. The first group consisted of Scandinavians, known to us as Vikings or Normans. From the late eighth century to the mid-tenth, the Christians of the West regarded these above all as violent invaders and pillagers, even though their raids were often accompanied by a certain amount of peaceful trading. In the tenth century, the Danes constituted a vast kingdom that incorporated Norway and dominated the North Sea all the way to Greenland. The earliest society that became established in Iceland clustered around a small group of Danish families and became a plutocratic oligarchy governed by its own newly created popular assembly, known as the Althing. The Icelanders converted to Christianity at the end of the tenth century and in 1000 elaborated a constitution. They remained largely independent from the Danes and, in the course of the Middle Ages, produced one of the most brilliant literary genres of the western world, the Sagas. On the extreme northwestern edge of the European space, there thus developed a society that lived off the sea and a civilization that enriched medieval Christendom in a remarkable manner. Meanwhile, in the late tenth century the Danes embarked on the conquest of Great Britain. For a while they were successful. From 1018 to 1035, Cnut the Great was king of both Great Britain and Denmark. In Denmark, he systematically promoted the monasteries and Christianity. In Norway, Saint Olaf, who reigned from 1015 to 1030, encouraged the Christianity that had been introduced by Olaf Tryggvason, who was king there from 995 to 1000. The canonization of Saint Olaf was in line with the papacy's practice of using sainthood to reward kings who converted their peoples to Christianity. This was but one of the many episodes in which converted and converting kings gained admittance to Christendom for their peoples. In Sweden, Olaf Skötkonung became the first Christian king at the beginning of the eleventh century. To complete this account of the entry of the Scandinavians into Christendom, it should be noted that the Normans who had settled in Gallic Normandy under the command of Rollo placed themselves under the domination of the

Carolingians and converted collectively to Christianity when they were offered and accepted the future duchy. It was with the blessing of the papacy that William the Bastard (William the Conqueror) seized Great Britain in 1066, after his victory at the Battle of Hastings put an end to Anglo-Saxon kingship. The Westerners of the North had now all acceded to Christendom, that is to say the future Europe.

In central Europe, the Hungarians' accession to Christendom was unusual. The Hungarians were peculiar in that their language was neither Roman, Germanic, nor Slavic. It has remained idiosyncratic right down to the present day, proving that, however important languages may be, linguistic differences are not insuperable in the constitution of a cultural and political entity. (We shall be returning to this subject, in which Switzerland provides another example.) At the end of the ninth century, after a long migration, the Hungarians, who originated in Asia, set up a seminomadic state in the Carpathians, under the leadership of Duke Arpad. From there, they launched murderous raids into central Europe, desisting only when, in 955, Emperor Otto I inflicted a bitter defeat upon them at Lechfeld. The Hungarians were then subjected to several campaigns of Christianization, some of which were initiated in the east, others in the west. The Roman missionaries – Germans, Italians, and Slavs – eventually prevailed. The example of Saint Stephen's upbringing testifies to the mixed nature of Christian Europe's constitution. He was influenced by the Archbishop of Prague, Vojtěch (later Saint Adalbert), by his own wife Gisèle, a Bavarian who was Emperor Henry II's sister, and also by Gellert, the Hungarian bishop of Csanàd, who had been trained in the Venetian monastery of San Giorgio Maggiore. Gellert organized the fledgling Church of Hungary and was martyred in the pagan uprising of 1046. In 1000, Stephen, who was baptized in 995, for his part created the Benedictine monastery of Pannonhalma at the supposed birthplace of Saint Martin. He organized the first ten bishoprics of Hungary, promulgated decrees obliging every village to build a church, and composed a prince's handbook entitled *Libellus de instructione morum* for his son Imre, who succeeded him and was likewise canonized. Finally, his descendant Ladislas (ruled 1077–95), also a member of this exceptional lineage of king-saints, was also canonized.

This great wave of Christianization around the time of the millennium also affected the western Slavs. We have already seen how the Croats established themselves in the northeastern region of the Adriatic. One other episode must also be noted, as it is extremely important for reasons both positive and negative. It involved an attempt to convert Slavs to the Greek Orthodox Christian religion. This was led by two brothers, Cyril and

Methodius. Both were Byzantine monks, who at an early stage began to work closely with Slavic communities, endeavoring not only to convert them but at the same time to strengthen their cultural identity. To this end they created a special writing for the Slavic language, using the Cyrillic alphabet. The principal field of their apostolic work was Moravia. But although their influence in the linguistic and liturgical domains was important and long-lasting, they failed to attach the Czechs and other peoples of Moravia to Greek Orthodoxy; and Bohemia and Moravia became part of Roman Latin Christendom. Nevertheless, this episode left a sufficient mark on the Slavs and other peoples of central Europe for Pope John-Paul II to proclaim Cyril and Methodius patrons of Europe, along with Saint Benedict of Nursia.

The period of the Christianization of central Europe was turbulent politically, quite apart from the emergence of Hungary. Prince Svatopluk (ruled 870–94) had created a state of Greater Moravia from which Bohemia broke away as early as 895. Around the year 1000, both Bohemia and Poland, both of which were now Christian, were laying claim to Moravia. In 966, Prince Mieszko of the Piast dynasty had himself baptized. Christian Poland's relations with the neighboring empire of Germany were half hostile, half friendly. In 999, an archbishopric that was strictly speaking Polish had been founded at Gniezno, the site of the tomb of Saint Adalbert. Emperor Otto III made a pilgrimage to it in the year 1000. Eventually, in 1025, Boleslas the Valiant had himself crowned king of Poland. In the course of the eleventh century the religious and political center of the country shifted southward and Kraków became the capital. This was the general pattern of Christianization at both the ecclesiastical and political levels. Usually, the promotion of archbishoprics was linked with the rise of particular kings. We shall be returning to the question of whether, in the Middle Ages and also in the longer term, central Europe possessed a distinctive character of its own. However that may be, in this construction of Christendom, the Europe that was emerging generally favored the institution of monarchical states as well as conversion to Christianity. Europe was represented by a collection of kings.

The establishment of Christianity in almost all of western and central Europe (by the end of the eleventh century, the only remaining pagans were the Prussians and the Lithuanians) was accompanied by widespread changes of toponymy. Baptizing places was almost as important as baptizing people. Networks of Christian place names, many of them linked with pilgrimages, thus left their mark on Christendom. At the end of the eleventh century, Martin was the most common toponym in Christendom, across the board from Poland to Spain.

A European "Peace" Movement

The world of AD 1000 was bellicose and violent. As fighting against pagans became a thing of the past, since the latter had all been Christianized, conflicts broke out between Christians at every level, even locally. At this point, in about 1000, a powerful peace movement developed in Christendom. Peace is one of the principal ideals promoted by Christianity and is embodied in its liturgy by the kiss of peace. Jesus praised peacemakers, and made peace one of the most important Christian values. The appearance, at the end of the tenth century, of a peace movement in southern France, which then spread throughout western Europe in the eleventh century, is historically linked to the rise of what is known as feudalism. The establishment of the power of feudal lords, a subject to which we shall be returning, was achieved by various means, but chiefly through violence that wiped out the central power of the last of the Carolingians, making way for the violence of the feudal lords. Christian peace was a sacred eschatological concept, a prefiguration of the peace of Paradise. The peace movement of around AD 1000 therefore found expression in demonstrations in which religious fervor was the key element. The foremost actors in the movement were the Church and the peasant masses. Some historians have considered the movement to have been a popular uprising exploited and taken over by the Church. The Church chose to back these gatherings, regarding them as councils in which laymen participated as well, and these helped to spread new religious features of Christendom, such as the cult of relics and miracles. But the movement also gave rise to an initial wave of rules for the protection of the weak: peasants, merchants, pilgrims, women, and (for the Church made the most of the situation) ecclesiastics. In short, in the face of the Europe of warriors, the movement stood for a Europe of the "unarmed." The feudal lords and political leaders then moved in to take over this peace movement. The measures that they took to favor peace consisted chiefly, not of banning violence altogether, but of channeling and regulating it. They introduced the idea of God's truce, according to which weapons had to be laid aside at particular moments. Respect for peace or, more modestly, for that truce was furthermore ensured by groups invested not only with considerable military power (which turned them into a police force) but also with governmental legitimacy and a role of pacification. In 1024, in an assembly that gathered on the River Meuse, Robert the Pious, the king of the Franks, and the emperor Henry II proclaimed universal peace. So at this stage peace was being imposed by the powerful. God's peace became the king's peace or, in certain regions such as Normandy, the duke's peace. Peace became one of the most important instruments that enabled kings to establish their own power firmly within their kingdoms. It lost the eschatological and sacred halo that had surrounded it in AD 1000. But it did remain a religious ideal. Even today, peace, first at a national, then at a European level, is one of Europe's major collective goals. The reason why, in the thirteenth century, the king of France, Louis IX (Saint Louis) was a successful arbiter, or what was called a pacifier, was that his saintly reputation enabled him better than most to accomplish a task that had initially been regarded as sacred.

A New European Sanctuary in Spain: Santiago de Compostela

It was also around AD 1000 that the first attempts were made to recover the Iberian peninsula from the Muslims. Later, this movement became known as the *Reconquista*. At the beginning of the ninth century, an important event had taken place. In Galicia, at Compostela (the "Field of the Star," *campus stellae*), at the site of an ancient Visigothic necropolis, a discovery was made, to the accompaniment of extraordinary lights and apparitions. What was found was the tomb of Saint James, the apostle, whose body, after his martyrdom, had apparently been brought by sea in a boat that had been wrecked there. Following its discovery in about 820–30, this tomb, over which a series of increasingly sumptuous sanctuaries were built, gradually became the center of a pilgrimage which, around the twelfth century, became the third greatest in Christendom (the other two being Jerusalem and Rome). In the course of the struggles against the Muslims, Saint James came to be regarded as the mainstay of the Christians. He was said to appear at their side in battle, and so was dubbed *Matamoros*, "killer of the Moors." Santiago (Sant'Iago) attracted pilgrims from every corner of Christendom in what became one of the greatest pilgrimages in Europe (although recently, it is true, it has been claimed that its heyday was not the Middle Ages, but the modern period). The fame of Santiago de Compostela confirms the importance of peripheral regions in the construction of Europe.

Meanwhile, the Christians who had maintained their position in northern Spain but were constantly raided by the Muslims, in particular by al-Mansur (responsible for the sack of Barcelona in 985, and Santiago de Compostela in 997), were organizing themselves and were not only resisting the Muslims, but attacking them too. In the kingdom of Pamplona, in the tenth century, definite progress was made in the military and political organization of the Christians. Following the death of al-Mansur and the

assassination of his grandson in 1009, they were ready to take advantage of
the crisis in Muslim Spain.

The Consolidation of Europe

Meanwhile, in the East, the gradual deterioration of relations with Byzantium had detached Latin Roman Christendom from the Byzantine Empire in
what was to prove to be a definitive fashion, although the Ottonian emperors were still endeavoring to avoid a break. Otto I had himself consecrated as emperor, in Rome. As mentioned above, in 972, as a gesture of
appeasement, he had married his son Otto II to the Greek princess Theophano. From 983 to 991, she acted as regent during the minority of Otto III.
Byzantine influence in the court of Otto III was in any case strong, so in AD
1000 Christian Europe was not yet completely detached either from Byzantium or from the Orthodox Slavic world. The king of the Franks, Henry I
(ruled 1031–60), the grandson of Hugh Capet, also married an Orthodox
princess, the Russian Anne of Kiev, in 1051.

Throughout the Carolingian and post-Carolingian period of the ninth
and tenth centuries, contemporary texts use the term "Europe" more often
than is sometimes recognized; and, contrary to certain claims, that was not
a purely geographical name. Besides, the expression, "a purely geographical
name" itself makes no sense. Such names are never innocent. The use of the
term Europe signifies a certain sense of community that antedated Christianization, but from the eleventh century on, although that sense of a
collective identity persisted and even strengthened among "Europeans," a
new word was mostly used to convey it, the word Christendom. The
ceremonial cloak of Emperor Henry II (1002–24), Otto III's successor,
which has been preserved in Bamberg, illustrates the cosmic dimensions of
the imperial dream. The zodiacal signs that adorn it are intermingled with
images of Christ, the Virgin, angels, and saints. The Latin inscription that
runs along the cloak's border salutes the monarch: "O thou, the honor of
Europe, blessed Caesar Henry, may the One who reigns in eternity increase
thy empire." (A picture of this cloak, and commentaries on it may be found
in Michel Pastoureau and Jean-Claude Schmitt, *Europe. Mémoires et
Emblèmes*, Paris: Éditions de l'Épargne, 1990, pp. 74–5.)

4

Feudal Europe (Eleventh and Twelfth Centuries)

The period in which Christendom became more firmly established witnessed the beginnings of a great surge forward in what was eventually to become Europe. But that surge forward might well have been frustrated in its early stages, for it was not a foregone conclusion that it should lead inexorably toward the unification of the future Europe. I shall concentrate particularly on the general features that these years bequeathed to Europe. This period may fairly be said to constitute its feudal stratum.

Agricultural Progress

Once again, let us start with fundamentals. Feudal Europe was rural, essentially a Europe of the soil. Today, even if the number and impact of the peasants in Europe have both greatly diminished, the rural economy nevertheless remains a fundamental factor and presents one of the most intractable problems facing the European Community. The world that the Common Agricultural Policy has to cope with is a legacy of the Middle Ages, when the cultivation of cereals became ever more important. Europe was to be a world of bread. It was also a world in which two beverages predominated. One was wine, whose importance had been strengthened since the Roman conquest by its use in the Christian liturgy. As a result of the demand for wine, vines spread as far as northern France and southern England, beyond what is considered to be their climatic limit. The other beverage was the ancestor of beer, ale. The distinction between a Europe of wine and a Europe of ale was so clear-cut that in the thirteenth century Franciscans tended to distinguish between the monasteries of their order by dividing them into wine monasteries and ale monasteries. In the West, a third drinking Europe also emerged, the Europe of cider. Despite such regional differences and variations, from AD 1000 onward, rural life was remarkably uniform, and its uniformity was marked by the progress of a number of important techniques. They indicated the growing efficacy of human labor, first and foremost in that fundamental activity, the preparation of the soil. The archaic swing-plow was superseded, particularly in the plains of northern Europe, by a plow equipped with an asymmetrical plowshare and a moldboard and – most important of all – that plowshare was made of iron rather than wood. Agriculture using the new type of plow also encouraged improvements in the means of traction. Donkeys and mules continued to be used as draft animals in the south, as did oxen in some parts of the north, but in the plains of the north horses began to replace oxen and, in the twelfth century, took over altogether in the peasant agriculture of Flanders. The importance of what is claimed to be the revolution introduced by the shoulder harness, which increases a draft animal's capacity so dramatically, may have been exaggerated, but at the very least its introduction and diffusion testify to a definite determination to improve agricultural methods.

In the north, there were also signs of an innovation that was to play an important part in the improvement of yields and the diversification of crops. This was a change made to the system of crop rotation, which was traditionally biennial, with half the land left fallow each year, to allow the soil to rest. Now, the designation of a third portion of the available land allowed the introduction of leguminous crops in a triennial rotation. This led to an increase in the overall yield, thanks to the possibility of producing two kinds of harvest a year.

Today, when we are increasingly sensitive to environmental problems and climatic variations, it is interesting to note, as some historians have, that the spurt of increased production after AD 1000 may have benefited from what Marc Bompaire has called "un coup de pouce du ciel" (a helping hand from heaven). Between 900 and 1300, Europe seems to have enjoyed optimum climatic conditions, with a rise in the average temperatures of one or two degrees and a drop in humidity that was favorable to the cultivation of cereals.

The Cell Structure of Society ("Encellment")

This period around AD 1000 and the decades that followed were a crucial time for the social and political restructuring of the space constituted by

Christendom; and the territorial organization of Europe was deeply marked by this restructuring. Given that the feudal castle played such an important part in this reorganization, to refer to the latter historians sometimes use an Italian word borrowed from Pierre Toubert's great work on medieval Latium: *incastellamento*. Seeking a word that could be extended to the entire territory of medieval Europe, Robert Fossier has suggested the alternative of the French *encellulement*, "encellment." What were the fundamental cells that formed the basis for this reorganization? One was clearly the castle, but there were three others: the feudal domain, the village, and the parish. The feudal domain designated the territory dominated by a castle and encompassed all its lord's land and peasants. It thus included land, men and the income obtained both from the cultivation of the land and from the dues paid by the peasants. In addition, as the master in command, the feudal lord enjoyed a number of rights, known as the "ban." Given that this system of organization operated throughout practically the whole of Christendom, some historians have suggested replacing the expression "feudal system" by "seigneurial system," for feudalism designates a more limited organization in which the lord was the master of a fiefdom that was ceded to him, as a vassal, by *his* overlord. Strictly speaking, the meaning of the term "feudalism" was of a legal nature.

Village and Cemetery

Most seigneurial domains contained settlements of peasants and subjects known as villages. The village, which replaced the scattered rural settlements of antiquity and the Early Middle Ages, became a major feature of eleventh-century Christendom generally. In the Europe of today, the status of castles in the landscape is simply that of a memory and a symbol, frequently in a state of ruin. In contrast, the medieval village, as a form of habitat, survives throughout western Europe. The village originated from houses and fields that were grouped around two essential elements, a church and a cemetery. Robert Fossier rightly believes that the cemetery was the principal element here and may in some cases have antedated the church. Here we have evidence of one of the most deeply rooted characteristics that medieval society has bequeathed to Europe. It concerns the relations between the living and the dead. In the West, one of the most important changes that distinguished antiquity and the Middle Ages was the way that the living took to making a place for the dead, first in their towns and later in their villages. The ancient world's attitude toward corpses was one of fear or even repulsion. Cults devoted to the dead were set up only in the intimacy of private families, or else well outside places where people lived, for example along the roads that led away into the countryside. With Christianity, the scene was totally transformed. Tombs holding the bodies of ancestors were integrated into the urban space. In the Middle Ages, the relations between the living and the dead became ever closer. This was achieved by the invention, in the twelfth century, of a third place in the Beyond, namely Purgatory. Even more importantly, in the eleventh century, the papacy, influenced by the monastic order of Cluny, instituted a day for commemorating the dead. This fell on November 2, the day following All Saints Day. In this way the saints, the dead par excellence, were brought together with all the other, ordinary, dead. In the upper levels of feudal society, the "cult" of ancestors became a fundamental social link upon which lineages were founded and thanks to which these were strengthened. In the late eleventh century, for example, the Count of Anjou, Foulque le Réchin, working back through the lineage of his ancestors and coming to a halt at the most ancient figures known to him, declared: "Before that, I know nothing, for I do not know where my ancestors were buried."

Royal dynasties hastened to create royal necropolises: Bamberg in Germany, Westminster in England, Fontevrault in Anjou for the early Plantagenets, San Isidoro-de-León for the kings of León-Castile, Saint-Bavon-de-Gand for the counts of Flanders, and Saint-Denis for the kings of France.

The Parish

Together with the cemetery, the church constituted the center of the village and in general it was also the center of another basic cell, larger than not only the village, but even the town: the parish. As an institution, the parish was not definitively stabilized until the thirteenth century, but most of the attendant problems that were resolved between the eleventh and the thirteenth century had already been sorted out in the context of the villages of the eleventh century. The main problem was one of territory. The establishment of parishes in the various town quarters and in rural areas was a delicate matter. In villages, the church naturally served the villages as a parish; that is to say, it gathered the faithful together under the authority of a parish priest. The parish established a number of rights, the right of the faithful to receive the sacraments, the right of the priest to receive certain dues. Just as it was the parishioners' right to receive the sacraments, it was the parish's monopoly to deliver them, so that in everyday life, right down to the day he died, a villager was closely linked with his parish church, his parish priest, and his fellow parishioners.

Society's Upper Crust: The Nobility

After AD 1000, an upper layer emerged within the group of seigneurial lords: the nobility. Nobility was linked to power and wealth, but was essentially a matter of blood. The nobility was a class with high prestige, intent above all on manifesting its rank, mainly through a pattern of social and religious gestures that involved the distribution of largesse. The most usual way of manifesting one's nobility was to shower benefits upon individuals, and in particular upon religious groups, abbeys and saints.

Where did nobles come from? One view is that nobility was a leftover from Roman antiquity; another, that it was a creation of the Middle Ages that stemmed from the status of a free man, which was reserved for a elite group.

Whatever the case may be, in the West, the Middle Ages saw the establishment of a superior social class which Leopold Génicot describes as "proud of its antiquity, with strength that stemmed from its wealth, its alliances, and the public role that it played, either to the detriment of the sovereign or with his aid." It enjoyed certain political and legal privileges and commanded great social respect. As has been noted above, its prestige was essentially based on blood. In consequence, ennoblement by kings and princes of men who were not born noble was a late and limited development that never bestowed upon the newly ennobled the respect granted to noble birth.

In Europe today, no more than scattered faint shadows remain of the nobility that emerged in the Middle Ages. However, the notion of what is noble and of nobility looms large among Western values. That is because, already in the Middle Ages, alongside the notion of noble blood there developed that of nobility of character and behavior, that is to say, virtue. Moralists would even draw a contrast between this acquired nobility and the innate nobility of a noble who did not necessarily live up to his name. "Nobility" is one of the key words used in Europe's debates on the question of how the value of men and women should be appreciated.

Chivalry and Courtliness

Around AD 1000, a more clearly defined social type appeared in large numbers, positioned in the social hierarchy immediately below the nobility. In the Roman Empire and among Romanized barbarians, *miles* was the word that designated a man's function: warfare (a *miles* was a soldier). But around 1000, this term evolved and came to designate an elite group of fighters, usually attached to a particular castle and its lord. These men specialized in combat on horseback and, as well as fighting genuine battles in the service of their lord, they would engage in what were called tournaments, which were designed partly for training purposes and partly for entertainment. These tournaments were regarded with hostility by the Church, which deplored the aggression of these men devoted to the second Indo-European function (that of the *bellatores*), particularly since that aggression was sometimes directed against the Church itself. In contrast to the clergy, for whom bloodshed was forbidden, these knights showed no compunction about shedding blood. It seems that their excesses may have been one of the chief reasons for the above-mentioned revolt that took the form of a peace movement in around AD 1000. Eventually the Church did manage to "civilize" the knights. It tried to channel their violence by deflecting it first toward pious ends such as the protection of churches, women, and unarmed people, and later, as we shall see, toward the fight against the infidels outside Christendom. Eventually, in the twelfth century at the latest, the Church carried off a relative victory in their struggle against the knights. At the end of a youth's adolescence, accession to knighthood was marked by a ceremony which represented at once an initiation rite and a rite of passage for the future knight. In it, the young warrior was presented with his weapons, as was customary among the Germanic peoples. While the Church did nothing to discourage the presentation of spurs, a purely secular rite, it did introduce a blessing of the panoply of weapons by which the knights were characterized – the spear with its banner, the emblazoned shield, and the sword. It also conferred the Christian symbolism of purity upon the bath taken before the ceremony. At the end of the twelfth century, it added to this ceremonial presentation of knightly equipment an armed vigil devoted to religious meditation. The most important development for the European future of the phenomenon of chivalry was the elaboration, already in the Middle Ages, of a knightly myth. It was, if not created, at least propagated by a special genre of literature. This is perhaps the juncture at which to point out the importance of the place of literature in the heritage bequeathed by the Middle Ages. The knightly myth began to take shape in the *chansons de geste*. As early as the late eleventh century, the two characteristic aspects of a knight, military prowess and piety, were embodied in the two heroes of the *Chanson de Roland* ("Song of Roland"), Roland and Oliver. In this work, the knights are praised as the greatest of the king's servants by virtue of their chivalric qualities: warrior valor, placed at the service of vassal loyalty. The knights of the *chansons de geste* were followed by others who enjoyed an equal success. These were the heroes of adventure

stories that stemmed from two major sources, on the one hand a transfig-
ured ancient history peopled with figures such as Aeneas, Hector, and
Alexander, on the other "stories from Brittany," relating the exploits of
Celtic heroes more imaginary than historical, chief among them the famous
Arthur. In the thirteenth century, this imaginary, fundamental to the future
imaginary of Europe, first produced the mythical hero known as a "knight
errant," then elaborated another theme that promoted the prestige of chivalry by bringing together heroes from a variety of backgrounds. They were
known as the "nine champions." This saintly history of chivalry featured
ancient champions (Hector, Alexander, and Judas Maccabaeus, as well as
Christian ones (Arthur, Charlemagne, and Godfrey of Bouillon). The imaginary world of chivalry, a combination of warrior exploits and devoted
service in defense of the weak (women, the poor, etc.) survived the Middle
Ages all the better because the epithet "chivalrous," although to a large
extent modeled by the Church, preserved secular values in a Europe that
progressively distanced itself from purely Christian ones. Conversely, in the
Middle Ages the Church, for its part, had persisted in dissociating itself
from chivalric values that it considered to be too barbarous. As Jean Flori
has observed, "Largesse is not charity, and gifts are not alms."

Chivalry was closely related to another form of feudal behavior, courtliness, and both have been handed down to modern Europe. As its etymology
indicates, courtliness was defined by the good manners said to have reigned
in the courts of kings and princes. An interesting point to note is that those
princely figures were just as likely to be women as to be men, for if chivalry
belonged to an essentially masculine world, courtliness characterized a
world in which women were omnipresent. They were perhaps expected to
set a particular tone or to attract writers and artists, like Marie, Countess of
Champagne (1145–1198), and – if we are to credit the legend – Eleanor of
Aquitaine, queen of England in the late twelfth century, or possibly simply
to elicit admiration and protection from the males who surrounded them.
These values and modes of behavior may reasonably be associated with the
good manners that originated in the Middle Ages, in the twelfth and
thirteenth centuries and whose importance the sociologist Norbert Elias
has underlined. The manners that he describes and illuminates in his work
The History of Manners (volume 1 of *The Civilizing Process*) to a large
extent consisted in better table manners, which introduced hygiene and
politeness to a society that did not adopt the use of the fork until right at
the end of the Middle Ages: for example, not eating from the same plate as
others, not spitting, washing one's hands before and after a meal...Good
manners could also be learnt in monasteries and convents. Hugh of Saint-
Victor, the great educator, who was a canon in the famous monastery on the

outskirts of Paris (1090–1141), composed a *De instructione novitiorum* which, as Jean-Claude Schmitt has skillfully shown, instructed young novices on how to behave, speak, and eat at table. The royal court may have been a fine cultivator of civilized manners, but we should not forget that the Middle Ages, following antiquity, always drew a contrast between the good manners of townsfolk and the uncouth habits of peasants. Urbanity and politeness (*urbs* is the Latin and *polis* the Greek for town) were opposed to *rus*, the countryside, the home of rusticity. Nor should we forget that the Romans customarily ate reclining on a couch, and that the Middle Ages introduced the dining table, both customs different from those of most Asians and Africans.

The Evolution of Marriage

In the evolution of sensibilities and customs that took place at the beginning of the feudal period, new attitudes to love hold a particularly important place. They were elaborated against the background of a decisive evolution in the concept of marriage. Marriage figured as an important element in the Gregorian reform (to which we shall be returning below) through which the Church bestowed upon it new characteristics that have remained for the most part constant throughout most of Europe, down to the present day. Marriage now became decidedly monogamous, whereas the aristocracy had thitherto practiced a de facto polygamy; it also became indissoluble. It was now difficult to repudiate a wife. The Holy See endeavored to monopolize judgment on this matter. Virtually the only justification for it that it accepted was consanguinity, closely defined down to the fourth degree and over which it maintained a strict control. At the same time and no doubt in reaction to these stricter rules on marriage, adultery, which seemed to be on the increase, was punished extremely severely. No doubt the most important point here is that marriage, which until then had been a civil contract, now increasingly became a religious matter controlled by the Church. The latter managed to reduce the number of "arranged" marriages by ruling that union must be by mutual consent, and thereby improved the status of women, even if the decisions made by families and men remained crucial. In the twelfth century, marriage was classed as one of the sacraments that only priests could administer. The Church's method of controlling marriage and avoiding unions between blood relatives was essentially by getting the Fourth Lateran Council (1215) to make it obligatory to publish bans that were posted up in the church where the ceremony was planned to take place. All the same, the celebration of marriage took some time to penetrate the actual edifice of the church. Right down to the sixteenth century, marriages usually took place outside the church rather than inside it.

Courtly Love

Most noticeable in the evolution of relations between the sexes was the appearance of new forms of love, generally designated by the expression "courtly love," or more restrictively, *fine amor*. These new forms of love were elaborated on the model of feudal rites. As we shall see, in feudality the fundamental rite was that of the vassal paying homage to his lord. In the case of courtly love, it was the woman or lady who held the position of the lord, while the man paid homage and swore loyalty to her. The inception and meaning of courtly love have been the subject of much discussion. It seems certain that the theme was first developed mainly by the Occitan troubadours and probable that it was influenced by Arabic love poetry. But I do not think that those influences should be exaggerated. What is remarkable is that *fine amor* and, to a lesser degree, courtly love can only begin and develop outside the framework of marriage. A typical example is the love between Tristan and Isolde. Courtly love therefore stands in contradiction to the Church's attitude to marriage. In fact, it is sometimes of a quasi-heretical nature. But the great question is whether this was Platonic love or whether it included sexual relations, and to continue that line of questioning, was courtly love real or imaginary, did it develop in real life as lived in medieval society or was it confined to literature? Courtly love undeniably did to some degree affect both the practices of love and the expression of feelings of love in real life. But in my view, it was basically an ideal that made scant impact on real life. Above all, it was an aristocratic kind of love that was most unlikely to be diffused among the masses.

One fundamental question raised by courtly love is whether it really promoted the position of the woman. On this matter, I am much inclined to agree with Jean-Claude Huchet and Georges Duby. Huchet suggests that *fine amor* was used as "an art of using words to hold the woman at a distance," while Georges Duby declares, "In this game, it was really the men who were in control." So it would seem that the homage that courtly love paid to women of the nobility was illusory. Later on, however, we shall be considering the position of the Virgin Mary and the cult addressed to her.

Courtly love was the subject of a handbook that was extremely influential. This was the Treatise on Love (*Tractatus de amore*) produced by André le Chapelain in 1184. Courtly love, and more particularly *fine amore*, may fairly be considered to be an effect of the efforts to civilize human *mores*, mentioned above in connection with table manners. Danielle Régnier-Bohler has even described *fine amor* as a "system for turning the control of desire into an eroticism." Interestingly enough, this civilizing of love clearly did not stop courtly love from making room for grossness and even obscenities, as can be seen particularly in the works of the first great poet of courtly love, William IX of Aquitaine (1071–1126). In a famous work by Denis de Rougemont, courtly love has, notwithstanding, been called a "modern love." The myth of Tristan and Isolde diffused by an abundant literature and also by musical works of genius has kept this prototype of courtly lovers alive in Europe for a very long time.

Abélard and Héloïse: Modern Intellectuals and Lovers

Those lovers include a famous couple that provides a rather different variant of courtly love, but then theirs is a true story. Their names were Abélard and Héloïse and their story is well known. Abélard, a philosopher and teacher nearing middle age, entered upon a passionate love affair with his very youthful pupil Héloïse. In due course their love produced a son. The story could not be more dramatic and romantic. The girl's vengeful family succeeded in having Abélard castrated, after which the lovers were imprisoned, Abélard in the monasteries of first Saint-Denis, then Saint-Gildas de Rhuys, in Brittany, Héloïse in Le Paraclet, an abbey dedicated to the Holy Ghost, in Champagne. The love between the former lovers endured to their deaths, as is testified by the collection of unique and moving letters that they exchanged. The story of Abélard and Héloïse provides answers to a number of questions, but whether these can be generalized is another matter. There can clearly be no doubt that this case of modern love was of a physical nature. It is equally clear that such love tended to develop outside marriage. Abélard did want to regularize his liaison with Héloïse but she, in astonishingly modern terms, argued that it would be too hard for an "intellectual" to work and fulfill himself within a marriage. At this point the problem of courtly love leads on to another twelfth-century question, the problem of the appearance of modern intellectuals. But certainly courtly love, that sentimental and existential creation of the Middle Ages, was one of its features that was to have a great impact on modern Europe.

Kissing on the Lips

Both courtly love and vassalage, the legal expression of feudalism, gave rise
to demonstrations of affection and gestures that created a new sense of ways
to behave that were also destined to persist down the ages in Europe. When
a lord grasped the hands of a vassal and the latter swore an oath of homage
and loyalty, and when a courtly lover expressed homage to his lady and
likewise swore fidelity, both situations involved patterns of behavior that
would be followed for a long time, not just within legal frameworks and in
specific rituals, but in society as a whole. The notion of loyalty would come
to express the strength of new types of personal relationships. They were
profoundly different from the personal connections of antiquity. The principal relationship between men in antiquity was that which linked to a
patron, a powerful figure, subordinates called "clients," who would be at
his service in certain circumstances. The patron–client relationship, which
for the most part was to be revived only in criminal and mafia circles, was
superseded by a system of loyalty. In modern Europe, it was this that would
make it possible for hierarchy and individualism to coexist. Let us not move
on from this world of loyalty and love without drawing attention to the
great future reserved in Europe for the rite that the Middle Ages found to
express such sentiments: kissing on the lips. Initially, such kisses were
exchanged between men, as they were still to be between the Communist
leaders of modern eastern Europe. The kiss of peace, of homage, always a
kiss on the lips, eventually also became the loving kiss, in which form it was
destined to enjoy a fine future in Europe.

The Military Orders: Militarism

It was also in the feudal Europe of the eleventh and twelfth centuries that an
innovation linked with the Crusades appeared in the monastic world: a
profusion of military orders, chief of which were the orders of the Knights
Templar and the Hospitallers of Saint John of Jerusalem, the German order
of Saint Mary of the Teutons, the English order of Saint Thomas of Acre,
and a number of others in the Iberian peninsula, in both Spain and Portugal.
The purpose of these orders was essentially to use the sword, prayer, and
conversion as means to combat infidels and pagans. Their actions represented a startling infringement of the rule according to which clerics were
forbidden to spill blood. The Cistercian Saint Bernard, not usually a man to
welcome innovations, nevertheless praised the knights of what he called the

nova militia engaged in the Crusades. But of course these specific military orders do need to be set within the general climate of a Christianization of military customs. Religion was not exactly military, but it was becoming generally militant. Militancy was another notion destined for a considerable future.

The Gregorian Reform: The Separation of the Clergy from Laymen

This great movement that fundamentally transformed both the Church and Christendom in the eleventh century has been mentioned above. It was named after the pope who inspired it, Gregory VII, pope from 1073 to 1087. Initially, the papacy considered the purpose of the Gregorian reform to be to free the Church from the domination and interventions of the laity, and in particular, to deliver the papacy from the pretensions of the Germanic emperor. But what it brought about, more generally, was a separation between the clergy and the laity, between God and Caesar, pope and emperor. This stood in total opposition to the solution adopted by the Greek Orthodox Christianity of Byzantium, which was governed by a form of Caesaro-papism in which the emperor himself was a kind of pope. It also stood in sharp contrast to the principle of Islamic government, in which no distinction at all was drawn between the religious and the political domains, for Allah dominated and decided everything. In contrast, Latin Christianity, especially from the time of the Gregorian reform on, defined a measure of independence for the laity and its specific responsibilities. The whole reorganization nevertheless remained within a religious framework: in other words, the laity remained part of the Church. However, the division that the Gregorian reform established was to facilitate the future emergence of a secular power over and above the laity, at the time of the Reformation and in late nineteenth-century Europe.

One of the principal directors of the Gregorian reform was Humbert de Silva Candida, who wrote as follows: "Just as the clergy and laymen are separated within sanctuaries by the places that they occupy and the offices that they perform, likewise they should be distinguished in the outside world, according to their respective tasks. Let the laymen devote themselves solely to their own particular task, secular affairs, and let the clergy devote themselves to theirs, that is to say the affairs of the Church. Both groups have been given precise rules." As well as establishing this general principle of a distinction between clerics and laymen, the Gregorian reform defined and established new ways of providing a social framework. Hervé Martin associates a number of essential institutions within that framework: the parish, the baptism of children, the family unit, Christian marriage, the discipline imposed by the acceptance of the Christian sacraments, the regulation of behavior by means of the threat of infernal punishment, and prayers for the dead. Jean-Claude Schmitt has even noted that, at this time, ghosts themselves were said to return in order to expound Gregorian theses. All this will give some idea of the power and depth of this movement, which may be counted among those that were to exert the most long-term influence on European Christendom.

The Battle between Virtues and Vices: The Devil at Large

The eleventh and twelfth centuries were also a period in which profound changes affected religious beliefs and practices. These too left lasting marks on Europe. We have already noted the spread of a combative spirit, and clearly the rise of the class of knights was largely responsible for this. The world of spirituality and piety was also affected, symbolically but deeply, by this spread of combativity. More than ever, the salvation of men and women depended upon the outcome of a conflict that was unceasing: the battle between virtues and vices. The virtues tended to be represented as strongly armed knights, the vices by disorderly pagan warriors. More than ever before, the world of sin was dominated by aggressive assaults on the part of the devil, the "enemy of the whole human race." He was extremely active in this period, when he acquired great popularity and gave rise to increasing fears. In the Early Middle Ages, the Church had banned theatrical performances and the theatre had still not made a comeback; dance, too, was considered as a definitely diabolical activity. Meanwhile though, wildly dramatic scenes were played out in the souls of Christians who were prey to the temptations and assaults of the devil and his demons. Satan led the dance. The devil could even insinuate himself into human beings' bodies and possess them. Manifestations of possession were the ancestors of the late nineteenth-century illnesses that the new exorcists, doctors such as Charcot, or psychologists become psychoanalysts such as Freud, described in scientific, secular terms. As Jérôme Baschet has observed, "The world of the devil allows the expression of hallucinations in many shapes." The devil terrified and tortured men and women with apparitions, hallucinations, and metamorphoses in animal forms – all phantasms that strove constantly to make them sink into sin and become the prey of Hell. The Church certainly took charge of the organization of the battle against the devil and Hell. Exorcism, prayers, and purgatory were all part of the defensive arsenal upon which it drew to fight against Satan. But in this world in which power invariably took imperial forms, Satan was well on the way to becoming what Dante was to call "l'imperador del regno doloroso" (emperor of the sorrowful realm).

Popular Culture

This devil-fixated Europe was also a Christendom in which popular culture was making a reappearance. Christianization had never impinged deeply on the bulk of new Christians, the peasants in particular. The Church had condemned and opposed a whole set of beliefs and patterns of behavior handed down either from Roman antiquity or from the barbarian past, lumping them all together and labeling them paganism. From the eleventh century on, the Church's battle turned into an attack on heretics, demographic and economic growth put more power in the hands of the laity, and seigneurial castles became cultural centers in which lords and peasants alike affirmed their secular identities in the face of the Church. All these factors combined in the emergence or reemergence of popular culture. Most of our knowledge of it is derived from the ecclesiastical texts that condemn it. The first great list of "superstitions" was the Decree produced by Burchard, who was bishop of Worms from 1000 to 1025. It describes the sexual perversions of peasants, their rainmaking ceremonies, and their traditions concerning children who died young, One example shows how old pagan customs and new Christian practices sometimes coincided: "When a child dies before being baptized, certain women take the little one's body, place it some secret place, and drive a stake through it, saying that if they did not do this, the child would rise up again and harm many people." Jean-Claude Schmitt has described how fear of ghosts gave rise to beliefs and rituals that involved ghosts both pagan and Christian. From the end of the twelfth century on, the Church endeavored to use Purgatory to sift out good ghosts from bad ones. In areas where the Church failed to offer cultural practices of a more satisfying nature, popular culture to some extent escaped destruction: dancing, for instance, and masked processions continued to take place. In many cases, though not in all, the Church managed to keep such practices out of the actual church, but they took place all around it. The legend of Saint Marcel of Paris, bishop of Paris in the fifth century, who slew a dragon in the Bièvre district (a Christianization of the old pagan theme of monster-slaying heroes) was still being reenacted in the twelfth century, in a procession that made its way round the church of Notre-Dame de Paris. Similarly, in a society in which the oral tradition was still dominant, popular stories, superficially Christianized, were absorbed into scholarly culture. In the nineteenth and twentieth centuries, eminent folklorists, working mainly in Finland, collected themes of European folklore whose existence, they say, goes back to the Middle Ages. Moving on to the thirteenth century, Jean-Claude Schmitt has described an astonishing belief in a Saint Guinefort, a dog-saint said to protect children, which is to be found in both central France and northern Italy. Pressure from the faithful was such that the Church found itself obliged to tolerate carnival processions. A good description exists of one that took place in thirteenth-century Rome. In the fifteenth and sixteenth centuries this popular culture was to grow richer and even more festive. In the period leading up to Easter it found expression in the carnivalesque and Lenten battles that are magnificently recorded in the paintings of Brueghel the elder. Modern folklorists have shown that this popular culture was certainly European but had absorbed a number of fundamental features from various pre-Christian cultures. It thus played an important role in the dialectic between unity and diversity which is fundamental to European history. A whole range of regional cultures have survived in the forms that they assumed in the Middle Ages (Celtic, Germanic, Slavic, Alpine, Mediterranean, and so on).

Money and Charters

Robert Bartlett has convincingly shown that what he calls medieval "Europeanization" was manifested not only by the cult of saints and their names (the "cultural homogenization of anthroponymy," as he calls it), but also by the diffusion of minting and charters. I imagine that, after Charlemagne's failure, the inability of medieval Christendom to impose the use of a single currency or even a small number of major ones in Europe must have been one of the main obstacles to the constitution of a unified medieval economic area. However, the diversity of currencies should not mask the importance of a recourse to the use of money on the part of many peoples who had never used it before they became a part of Christendom. The minting of coins began east of the Rhine sometime after 900. In the mid-tenth century, the dukes of Bohemia followed suit, as did the Polish princes from about 980 on. Money was introduced in Hungary at the time when the Christian hierarchy was first established (1000–1). Bartlett tells us, "The year 1000 saw the introduction of new currencies across the board from the middle reaches of the Danube to the Baltic and the North Sea." Another means of communication and the diffusion of power throughout Christendom was the production and circulation of charters.

The use of writing played a major role in the process whereby Christendom became unified. We shall later be returning to the subject of a Europe of books. For the moment, following Robert Bartlett, let me simply draw attention to the importance of charters in Christendom. These texts carried a legal authority that was the basis of rights held over land, buildings, individuals, and income. They constituted an essential instrument at the service of the law, wealth, and power, and were produced and circulated throughout Christendom. Most of those who used and drew up these charters were, to be sure, members of the clergy, but the rise of towns and the appearance, initially in southern Christendom, of notaries, now promoted the role of qualified laymen. The use of charters gave rise to institutions that were to play an important role throughout Christendom. These were the chancelleries. The importance of charters can be gauged by the panic that seized King Philip Augustus of France when, at the battle of Fréteval (the town where the charters were stored), the king of England, Richard the Lionheart, took possession of the coffer containing the charters of the French monarchy. It was decided to find a permanent home for such archives, and Saint Louis ordered them to be deposited in a holy place, initially the chapel of Saint-Nicolas, later the Sainte-Chapelle of the Palais Royal. Bartlett draws attention to the fact that charters soon spread to and abounded in the peripheries of Christendom. We find a parallelism between writing and money. The widespread diffusion of charters included cartularies, which were rational collections of charters for practical use, and also collections used as records. The diffusion of these and money was to lead to a shift from a period in which such items were restricted to a sacred use to one in which they were used for general practical purposes. Paradoxically enough, it was Christendom that secularized these instruments of wealth and power in what was to become Europe. In 1194, other means of development and power appeared – means that Charlemagne had envisaged only dimly: urban schools and those new centers of learning, the universities.

Pilgrimages

This Christendom on the move was encapsulated by the extraordinary development of pilgrimages. Traditional historiography portrays the Middle Ages as a static time when peasants stayed attached to their plots of land and most men and women never ventured far from their little native realm, the only exceptions being a few itinerant monks and adventurers who set off for the Crusades. However, recent historiography has replaced this image with one that is certainly more accurate, that of a mobile medieval population, frequently on the road, *in via*, the very embodiment of the Christian definition of man as a traveler, a pilgrim, *homo viator*. Pilgrimages frequently paved the way for new trading activities, but little by little both functions came to be carried out by the same men, or at any rate, pilgrims and traders traveled the same routes, side by side.

As Michel Sot has rightly observed, a pilgrimage was first and foremost an experience involving physical effort, "a journey to somewhere else." But the objectives of that effort were of a spiritual nature; it was a quest for salvation, for forgiveness for one's sins, or for a miracle cure. A medieval pilgrimage was also a penance. After the year 1000 and above all in the twelfth and thirteenth centuries, when Christendom was swept by a wave of penitence, pilgrimages caught a second wind. A pilgrim was an expatriate, a voluntary exile, and that ascetic aspect conferred a spiritual quality upon the earliest of these figures, initially regarded as suspect but later much appreciated, such as merchants and the students who were always moving on from one school or university to another. Of course, the traveling in itself was not enough to justify a pilgrimage; it had to have a sacred goal. A widespread network of pilgrimages developed throughout Christendom, as did a hierarchy of the destinations to which pilgrims would make their way, seeking spiritual contact with the god or saint that they went to revere, along with a physical contact with his tomb or place of death. As early as 333, Gallic pilgrims had produced *An Itinerary from Bordeaux to Jerusalem*, and in 384 the Spanish nun Egeria dictated a journal of her own voyage to the Holy Places. Jerusalem was thus the first major place of pilgrimage. Who, after all, could deny the position of the greatest importance to Christ who became man and to his Holy Sepulchre? However, a journey to Jerusalem was not within everyone's means. It was so far away, it took so long to get there, the cost of the journey was so high, and Palestine was constantly ravaged by outbreaks of violence against those who had laid claim to it, first the Romans, then the Byzantines and the Persians, and finally the Muslims.

There was thus a second fundamental place of pilgrimage, Rome, where lay the bodies of the Church's two founding saints, Peter and Paul. Rome could also offer pilgrims the tombs of martyrs and of other Christians in its catacombs and the cemeteries outside the city, as well as churches of great beauty, many of them adorned by superb frescoes. Beyond the city walls were Saint Peter's in the Vatican, Saint Paul's positioned on the road leading to Ostia, and the churches of Saint Lawrence and Saint Agnes bordering other major Roman roads. Within the walls too, the churches of Saint Saviour of Lateran and Santa Maria Maggiore on the Esquiline had already been built. Speeding up the movement of urban burials, which was a major characteristic of Christianity, right down to the mid-ninth century popes were arranging for the bodies of saints to be brought to Rome to be reburied there, inside the city. They actively encouraged pilgrimages to Rome, and had buildings specially erected to house the pilgrims who flocked there. In the Early Middle Ages many of them were Irish or Anglo-Saxon. (Making a chronological jump, this seems the point at which to mention that the medieval high point of pilgrimages to Rome was, with the encouragement of the papacy, to be 1300, when Pope Boniface VIII instigated Jubilee celebrations. On this occasion, the great press of pilgrims, who were attracted by the promise of indulgences and remission of punishment for their sins, marked the climax of the medieval enthusiasm for pilgrimages, and possibly also a presentiment of the attacks to which the Church would be subjected by the Reformation in the sixteenth century.)

The third major holy place that was a focus of medieval piety was also in a peripheral region of Christendom, Santiago de Compostela, in Spanish Galicia. The saint's body, carried from Palestine in a boat that was shipwrecked on the Galician coast, was discovered there in the early ninth century. Not until the tenth century did the pilgrimage really take off. It was encouraged by Christendom's greatest religious order, that of Cluny. A work of exceptional interest, a *Guide for Pilgrims of Saint James*, was composed between 1130 and 1140.

The whole of Christendom was crisscrossed with pilgrimage routes, and the fame of a number of other sacred places should not be forgotten. One was Tours, where Saint Martin, who had died in 397 and was extremely popular throughout Christendom, was entombed. It attracted a number of the greatest of figures ranging from Charlemagne to Philip Augustus to Richard the Lionheart. Saint Louis came here three times. Other great pilgrimage centers were places where Saint Michael, the bodiless archangel who left no relics, was said to have appeared, Saint Michael being the archangel of high places and symbolizing flight up to Heaven. By the fifth century his cult was well established at Monte Gargano in southern Italy. In Normandy, one popular pilgrimage was to the Mont Saint-Michel, a site that was most impressive to a society that feared the sea. The pilgrimage became known as that of Saint Michael-in-peril-of-the-sea. In the fifteenth century, Mont Saint-Michel, where the French garrison had resisted the English throughout the Hundred Years' War, turned Saint Michael into a kind of French national saint. Mont Saint-Michel was also well known for its children's pilgrimages from the fourteenth century on, at a time when the idea of the child and the cult of the Infant Jesus were very popular in medieval society. From the eleventh century on, the Virgin Mary became the object of veneration in the many pilgrimages inspired by the extraordinary popularity of the cult devoted to her. In Chartres, her shift was an object of devotion. Sanctuaries consecrated to the Virgin Mary appeared in Boulogne and Liesse in France, in Montserrat in Spain, in Hal in Belgium, in Walsingham in England, in Aix-la-Chapelle in Germany, and in Mariazell in Austria. The huge success of the pilgrimage to Rocamadour in the diocese of Cahors, in the twelfth century, provides a good example of the popularity of pilgrimages consecrated to the Virgin. The chapel was situated on an impressive site, at the top of a rocky cliff overlooking a narrow valley 120 meters below, from which, in the thirteenth century, pilgrims on their knees climbed the 197 steps to the top, meanwhile reciting the rosary. This pilgrimage owed its success partly to King Henry II Plantagenet of England, who visited Rocamadour twice, in 1159 and 1170, and partly to a record of the miracles performed by the Virgin, produced in 1172. This was a royal pilgrimage that also attracted a number of French kings. Louis IX (Saint Louis) came in 1244, accompanied by his mother Blanche of Castile, and his brothers Alphonse of Poitiers, Robert of Artois, and Charles of Anjou; Philip the Fair came in 1303, Charles the Fair and Queen Marie of Luxemburg in 1323, Philip VI in 1336, and Louis XI in 1443 and 1464. It also attracted the piety of the kings of Castile, in particular Alfonso VIII, Blanche of Castile's father, and his wife Eleanor of England, the daughter of King Henry II Plantagenet. In 1181, Alfonso and Eleanor presented the Blessed Mary of Rocamadour with two villages situated near Burgos. By the twelfth century, pilgrims were flocking to Rocamadour from all over Europe and from as far afield as the Baltic States.

Feudal Fragmentation and Monarchical Centralization

In the political domain, eleventh- and twelfth-century Christendom presented an apparently contradictory spectacle, traces of which nevertheless survived almost down to the present day in Europe and are to a certain extent now reappearing in conjunction with contemporary policies of decentralization. On the one hand, a feudal society was becoming established that was partly characterized by a weakening of the central power. The latter had seemed impressive in the Carolingian period, but now the exercise of authority was fragmented thanks to the seigneurial lords, who were usurping so-called regal rights. One was the right to mint coins (although in this particular period, this was not yet a very important issue), but others, more importantly, were the rights to administer justice and to levy taxes. On the other hand, after the short-lived Carolingian experience, the people of Christendom were trying to regroup around central leaders who were finding ways of reconciling the power that remained to them with the feudal fragmentation. Historians have traditionally been inclined above all to stress the apparent incompatibility between a centralized state and a feudal system. The more subtle reality is that compromise political systems were introduced: these may be called feudal monarchies. The existence of these monarchies, which left the future Europe many legacies, presupposed a number of fundamental factors. In the Christendom of the feudal period, two powers were recognized to be superior to the kings who headed the monarchies. One was that of the pope, the other that of the emperor. Here, another apparent contradiction arises, this time in connection with papal power. This was a period during which papal power was on the increase. It would even be fair to say that by the end of it, under Pope Innocent III (pope 1198–1216), the papacy had become the most powerful of all the Christian monarchies. It had a vast network at its disposal: the central agencies of the Holy See, which throughout Christendom obeyed the papacy, had grown increasingly strong, and most importantly of all, perhaps, throughout Christendom the Holy See levied dues that assured it of financial means greater than those of any other monarchy. On the other hand, the Holy See and the Church respected the outcome of the Gregorian reform, which proved definitive despite all Gregory VII's attempts to impose the domination of the Church upon the secular states. The separation between spiritual and temporal power truly held, even though, in certain cases, as for example marriages considered to be incestuous, the Church did in general impose its will. Furthermore, the Holy See and the Church had rapidly elaborated a policy of collaboration with those monarchies and lent their regimes important support.

The Prestige and the Weakness of the Emperor

The development and power of these feudal monarchies might, equally, have been limited by the existence of another superior, but in his case, secular figure, namely the emperor. But the emperor of the Germanic Holy Roman Empire was not powerful enough to impose his domination upon those young and vigorous monarchies. The new kings paid him homage in a number of theoretical respects. But independence from the empire and the emperor was a major political development in this period. Eventually, the situation was clarified by a number of significant statements such as the following declaration made by Philip Augustus, in France, in the thirteenth century: "The king of France recognizes no superior within his kingdom." A century later, Philip the Fair confirmed this, specifying,

"A king is emperor in his own kingdom." The kings of France may have insisted upon the independence of their monarchy vis-à-vis the empire in the most trenchant fashion, but from the twelfth century on the same situation obtained generally, throughout Christendom.

The Medieval King

It is important to have a clear idea of the characteristics of the medieval king not only in order to understand this period, but also because many of those characteristics were transferred to republican and democratic rulers and were to survive either as functions or at least as images. A feudal king was a human image of God, *Rex imago Dei*. Obviously, this aspect was to fade away between the nineteenth and the twenty-first centuries, but many modern European governments preserved certain privileges that stemmed from the sacred position of kingship, such as the right to grant pardons and the right to legal immunity. The medieval kings were trifunctional, that is to say they concentrated in their persons the three Indo-European functions that defined the overall functioning of a society by dividing it into three different categories of people. The king embodied the first function, namely the religious one, in that, although he was not a priest, he did exercise one essential part of that function, the dispensation of justice. As king, he also possessed the second, military, function, for he was a noble and a warrior (today's president of the French Republic is the supreme commander of its armies, admittedly more in a political than in a military capacity). Finally, the king also fulfilled the third function, although in a way that is harder to define. This third function, characterized by work according to the medieval formula, affected the prosperity and beauty of a society. The king was thus responsible for the economy, that is to say the prosperity of the kingdom, and was personally obliged to perform acts of compassion, which involved abundant distributions of alms. Finally, presumably this third function also bestowed upon the king a special duty to encourage the construction of churches, although this aspect is perhaps less clear.

A medieval king also had to make his mark in the domain of learning and culture. John of Salisbury, the future bishop of Chartres, when defining monarchy in his important treatise *The Policraticus* (1159), repeated an idea already expressed by William of Malmesbury in 1125: Rex illiteratus quasi asinus coronatus (an illiterate king is little more than a crowned ass).

The position of a feudal king was also affected by other important developments in this period. From Roman law and Roman history, he had inherited the powers constituted by *auctoritas* and *potestas*, which, respectively, defined the nature of his power and the means to exercise it. To these, Christianity had added the *dignitas* that characterized all ecclesiastical or other eminent functions. The feudal period, possibly in reaction, witnessed a revival of Roman law and resuscitated the Roman notion of *majestas*, to the advantage of the new kings. *Majestas* made it possible to define two of the powers held by these kings. One, the right to grant mercy, has been mentioned above. The other, even more important, was the right to protection against the *crimen majestatis*, treason. However, a medieval king was not an absolute ruler. Some historians have wondered whether he was a constitutional king. But that is not the case, for there is no known text that can be considered to be a constitution. Perhaps the closest to come to such a text is Magna Carta, which the nobility and ecclesiastical hierarchy imposed upon John Lackland, king of England, in 1215; but it is unique. Magna Carta certainly represents one of the stepping stones that led Europe to constitutional regimes. The important truth of the matter is that a medieval king was a contractual monarch. In the oath that he swore at his consecration and coronation, he committed himself to God, the Church, and his people. As history has evolved, those first two contracts have become null and void, but the third marks another stepping stone on the way to the establishment of power for the people, or at least for the organ that represents them. Finally, both in theory and in practice, the king was above all responsible for a twofold function, that of justice and peace. The second of those two terms might be translated, rather, as order, but this was an order that was not concerned solely with tranquility here on earth; it also covered the onward march to salvation. At any rate, feudal monarchy set Christendom on the path leading toward what we today call the law-governed state. Less important in the long term is the fact that feudal monarchy was aristocratic, so that, since the king was the first of all the nobles, it helped to legitimate blood nobility. Today, that aspect plays no more than an anecdotal role; but in the Middle Ages it was factor of continuity and stability, since it favored the existence of royal dynasties. Moreover, in a kingdom such as France, the exclusion of women from the throne – which came to be known only in the fourteenth century, in a spirit of antiquarianism, as the Salic Law – contributed to the solidity of the monarchy, since, by biological chance, an unbroken string of royal sons was produced from the end of the tenth century right down to the fourteenth.

It is thanks to this last aspect that feudal monarchy can be placed within a long-term view of Europe. The twelfth century was a *great legal century*. Even more important than the revival of Roman law, of which we have all along been aware, was the definitive elaboration of canonical law, based on a Decree produced by the monk Gratian of Bologna between 1130 and

1140. This law not only reflected the Christianization of the spirit and apparatus of the judicature and the role that the Church played in providing a framework for society; it also legitimated certain legal innovations that had been introduced in response to the evolution of society and the problems that this had raised (problems to do with marriage and economic matters, for example).

The Feudal Monarchies

Not all these monarchies achieved the same degree of development and stability, so the bases of the future nations were not established equally solidly throughout Europe. In the world of northern, Scandinavian Christendom and in the Slavic and Hungarian Christendom of central and eastern Europe, the monarchies lacked solid territorial bases. Germany and Italy were split up into many different powers, the most important of which were based on towns. (We shall be returning to these.) That leaves England, France, and, in the Iberian peninsula, Castile. To these we may add another monarchy, of an unusual nature, which only survived until the nineteenth century but the memory of which is part of the long-term image of Europe. This was the kingdom of southern Italy and Sicily, which was formed, precisely, in the medieval period.

In England

In the eleventh and twelfth centuries the kingdom of England experienced changes of fortune which, far from weakening it, strengthened its institutions. Thanks chiefly to the intellectual and literary activity of King Alfred in the ninth century, and the exceptional personality of Edward the Confessor in the eleventh (ruled 1042–66), the Anglo-Saxon period laid a number of institutional bases. Duke William of Normandy's conquest of England in 1066 marked the beginning of a significant strengthening of the English monarchy. The government of the Norman kings of England drew support from an extraordinary text, The Domesday Book (or, more accurately, The Domesday Survey), which contained a detailed and precise inventory of the possessions of the English crown. The very name underlines the exceptional character of this work, which describes England at the end of the eleventh century, laying emphasis on the accountability of the monarchy, set on its course to the Last Judgment and Salvation. This text made possible a rational distribution of lands and revenues to the conquering Norman aristocracy, and thereby sustained the economic development that helped to turn England into the foremost great European monarchy. Over the tenth and eleventh centuries the Duchy of Normandy had developed an administrative system remarkable for its time, and the Norman kings who inherited the duchy transferred this to England, as a means of implementing the king's determination to exercise a centralized control there. Royal agents, in the form of sheriffs, now appeared in the English counties, while around the king a bureaucracy of specialists was set up, most notable for the activities of financial officers centered on the Exchequer, where they kept the kingdom's accounts.

In the mid-twelfth century, the development of the English monarchy received a second stimulus. Following a troubled period after the death of Henry I in 1135, his daughter Matilda married Geoffrey Plantagenet, the count of Anjou. Their son, Henry II (ruled 1154–89) became king of England and also controlled a vast territory in France, composed of Anjou, Poitou, Normandy, and Guyenne. Henry II's England was the first "modern" kingdom of Christendom. The terms "Angevin empire" and "Plantagenet empire" have sometimes been used, but this was no empire. This remarkable king clashed not only with his wife, Eleanor of Aquitaine, but also with his sons, Richard the Lionheart and John Lackland. (The latter was born after the royal estates had already been divided between his elder brothers, Henry the Younger, who died before his father, and Richard. The feudal custom of dividing up property between the king's sons had been retained in England, whereas in France the Capetians resolved the problem with a system of appanages whereby property reverted to the royal domain when a prince died.) Thanks to the heavy hand of the royal administration, Henry II became known even in his lifetime as a monarch whose court, extremely well organized and flocked to by the entire nobility, now brought to heel, was described as a very hell. It was the beginning of a Europe of monarchies and courts, with all their attendant prestige, intrigues, and conflicts. This was the image of monarchy in Europe for centuries to come.

In France

The other monarchy that became as stable as the English monarchy and at an equally early date was the French one. Its stability stemmed, in the first place, from the dynastic continuity of its kings: the Capetian dynasty had reigned in France ever since 987. It was strengthened by the fact that women were excluded from the throne, and that, by a biological fluke, the kings of France produced a continuous string of male heirs right down to 1328. This was a Europe where primogeniture reigned. At first, the French kings were mainly occupied in stamping out disobedience among the minor lords within the royal domain. Next, they made sure of the support of councilors selected from the clergy and the minor nobility, who managed to keep the higher aristocracy away from power. Eventually the Capetians stabilized their seat of power by building a royal palace in Paris and making this town their capital. This was a Europe of capitals. The Capetian monarchy was also strengthened by the support of a powerful Benedictine abbey situated close to their palace. The abbey of Saint-Denis was a great historiographical center, which devoted itself to the Capetian cause. In the thirteenth and fourteenth centuries it produced a series of great national chronicles. This was a Europe of history and historiography.

The Capetian monarchy made the most of a number of trump cards. The first was the consecration of the king in Reims, at the beginning of his reign. This ceremony brought to mind the exceptional character of the Frankish monarchy, which had been baptized in Reims, in the person of Clovis, by a miraculous oil brought down from heaven by the Holy Ghost in the form of a dove. This miraculous liquid then became the oil of consecration. The Capetians also cashed in on the growing prestige of the Virgin. The symbolic fleur-de-lys and the color blue of the king's cloak had been borrowed by the kings of France from the Virgin Mary, whose cult took off in spectacular fashion between the eleventh and the thirteenth centuries. Already at the time of Robert the Pious (ruled 996–1031), the fleur-de-lys figured on the royal shield. Whereas the kings of England had alienated the Church by the murder of Thomas Becket, the archbishop of Canterbury (1170), in France the alliance between Church and king, throne and altar, was the abiding basis of political stability.

In Castile

In the Iberian peninsula a third monarchy emerged among Christendom's various powers. In the course of the *Reconquista*, the mosaic of kingdoms that appeared as the Christians chased the Muslims further and further south underwent a simplification. Castile, above all, benefited from this. First it fused with Navarre; then when, in 1017, Ferdinand the count of Castile defeated the king of León, it took possession of León. When León became part of Castile in 1037, Ferdinand assumed the title of king of Castile and León (although this union did not become definitive until 1230). The kings of Castile had to cope with the warrior nobility, which produced a figure characteristic of the ambiguity of the situation in the peninsula. Sometimes he fought in the service of the Christian kings, sometimes for the Muslims. His name was Rodrigo Díiaz de Vivar. He was brought up with Sancho II, the future king of Castile and, as the Cid (1043–1099), became a legendary hero of warrior and chivalric mythology. We shall return to him later.

The kings of Castile nevertheless gradually built up their power by looking beyond the aristocracy and winning over the urban oligarchy of the towns of Castile, by creating assemblies (known as Cortés) and by the concession of local rights (fueros) to communities of city-dwellers and non-nobles. At the expense of Toledo, which Alfonso of Castile won from the Muslims in 1085, the kings of Castile tried to impose a capital at Burgos, where the bishopric had enjoyed exemption from direct dependence on the pope since 1104. In the mid-thirteenth century, Burgos received the official title of "head of Castile and the king's chamber" (cabeza de Castilla y de los reyes).

The Normans

To those three principal monarchies that prefigured the monarchical Europe of the future, an unexpected fourth should be added: it was constituted by the diaspora of the Normans, the medieval name given to the Scandinavians, who represented one of the period's important elements. A few, in truth somewhat unstable, monarchies had been established in Scandinavia (a handbook for a royal prince was produced in Norway in the thirteenth century); and a group of Vikings had established themselves in French Normandy, from where, in the first half of the eleventh century, they proceeded to launch a partial and ephemeral conquest of England, under Cnut the Great (who died in 1035). But furthermore, at the end of the eleventh century this astonishing diaspora also created a kingdom in southern Italy. Between 1041 and 1071, they seized Calabria and Apulia from the Byzantines. Then in 1071, Robert Guiscard captured Bari, to which, in 1087, sailors brought the body of Saint Nicholas. It was placed in a superb basilica from which the cult of the saint, the patron of infants and school-children, spread throughout Europe. By 1137 the kingdom extended to Naples and to Sicily, where, by 1072, the Normans had conquered Palermo and by 1086 had also seized Syracuse.

A period of bitter conflict with the papacy followed, earning Roger I (1031–1101) the label of tyrant, which was at this time bestowed upon bad kings, in memory of the tyrants of antiquity. Thereafter, however, the Norman kings of Sicily became reconciled with the papacy and this became one of the most brilliant of all the Christian kingdoms. It had been wrenched from the Byzantines and the Muslims and at last restored southern Italy and Sicily to European Christendom. Roger II (ca. 1095–1154) was crowned king in 1130, after transferring the seat of power to Palermo.

The last Norman king of Sicily, William II (1154–1189), died childless, and the crown passed to his aunt Constance, along with her husband, the son of Frederick Barbarossa, who in 1191 became Emperor Henry VI. When he died prematurely in 1197, he left the kingdom of Naples and Sicily to his son, the future Frederick II. Continuing and even surpassing the efforts of his Norman ancestors, Frederick turned his kingdom into one of the best organized of the feudal monarchies. Palermo became the only town in Christian Europe that could compete with the great Byzantine and Muslim towns. From a cultural and artistic point of view, much translation work was done, with Christians, Jews, and Muslims all in constant collaboration, making Palermo not only an exemplary but also an exceptional capital of Christian Europe. At the end of the thirteenth century, the kingdom of southern Italy and Sicily was briefly conquered by the French (Saint Louis's brother Charles of Anjou (1227–1285) became king in 1268), then in 1282 it was conquered, more lastingly, by the Aragonese, after a massacre of the French known as the "Sicilian Vespers." Had those conquests not taken place, this unusual section of Mediterranean Christendom might well have become either independent or else an integral part of the Byzantine or Muslim world. Its example shows that the geography and history of Europe were not necessarily a foregone conclusion.

The Twelfth-Century European Renaissance

The period from the eleventh to the twelfth century was marked by an essential transformation in Christian Europe. This renaissance of the twelfth century has been generally recognized since the publication in 1927 of a work by the American historian Charles Haskins. Although, as we have seen, the people of the Middle Ages tended generally to camouflage their innovations by speaking of them in terms of a renaissance of ancient culture, the changes that took place in Christendom at this time in truth amounted to very much more than this. Taking a long-term view of European history, I should like to draw attention to the importance, during this period, of the birth or decisive development of a new culture and new attitudes. The first features to mention are the feminization and, as I shall explain, the "dolorization" of Christianity. These were accompanied by the extraordinary rise of the cult of the Virgin Mary and a new prevailing emphasis in the cult of

Christ, who was now regarded not as the Christ who overcame death, but as a Christ of suffering, the Christ of the Passion and the Crucifix.

I shall endeavor to show how a new, positive, Christian humanism emerged and came to constitute a new layer in the long elaboration of western European humanism. This humanism affirmed the standing of man. Made in the image of God, he was no longer just a sinner crushed by original sin. The eleventh and, even more, the twelfth centuries redefined not only the Christian faith, transformed but as ever vital and vibrant, but also two other essential concepts that were to provide the framework for western European thought: the notion of nature and the notion of reason.

Finally, I shall consider the recent ideas of Robert I. Moore, who detects in this period an affirmation of what he calls "the first European revolution." It was manifested positively by a surge forward in the economy of society and in learning, and negatively by efforts to restore order, which revealed an underlying Europe of persecution and exclusion.

The Rise of the Cult of the Virgin Mary

Between the eleventh and the thirteenth centuries Europe was deeply affected by the extraordinary development of the cult of the Virgin Mary, the "Mother of God." In Greek Orthodox Christianity the cult had developed at a very early date. In the Christian West it made its way more slowly. Mary had certainly been present in western Christianity even in the Early Middle Ages, particularly during the Carolingian period. However, not until the eleventh century did she acquire a place of central importance in the beliefs and practices of western Christianity. Between the mid-eleventh century and the mid-twelfth, the cult of the Virgin lay at the heart of Church reform. It was linked to an increasingly fervent devotion to Christ and particularly to the Eucharist. The Virgin was, of course, essential to the Incarnation and over the years she came to play an ever more important role in relations between human beings and Christ. She acted as the almost exclusive intermediary between human beings and her son. Whereas most saints specialized in the healing of specific illnesses or in one particular social function, the Virgin performed every kind of miracle. She could deal most effectively with all the problems that beset men and women. In fact, she was such a key figure in procuring the salvation of human beings that she was said even to offer her protection in shocking or scandalous circumstances. She protected criminals and sinners whose crimes and sins seemed inexcusable. She pleaded for them and Christ acceded to his mother's intercessions, however exorbitant they might be.

The Virgin thus seems to me to have acquired a quite exceptional status, almost becoming a fourth element in the Trinity. Three major Christian festivals were devoted to her: the Purification (Candlemas), the Annunciation, and the Assumption. Candlemas, celebrated on February 2, masked an old pagan festival devoted to the revival of nature and the end of the bear's period of hibernation. It also marked the churching of women and prolonged the Jewish rites of lying-in forty days after giving birth to a child. This festival was also linked with the presentation of the child Jesus in the Temple. But there was more to it still: this was a festival of purification and, as such, it posed a problem that was disturbing both to the Church and to Christians generally, particularly in the fourteenth century. Could it be that Mary, as a human creature, a woman, defiled by pregnancy and childbirth, was tainted by original sin? Belief in the immaculate birth of Mary herself did not triumph until the nineteenth century; but I think that it reflects the tendency of men and women of the Middle Ages to promote Mary to a status equivalent to that of her divine son.

The Annunciation (Lady Day, March 25) brought Mary, and through her, humanity in general, the news of the imminent Incarnation of the son of God. This prophetic dialogue between the Virgin and the Angel Gabriel also established a prototype. It was one of the great moments in human history and for painting, as Erwin Panofsky demonstrated in 1927, as did Daniel Arasse, in greater depth, in 1999. The Annunciation launched the subject that was represented in European painting for the first time in 1344, by Ambrogio Lorenzetti of Siena.

The third great festival in honor of the Virgin Mary was that of the Assumption (August 15). This constituted an echo of the Ascension of Christ. Here again, from the moment of her earthly death, Mary is elevated not just to Paradise but to the zenith of the heavens, where God is enthroned and she is crowned by her son.

The twelfth century onward produced a great surge of pious literature dedicated to Mary. A twelfth-century prayer, the *Ave Maria*, acquired a status comparable to that of "Our Father." The subsequent more or less constant inclusion of this prayer, from 1215 on, in the penances assigned to sinners making their annual confession, made the cult of Mary a part of the fundamental piety of Christians. Of the many works dedicated to her, two were exceptional: one was a collection of miracles assembled by Gautier of Coincy (1177–1236), containing 58 miracles, several pious songs, and a number of sermons composed in verse; the other was an illustrated collection of remarkable miniatures which the king of Castile, Alfonso X the Wise, offered to the Virgin, together with a pious poem entitled *Las Cantigas de Santa Maria*, composed in Galician, the poetic language of the Iberian peninsula.

It is important to note how greatly the cult of the Virgin Mary benefited from the extraordinarily dazzling iconography of the period. Miniatures and sculptures introduced a whole treasury of images of the Virgin Mary to the eyes and hearts of the men and women of the Middle Ages. The principal themes for the representation of the Virgin evolved in the course of the Middle Ages. The Romanesque Virgin was above all a mother, with her divine child seated on her knees. She then became an icon of feminine beauty. She was also a key element in the "dolorization" of Christianity, a *pietà* holding her dead son, Christ, across her knees, and a Virgin of mercy who protected individual figures, or frequently groups, within the folds of her vast cloak. Despite the check to the cult of the Virgin Mary effected by the Reformation, for centuries the Virgin has been the mother and advocate of the human race throughout Europe. A whole cycle of artistic works devoted to the Virgin was produced, linked with those devoted to Christ, but in which the figure of the Virgin became increasingly dominant. The cult of the Virgin Mary produced many Books of Hours, chiefly intended for the private devotions of women. The Virgin became the foremost revered player in the greatest event in history, the Incarnation. As with all important historical phenomena, her cult took root in a whole network of places. These were not constituted simply by the places of pilgrimages where the relics of saints lay, mentioned above, but included places of worship newly dedicated to "Our Lady," *Notre Dame*, the name that was now given to the majority of Christendom's cathedrals. In most cases the dedication was quite simply changed, as in the case of the cathedral of Paris, which abandoned the original dedication to Saint Stephen and became Notre-Dame de Paris.

The cult of the Virgin Mary presents the historian with one more problem. Did its popularity benefit the position of women on earth? Did it turn out to be the basis and inspiration for the promotion of women in the medieval West? That is not an easy question to answer and the opinions of historians on this matter remain divided. But in my view, the Virgin, set in opposition to Eve, the sinner, has indeed become the image of woman rehabilitated and dispensing salvation. Bearing in mind that the cult of the Virgin Mary arose at about the time when marriage was transformed into a sacrament, and a greater value came to be placed on children and closely knit families, as they are portrayed in pictures of the Nativity, one cannot but see the Virgin as a great promoter of a woman's earthly lot. The status of women *was* improved thanks to this cult, just as it was by the rise of courtly love. "Our Lady" was, in the highest degree, also the knight's lady, the "lady" of men in general, a shimmering feminine figure in the divine and human world of medieval society.

The "Dolorization" of Religious Devotion to Christ

The cult of the Virgin Mary had led to a feminization of piety and this was combined with what I have called its "dolorization." In the historical evolution of the image of God, Christ had for many years been represented, in the tradition of the heroes of antiquity, as the conqueror of death, a Christ triumphant. Now he was replaced by a suffering Christ, a Christ of pain. It is not easy to follow this evolution or to understand its causes. However, there can be no doubt that, now that military victory was not regarded as a sign of the elect, whatever contributed to this, so to speak, demilitarization of the figure of Christ certainly stripped the image of Christ of its triumphal aspect. Meanwhile in what seems to me to have been a continuing tendency to distinguish between the respective roles of the three persons of the Trinity and the Virgin, God the Father, who absorbed the image of majesty, also became associated with the evolution of the powers of earthly kings. At the same time, influenced in particular by the mendicant orders of the early thirteenth century, the Church, through its works of compassion, brought a more fraternal gaze to bear upon the humble, the sick, and above all, the poor. The rallying cry of the evangelical reawakening that now made itself felt within the Church and was communicated to certain of the laity was "naked, follow the naked Christ." Here again, iconography both bore witness to this development and played an active part in it. The Cross had been the emblem of Christians ever since the earliest days of Christianity, but the eleventh century saw the beginning of the spread of the image of the crucifix.

The Christ now most revered was the Christ of the Passion, a suffering Christ. Iconography diffused new images of that Christ, images which, in a mixture of symbolism and realism, included representations of the instruments of the Passion. Images of not only the crucifixion but also the deposition and the entombment prepared the way for the meditations on death that fueled the fourteenth-century human fascination with the macabre. A Europe of corpses and, slightly later, skulls encompassed the whole of Christendom.

Man in the Image of God: Christian Humanism

Meanwhile, in the twelfth century and after, Christianity was ever more energetically purveying a new image of man in relation to God. In the Early Middle Ages man felt annihilated before God. Man's best symbol was Job, humiliated and prostrated, as Gregory the Great had described him in the sixth to seventh century. Now a great theological work written by Saint Anselm of Canterbury (1033–1109) marked a turning point: this was *Cur deus homo?* (Why was God made man?). New interpretations of the Bible prompted reflection on the text of Genesis. Theologians, canonists and preachers were all struck by the text in Genesis which declares that God made man in his own image, to resemble him. This human image of God survived the defilement brought about by original sin. The objective of salvation was now preceded by the efforts that human beings made, already here on earth, to embody that resemblance to God. That resemblance now became the basis of Christian humanism, which appealed to two elements that had been more or less confused ever since the beginnings of Christianity even by the Church Fathers and Saint Augustine himself. Those two elements were Nature and Reason. In the Early Middle Ages, a symbolic concept of nature predominated. Saint Augustine tended to absorb the natural in the supernatural, and still in the twelfth century, jurists such as Gratian assimilated Nature to God ("Nature, that is to say God"). The distinction between the natural and the supernatural, and the definition of nature as a specific physical and cosmological world developed in the twelfth century. It was strongly influenced by the ideas of Jews and Arabs, in particular by their introduction into the West of works of the forgotten Greek antiquity, above all those in which Aristotle expounds his notion of the sublunary region. The idea of nature pervaded the whole of human thought and behavior. For example, homosexuality was condemned all the more strongly because it was said to be "a sin against nature" (a subject to which we shall be returning).

In the twelfth century, along with Nature, Reason, even more characteristic of the human condition, was promoted. For the Church Fathers and particularly for Saint Augustine, the concept of reason was likewise vague, confused and polysemic. It was again Saint Anselm, at the dawn of the twelfth century, who called for a better definition of reason. What he proposed to Christians was "fides quaerens intellectum" (faith in quest of intelligence). In the early twelfth century, the great theologian Hugh of Saint-Victor divided reason into superior reason, directed toward transcendent reality, and inferior reason, directed toward the material, earthly world. Father M. D. Chenu has shown that the evolution of twelfth-century theology followed the general evolution of methods of textual analysis (grammar, logic, and dialectic). Christianity was moving toward scholasticism.

Twelfth-century humanism was also founded on a development of introspection. The elaboration of the theme "Know yourself, Christian" has sometimes been called Christian Socratism. Scholars have noted that this Socratism was based on a new concept of sin, a morality of intention, and that this led to the kind of introspection instituted in 1215 by the Fourth Lateran Council. Taking a variety of sometimes opposed forms, this humanism is an element in the thinking of nearly all the great minds of the thirteenth century, across the board from Abélard to Saint Bernard, William of Conches and John of Salisbury.

This humanism took shape at the heart of an upheaval that Robert I. Moore has described as "the first European revolution," which seems to have developed between the tenth and the thirteenth centuries. Moore maintains that Europe was born in the second millennium, not the first. In my opinion he exaggerates the importance of the Europe of the eleventh to thirteenth centuries, at the expense of the Early Middle Ages. I hope to show that the two periods produced two strata that were equally important, even decisive, for the elaboration of Europe. According to Moore,

> it was the consequent combination of rapacity, curiosity, and ingenuity that pushed these Europeans to exploit their lands and their workers ever more intensively and ceaselessly to extend the power and influence of their governmental institutions, thereby eventually creating the conditions necessary for the development of capitalism, industry, and their empires. For better or worse, that was the central event not only for European history but for modern history as a whole.

I believe that, for all the obvious exaggeration, Moore does put his finger on an important idea that draws attention to a great turning point in the construction of Europe. I shall be analyzing that turning point in the next chapter, which is devoted to the thirteenth century, for I think that it is only in the thirteenth century that one can really appreciate the full scope of this construction of a Europe that was based mainly on towns but at the same time now witnessed the beginning of a slowdown in the lively surge of activity of the twelfth century, when western Europe was really bubbling over.

The Birth of a Europe of Persecution

We must now tackle the dire consequences and adverse results of that buoyancy and effervescence. Here again, Robert I. Moore has lucidly identified what he calls the birth of "persecuting society." What happened? The Christians of the West, who for many years had been in a fragile position and had suffered from a sense of insecurity, became more assured both materially and from an intellectual and religious point of view. They may not all have believed, as Otto of Freising did, that Christendom had reached a state of quasi-perfection, but they had become sure of themselves and, consequently, expansive and even aggressive. Above all, they wished to eliminate any burgeoning defilement that would threaten the solidity and success of Christendom. Hence a concerted series of operations, initiated by both the Church and the secular authorities, which were designed to marginalize and, in the last resort, exclude from Christendom all those who sowed seeds of dissent and impurity. The principal victims of these persecutions were in the first instance heretics, but also Jews, homosexuals, and lepers.

The Heretics

From virtually the very start, the history of Christianity was accompanied by that of heresy. Little by little, the new religion, chiefly by means of ecclesiastical councils, defined its official doctrine. In the face of this orthodoxy, a number of different "choices" (which is the meaning of the word "heresy") developed, and sooner or later the Church condemned them. Some of these heresies concerned the Christian dogma. That was particularly the case of opinions that did not place the three persons of the Trinity all on the same level, for these failed to recognize either Jesus' divine nature or else his human nature. Other heresies concerned ecclesiastical *mores* and were of a markedly social nature. One example is provided by Donatism, in North Africa, which Saint Augustine fiercely opposed. In the Carolingian period, a number of trinitarian heresies still existed. But after AD 1000 there developed a great wave of heresies amid which a distinction is customarily drawn between those of a popular nature and more learned ones. This wave of heresies is generally attributed either to an aspiration on the part of the faithful toward a greater purity of *mores*, or else to the general desire for change that paved the way for the Gregorian reform of the eleventh and twelfth centuries. After many years of political and social stability in the Carolingian period, came a time of instability and upheaval characterized by a twofold movement. On the one hand, the Church was endeavoring to escape the domination of powerful laymen; on the other, laymen were seeking greater independence from the clergy. Medieval society and civilization rested upon the power of the Church, a power at once spiritual and temporal. What the Church could not accept were heresies that brought its power into question, as can be seen from the events that occurred in

Orléans, Arras, Milan, and Lombardy at the beginning of the eleventh century. The regions where protest movements were strongest, either remaining bent on reform or becoming heretical, were Lotharingia (the modern Lorraine), the southwest and southeast of present-day France, northern Italy, and Tuscany. A Europe of protest now appeared. It was difficult for the Church to move forward, swinging as it did now toward reforms necessary within the clergy, now toward the repression of heresy. The reform of clerical behavior included condemnation of the sale of sacraments, simony, and the nonobservance of priestly celibacy (for most priests were living either in a state of marriage or with concubines). Meanwhile, a growing number among the laity were refusing to accept the sacraments from priests who behaved incorrectly, or even, quite simply, from any clergy at all.

Some heretics also refused to revere the crucifix and even the Cross itself. Influenced by the monks of Cluny, the Church was ascribing an increasing importance to prayers, to services to honor the dead, and to remuneration for the clergy who presided over such rituals. Many laymen rejected this new pattern of behavior. Such protests also affected cemeteries in that these laymen refused to regard them as sacred simply because they had been consecrated by the Church. Laymen similarly challenged the Church's monopoly over the interpretation of the Gospels and the way that they used them in their preaching. Finally, the increasing wealth accumulated both individually and collectively within the Church attracted virulent criticism. The Church soon came to feel that it was a fortress under siege. Its first move was to try to name these heresies and distinguish between them, the better to oppose them. But in many cases the names that it found for them were those of heresies of late antiquity, which it discovered in old texts, names that in no way corresponded to the real heresies by which it was now threatened. In general, it regarded all these as Manichean heresies that drew a radical distinction between Good and Evil. The people who believed in them were called "Integrists."

The struggle against such heresies was prepared by the great institution that dominated Christendom, namely the order of Cluny, which also organized the Crusades. Peter the Venerable, the great abbot of Cluny from 1122 to 1156, wrote three treatises attacking what he called the major threats to Christendom. They became to some extent the textbooks on Christian orthodoxy. One attacked the heretic Pierre de Bruys, the parish priest of a village in the High Alps, who rejected sacraments and prayers for the dead and preached horror of the Cross; another was the first treatise in Christendom to attack Muhammad and all his disciples, in which Muhammad was presented as a sorcerer; the third attacked the Jews, condemning them as deicides. After 1140, the offensive became general and, in conformity with the new concepts of nature, heresy was regarded as a disease: a leprosy or a plague. The Church also spread the idea of contagion, so that heresy was made to seem a terrible threat to all and sundry.

In southern France, the term "Cathar," which meant "pure" in Greek and produced the German derivation *Ketzerei*, meaning heresy, became a particularly key word. In 1163, Cathars were discovered in both Cologne and Flanders. In 1167 a heretical assembly, in the form of a council, apparently met on land belonging to the count of Toulouse, at Saint-Félix-de-Caraman. The Cathar heresy more or less won over part of the nobility and even the Languedoc and Occitan upper nobility. This was chiefly on account of the Church's prohibition of marriages of so-called consanguinity, which led to the fragmentation of rural patrimonies. Catharism, in the strict sense, truly was a form of Manicheism, which favored a rejection of the material and the flesh and the substitution of behavior and rituals very different from those of the Christian Church. One feature of Catharism was the distinction of an elite category of the "pure," known as the "Perfect Ones," who, toward the end of their lives, received a kind of sacrament known as the *consolamentum*. I believe that Catharism was not, in truth, a Christian heresy, but an altogether different religion. In my view, its importance was exaggerated both by the Church, which wished to destroy it, and also, in the twentieth century, by regionalist militants who considered it a very specific heritage. To believe that, had Catharism triumphed – a most unlikely eventuality, in any case – it would have created an "Integrist" Europe is in no way to minimize the cruelty of the ecclesiastical repression that it evoked.

Amid the seething heretical upheaval of the second half of the twelfth century, there appeared in Lyon a merchant by the name of Pierre Valdès (also called Peter Waldo) who, while remaining a layman, preached in favor of poverty, humility, and an evangelical life. In the first instance, the Waldenses seem to have been, not a heresy but rather a movement of reform in which laymen, without challenging the authority of the Church, simply aspired to play a more important part. In 1184, Pope Lucius III, with the support of the emperor, launched a decree from Verona, *Ad abolendam*, which introduced violent repression against *all* heretics. They were all lumped together ("Cathars, Paterins, those who, under a false name, have called themselves the humble and the poor of Lyon, the Passagians, the Josephins, and the Arnaldists") in an amalgamation that in truth failed to conceal the disarray of a Church that was overwhelmed by "the opacity of heresy" (as Monique Zerner puts it).

The great organizer of antiheretical oppression was Pope Innocent III (pope 1198–1216). As early as 1199, he assimilated heresy to the crime of treason, in consequence of which a heretic could be sentenced to have his possessions confiscated, to be excluded from all public functions, and to be disinherited. Innocent III redirected the idea and reality of the Crusades, turning them against the heretics. In 1208 he launched against them a war in which he appealed to lay crusaders to come forward to fight. The war started off with the sack of Béziers and the massacre of the Biterrois in their town church. From northern France it attracted numerous petty lords who were short of land. The so-called Albigensian Crusade did not come to an end until 1229, when the Count of Toulouse capitulated, along with all the lords and towns of southern France.

In the meantime, the Fourth Lateran Council (1215) had imposed an antiheretical oath upon the Christian princes. It had also condemned Jews to be distinguishable by a sign, usually a red disk, sewn on to their clothes. This constituted the birth in Europe of the future yellow star. Most secular governments chose to ignore that decision, although in 1269, at the end of his life, Saint Louis was obliged, apparently against his will, to observe it. In 1232, Pope Gregory IX set up, alongside the episcopal Inquisition, a pontifical Inquisition which passed judgment on heretics throughout Christendom, in the name of the Church and the pope.

The Inquisition adopted a new judicial method, known precisely as "inquisitorial" rather than "accusatorial." It consisted in interrogating the accused in order to obtain a confession of his or her culpability. It thus instituted a Europe of confessions, and it was not long before those confessions were being extorted under torture. Torture had been used very little in the Early Middle Ages, for in antiquity it had usually been limited to slaves. Now the Inquisition revived it and extended its application to lay men and women. It constituted one of the most abominable aspects of the Europe of persecution that is exposed by Robert I. Moore.

The Inquisition sentenced a large number of heretics to be burnt at the stake, although it is not possible to quantify this. The execution of the heretics condemned by the courts of the Inquisition was carried out by temporal authorities acting as the Church's secular arm. From a social point of view, Catharism was initially widespread among the nobility in the towns and among certain craftsmen such as weavers. By the second half of the thirteenth century, the severity of the repression had reduced the Cathars to a scattering of mountain communities, such as the inhabitants of the village of Montaillou in the Ariège region, to whom Emmanuel Le Roy Ladurie has devoted an exemplary study.

The Persecution of the Jews

The Jews constituted the second group persecuted by the Church and the Christian princes. For many years the Jews had not posed serious problems for the Christians. Before the tenth century, Jewish communities were not numerous in the West and consisted essentially of merchants who, along with other people from the East (Lebanese, Syrians, and so on), carried on most of the small amount of trading that took place between Christendom and the East. The Church nevertheless elaborated a code of relations between Christians and Jews that was both theoretical and practical. Visigothic Spain constituted an exception, for here the kings, in association with the bishops, introduced violently anti-Jewish legislation, which Leon Poliakov has considered to have been the origin of anti-Semitism. However, the conquest of the greater part of the Iberian peninsula by the Muslims then led to a new situation in which both Jews and Christians were more or less tolerated by their conquerors.

Charlemagne and his successors did not persecute the Jews, although Jews were the object of vicious attacks by Agobard, the archbishop of Lyon. Following Saint Augustine, the Christians observed a precept from Psalm LIX in their dealings with Jews: "Slay them not, lest my people forget: scatter them by thy power and bring them down." In this way they somewhat hypocritically manifested a kind of tolerance, or even protectiveness, which, however, they justified by converting it into an undying memory of the pre-Christian past and a pretext for expelling and subordinating the Jews. When feudalism became established in Christendom, the status of the Jews was assimilated to that of the serfs. This state of servitude placed them under at once the domination and the protection of their lords, and of the Christian princes in particular. The latter mostly oscillated between, on the one hand, tolerance and protection, and on the other, persecution. Popes, emperors and kings such as Saint Louis all acted in this way, detesting the Jews but nevertheless considering themselves their "bishops from outside," as Saint Louis put it.

Medieval Jewish literature and Christian literature alike attribute a special, legendary place to Charlemagne in this respect. Around AD 1000 there were probably about 4,000 Jews in the Germanic countries, and by the end of the century, on the eve of the first crusade, their number had grown to close on 20,000. Jews were sometimes summoned to the courts of Christian rulers and were privileged on account of their special economic skills and services, which the Christians could not rival. The increasingly buoyant economy of Christendom after AD 1000 was thus one of the causes of the increase in the number of Jews living in Christendom, but it was not long before it gave rise to the beginnings of Jewish persecution. All the same, in the eleventh century, Christians and Jews still continued to coexist more or less in peace. Only the Jews were recognized by the Christians as possessing a legitimate religion of their own, even if no name for it existed, whereas the Muslims, for example, were simply assimilated to pagans. Some scholarly clerics maintained relations with rabbis in order to exchange views on biblical exegeses; and Jews were permitted to build themselves not only synagogues but schools too. The first crusade marked a serious turning point in this situation.

In the course of the tenth century, Christians became more and more obsessed by the image of Jerusalem. This was an all-important factor in the crusade in favor of which the Christian pope Urban II preached in Clermont in 1095, and which led to the capture of Jerusalem in 1099. The fall of Jerusalem was followed by a huge massacre of Muslims by the Christians. The enthusiasm for Jerusalem and its evocation of Christ's Passion as a victim of the Jews produced a huge wave of hatred and hostility directed against the latter. The hostility was all the greater given that Christians of the late eleventh century possessed an extremely tenuous grasp of historical time. They imagined that Christ's Passion had been a contemporary event and were determined to punish his tormentors. The more powerful and wealthy crusaders traveled by sea on ships that they hired in Marseille or Genoa, but the mass of poor crusaders lacked the financial means to do this. They were frequently led on by fanatics such as Peter the Hermit, and reached the Near East by crossing central Europe. On their way, they came across numerous Jewish communities, many of whom they massacred. This was the first major wave of pogroms in Europe.

In the twelfth and thirteenth centuries, other motivations led to the persecution of the Jews. Two myths were invented. The first took the form of a rumor that was believed to be true, according to which the Jews would kill a young Christian boy in order to use his blood in their rituals. This rumor nearly always led to pogroms. The first such accusation seems to have been made in 1144, in Norwich, and in the second half of the twelfth century and the first half of the thirteenth there were many other cases of similar accusations and massacres in England. In 1255, there was yet another case in Lincoln where, following the death of a young boy and a rumor that he had been tortured to death by the Jews, the latter were taken to London and 19 of them were hanged. Only the intervention of the king's brother, Richard of Cornwall, saved 90 others from the same fate.

Similar accusations, executions and massacres also spread through the continent, although no pogrom is known to have taken place on French territory during the reign of Saint Louis (1226–70). Another rumor was also spread during this period when Jews were beginning to suffer persecution at the hands of Christians motivated by a desire for purity. It was said that the eucharistic host was being profaned by Jews, who defiled the consecrated wafers. The accusation was clearly prompted by a growing devotion to the eucharistic sacrament, which eventually culminated in the establishment of the festival of Corpus Christi, in 1264.

The persecution of the Jews often involved massive expulsions. Many Jews were expelled from England in 1290, and from France in 1306. Some of the latter having gradually trickled back, a would-be definitive expulsion from the kingdom of France took place in 1394. In the fourteenth century, successive waves of violent Jewish persecution broke out at times of major calamities. In 1321 the Jews, along with lepers, were accused of poisoning the wells, and pogroms ensued. Worse still, in Germany in particular, between 1348 and 1350, while the Black Death epidemic was raging, the Jews were held responsible for it. Throughout Christian Europe, the idea of this kind of contagion was spreading.

In the twelfth and thirteenth centuries the isolation of the Jews increased, making them ever more vulnerable to persecution. They were prohibited from owning property, from working on the land and from most professions. The greatest expulsion took place in the Iberian peninsula in 1492, at the time of the destruction of the last of the Muslim kingdoms in Spain, the kingdom of Granada. The Catholic monarchs went further in the pursuit of blood purity (*limpieza del sangre*) than any other Christian sovereigns. In places from which they had not yet been expelled, such as the Papal States and the imperial possessions in Germany, the Jews were later confined to ghettoes that at once protected and imprisoned them.

Amid so many prohibitions, many Jews had continued to act as moneylenders, if only on a small scale, for domestic purposes. As a result, they were persecuted as usurers by the Church, and furthermore, they attracted the hatred of Christians who could not manage without their financial aid. Other Jews, who still possessed great medical skills, became doctors to the rich and powerful. Most popes and Christian kings (Saint Louis included) were attended by Jewish doctors.

Within this Europe of emerging and spreading persecution, the persecution of the Jews was without doubt the most persistent and the most abominable. I hesitate to use the word racism, which, it seems to me, implies not only the notion of race but also certain pseudo-scientific allegations that were not a feature of the Middle Ages. However, the starting point of the Christians' hostility toward the Jews based essentially on religion (but then, in the Middle Ages, religion was everything, so much so that the actual concept of what was religious did not exist, nor would it before the eighteenth century), anti-Judaism, does not suffice to explain the Christians' attitude. The truth is that the Christian society of the Middle Ages laid the earliest foundations in the construction of European anti-Semitism.

Sodomy

The third category of people persecuted and excluded was that of homosexuals. Christianity took over the Old Testament's taboos that so severely condemned homosexuality, and the vice of the inhabitants of Sodom was regarded as a sexual deviation. Nevertheless, sodomy was tolerated up to a point, particularly in monasteries. However, the twelfth-century wave of reform affected sodomites, the more so because the evolution of the notion of nature had made sexual sins seem worse because they were sins against nature. Homosexuality was now not only condemned but relegated to the realm of silence: it became the vice that could not be named. Sodomy was a sin frequently ascribed to men (women are hardly ever mentioned) by enemies bent on dishonoring them and having them condemned to the most severe of punishments, even death. Muslims were accused of practicing homosexuality. So were soldier-monks such as the Knights Templar, and they were condemned and wiped out. Even their leader, Jacques de Molay, was burnt at the stake at the beginning of the fourteenth century. On the other hand, among the high and mighty, sodomy was more or less tolerated. Two kings of England were homosexual, possibly three, if the rumor about Richard the Lionheart was true (but that was never proved). In the case of William Rufus (ruled 1087–1100) there seems to be no doubt about it, and even less in the case of Edward II (ruled 1307–27), who was deposed and then assassinated along with his favorite.

From the mid-thirteenth century on, cases of sodomy, like many other forms of deviant behavior, were handed over to the Inquisition, and relatively large numbers of homosexuals were burnt. Flashes of tolerance reappeared here and there, particularly in the fifteenth century and principally in Italy, above all Florence.

The Ambiguity of Leprosy

The inclusion of a fourth category of individuals who, from the twelfth century on, were persecuted and disadvantaged may cause surprise. These were the lepers. The attitude of medieval Christians toward lepers was twofold. The image of Christ kissing the leper certainly affected them. Great saints were praised for having emulated Christ by offering food to lepers and even, on occasion, kissing them. The most famous of these was Saint Francis of Assisi, but Saint Louis was another. Leprosy seems to have spread to the West only in the fourth century, and lepers became, on the one hand, objects of pity and compassion; on the other hand, however, they were simultaneously objects of horror, both physical and moral. In this society, in which the body was believed to reflect the soul, leprosy seemed to be a sign of sin. In courtly literature, the leper is often portrayed as a repulsive figure, as in the terrible episode of Isolde among the lepers. It was believed that lepers were marked as the children of sin, having been conceived by parents who did not respect the periods when sexual relations were forbidden. As Michel Foucault has shown, the general reaction to them was to shut them away. From the twelfth century on, many leper-houses were built in which to confine them. In theory, these were hospitals of a sort, but in truth they were prisons, situated on the outskirts of towns in districts named after Mary Magdalene, La Madeleine, the saint who became their protectress. Only rarely were they allowed out, when they kept Christians away from them by ringing their little bell. Leprosy was the disease most typical of medieval Europe, charged as it was with terrifying symbolism. The climax of this fear of leprosy was reached in the early fourteenth century, when lepers were accused of poisoning the wells. Subsequently leprosy seems to have been considered the foremost of all Western symbolic illnesses. The plague was soon to take its place.

The Unleashing of the Devil

Eventually all these different types of pestilential beings came to form a countersociety that threatened the purity and salvation of good and faithful Christians. The leader of them all was Satan, whether they were actually *possessed* by him or were simply his subjects. The Devil entered Europe at the same time as Christianity, and under his rule he unified a multitude of different demons who had originated either in Greco-Roman paganism or else in one of the many popular beliefs. But it was only from the eleventh century on that he was recognized to be the commander-in-chief of all the cohorts of evil. From then on, he led the dance of the future damned. Not every man and woman succumbed to him, but all were threatened, all tempted. Unified Christendom conferred a unified power upon "the enemy of the whole human race," with heresy as its instrument. The Inquisition was to be the Church's instrument in the fight against it. But the devil's presence and actions were to be long-lived. The Europe of the Devil had emerged.

The Peripheries of Feudal Europe

By the late twelfth century feudal institutions had, to varying degrees, taken over the whole of Christendom. It is interesting to note that there were some outlying fiefdoms that more or less preserved the original character of those peripheries of Europe, yet continued to play an important role in the Christian world as a whole. One example is provided by Ireland, the great center of Christianity and civilization in the Early Middle Ages. It preserved its own form of Christianity, allowing the Gaelic culture to remain rich and vibrant and even influencing the Welsh and the English who, despising these so-called barbarian Christians, sought in vain to conquer and despoil them. Ireland was a part of Europe.

The case of Brittany was at once comparable yet different. Ever since the fourth century it had been occupied by Britons from Great Britain. In the course of the Middle Ages it acquired a considerable measure of political emancipation, as a kingdom during the Carolingian period, then as a duchy in the Capetian period. The policies of the dukes of Brittany constituted a complex balancing act between the French and the English. The duke of Brittany received the ambiguous title of peer of France and, by the fifteenth century, seemed well on the way to winning true independence. Meanwhile, making the most of its geographical situation, Brittany developed its fleet and came to count increasing numbers of sailors and traders among its inhabitants.

Turning from those Celtic lands to Mediterranean ones, we find that the end of the twelfth century was a decisive time not only for the Iberian peninsula but also for Sicily and northern Italy. In Spain, the *Reconquista* had speeded up. The capture of Toledo in 1085, by Alfonso VI of Castile and León, marked a crucial point: the widespread influence of this town, a meeting place for Christians, Muslims, and Jews, which produced many translators of Greek, Hebrew, and Arabic, made it one of the great poles of the intellectual activity of Christian Europe. In Sicily and southern Italy, the Norman sovereign was succeeded by German monarchs (Henry VI in 1194, then Frederick II in 1198) and this reinforced the region's position in Christendom and made Palermo a remarkable multicultural capital.

In central and northern Europe, Hungary was consolidated as a Christian kingdom, now united with Croatia. King Bela III (ruled 1172–96) remained on good terms with the Byzantines, and at the same time reinforced the eastern frontier against nomads and strengthened his links with Latin Christendom by taking as his second wife a daughter of King Louis VII of France. Bohemia and Poland similarly reaffirmed their respective positions as a Christian principality and a Christian kingdom. With the support of the emperor, the Przemyslid dukes demonstrated their power by establishing abbeys and assuming the prerogatives of Moravia. In Poland, Boleslav III "Crooked Mouth" (ruled 1102–38) improved the Piast monarchy's economic exploitation by setting up a string of villages, each specializing in a particular domain. This enabled him to strengthen his power, and he went on to conquer Pomerania and to create the new bishoprics of Wloclawek, Lubusz, and Wolin. He also lent his support to the Benedictine and Premonstratensian religious orders. However, in his will, he divided Poland into separate provinces, which he distributed among his sons. This was the beginning of the weakening of the monarchy in Poland. Some historians reckon that after the collapse of the Soviet Union in 1989, the central Europe that had been formed in the Middle Ages reappeared. One is the Hungarian medievalist Gabor Klaniczay, who has helped to organize a department of medieval studies in the new Central European University. It has introduced courses of comparative studies on the Latin, Greek, Slavic, and eastern Christendoms of the Middle Ages and on the gradual spread of European civilization in those regions. What he has revealed is a central Europe which, as in the Middle Ages, constitutes an open, diversified and creative laboratory for a vast and limitless area extending from west to east: in his own words, a veritable European "Utopia."

In the north, Scandinavia similarly consolidated its position in the Christian world. At the end of the eleventh century, Iceland began to produce its sagas, those extremely original epics that were to be one of the flowers of medieval Christian literature.

The political and administrative stability of Scandinavia was by no means assured in the Middle Ages. Denmark, Norway, and Sweden were not clearly distinguishable states, and for a short while in the early eleventh century the Danes were even the masters of England at the same time as they endeavored to dominate the two other Scandinavian kingdoms and also Iceland.

The religious metropolis was at first the archbishopric of Lund, at that time Danish, which from 1103 to 1104 exerted its authority throughout Scandinavian territory. Then in 1152, an archbishopric was established at Nivados (Trondheim), in Norway, where the most glorious time was the Valdemar period (1157–1241). In Sweden, Uppsala was elevated to the rank of a metropolitan see in 1163–4 and, thanks to the efforts of Cistercians, a number of monasteries were established. However, political instability grew ever worse. Between 1156 and 1210, five kings were assassinated. Eventually, as the military art was transformed (by the introduction of heavy cavalry and fortified castles), a veritable nobility became the dominant class. Conversion to Christianity brought access to a superior culture that offered writing and a knowledge of Latin, which could be obtained by going to study abroad at Hildesheim in Germany, Oxford in England, and above all in Paris. The Scandinavian countries nevertheless remained somewhat archaic and marginal compared to the rest of Europe.

Crusading Europe

The Crusades constituted a spectacular phenomenon that disrupted Christian Europe from the eleventh to the thirteenth centuries. History textbooks devote considerable space to them. The term "crusade" itself is not medieval, for it was invented at the end of the fifteenth century (although the expression "to cross oneself" already existed in the twelfth century). The word "Crusades" designates the military operations in Palestine undertaken by Christians in order to wrest from the Muslims the Holy Sepulchre, Christ's tomb in Jerusalem, and also the territories said to be where Christianity first began. Medieval Christians considered the Crusades to constitute a reconquest similar to the *Reconquista* in the Iberian peninsula. Jerusalem had passed from Roman domination into the hands of the Byzantines (its only Christian occupiers), and thence into the hands of the Muslims. No unified Christian political institution was ever established in the places considered holy by Christendom. These were also considered sacred by Judaism (although the Roman conquest and the Jewish diaspora that followed had reduced the Jewish population of Jerusalem to a small minority). They were also considered holy by Islam, as Jerusalem was where Muhammad flew up to Paradise from the Dome of the Rock. As has been noted above, for western Christians, Jerusalem at a very early date became the pilgrimage destination par excellence. The Turks' invasion of the region from the tenth century onward provided a pretext that legitimated a change of attitude on the part of the western Christians. But that was not really the essential point. The religious and ideological motivation of the Crusades may be traced to the convergence of two long evolutions.

The first, and probably the more important, was Christianity's conversion to warfare. The Christianity of the New Testament, like Jesus himself, was pacifist and deeply hostile to war. One of the principal reasons for the Roman emperors' persecution of the Christians was their refusal to serve as soldiers. This was prompted not only by a reluctance to swear loyalty to the emperor but also by a hostility to the very idea of shedding blood. By the end of the fourth century, when the empire became Christian, the attitude of Christians was already beginning to change. Now all subjects of the empire (soon all to be Christian) were called upon to defend their Christian empire. Christian hostility to the notion of war nevertheless persisted for a long time. Even when attitudes toward warlike practices changed, the bearing of arms and the bloodshed to which it led was forbidden for bishops and for the clergy generally. There were few exceptions. The only one that the Church accepted and even praised was that of the military orders. From the twelfth century on these took to forming groups of monk-knights, to fight in defense of the Christian Holy Places and, in some circumstances, also in the West itself – in the Iberian peninsula for example and, in the case of the Teutonic knights, in Prussia and Lithuania. However, the most important development was the establishment of the theory of a just war, the bases of which were laid by Saint Augustine. A just war was one decided upon and waged not by an ordinary individual but by a leader invested with supreme authority, such as that of the Christian emperor, and later the princes and kings of the Middle Ages. In theory, such a war was supposed never to be aggressive. Christianity always rejected the notion of preventive warfare; warfare had to be a response to aggression or injustice. It was supposed not to be waged with an eye to conquest and booty, and always to respect the lives of the unarmed (women, children, monks, traders, etc.). But Christians considered war to be particularly justified when waged against pagans and those assimilated to them, such as Muslims.

But before a just war could become a holy war, there had to be another important change. It resulted largely from the papacy's appeal for help to warriors such as the Franks who, under Charlemagne, protected it against the Lombards, or to those who, in the eleventh century, came to its defense against the Normans of Sicily. More generally, the papacy also tended to transform into a holy war any military resistance on the part of Christian peoples who deplored all forms of imperial aggression against the papacy. However, as Paul Alphandéry and Alphonse Dupront have shown, in the course of the eleventh century it was the image of Jerusalem that increasingly aroused passions in Christendom. A combination of causes and motivations led to the organization of a crusade at the end of the eleventh century. Christendom had just experienced a remarkable demographic and economic expansion. The demographic growth had produced a large number of young men, mostly from knightly backgrounds, without either land or women of their own. Georges Duby has produced a fascinating study of them. At the same time, the increasing wealth of the nobility provided it with the means of arming itself better and undertaking military expeditions.

Even after the conversion of the barbarians, the Christianization of warfare went on. Once baptized, a sword could continue to do its work with the blessing of the Church. Paradoxically, the Crusades resulted in large part from the peace movement that marked the year 1000. That was in the first place because, as the Church saw it, a just war was a way of reestablishing justice and peace; secondly, a just war seemed the best way of overcoming violence. The papacy played a crucial role here. It detected multiple advantages to be gained by directing the military force of the Christians against the Muslims. This policy was no doubt partly an outcome of the growing fervor aroused by current perceptions of Jerusalem and Christ. But it was also a way of channeling the bellicose frustrations of those young knights and directing them against the Infidels. Finally, it was a way for the papacy to set itself firmly at the head of the whole of Christendom, for the leadership of a war such as this, in which religious and political aspects were closely intermingled, could only belong to the supreme religious leader that the pope aspired to be. That the crusading pope, Urban II, happened to be a Cluniac monk was no mere chance. A crusade fitted in very well with the kind of Christendom envisaged by the great community of Cluny.

The papacy thus favored the emergence of the notion of a holy war, the symbol of which was the cloth cross displayed on the chests of the crusaders. Christian Europe had thus followed in the footsteps of Islam, which, from the very first, when the Koran appeared, had established holy warfare, the *jihad*, as a major obligation for the Muslim faithful.

I will not embark upon a history of the Crusades. Suffice it to note that the first crusade eventually, in 1099, achieved the capture of Jerusalem, which was marked by a terrible Christian massacre of Muslims and the establishment of Christian states in Palestine, foremost among them the Latin kingdom of Jerusalem.

Following the Muslim capture of Edessa in 1144, a second crusade, encouraged by the preaching of Saint Bernard, was undertaken by Emperor Conrad III and King Louis VII of France. It was a failure. In 1187, the Kurdish sultan Saladin, at the head of a great Muslim army, destroyed the forces of the king of Jerusalem at Hattin, and seized not only that town but the entire kingdom except for Tyre. A third crusade was undertaken by Emperor Frederick Barbarossa, King Richard the Lionheart of England, and King Philip Augustus of France. Frederick took the overland route and was accidentally drowned while crossing a river in Anatolia. Richard the Lionheart and Philip Augustus traveled by sea. But this crusade too was a failure and the Christians lost Jerusalem forever.

In the thirteenth century, the crusading spirit very much cooled down. In 1228–9, Emperor Frederick II brought the sixth crusade to an end by signing with the Muslims a treaty that most Europeans considered to be shameful. An anachronistic resurgence of crusading fervor aimed at conversion rather than conquest inspired two disastrous crusades led by King Louis IX (Saint Louis) in Egypt and Palestine (1248–53); the king died before Carthage in 1270. The last remaining Christian fortresses in the Holy Land then fell into Muslim hands, Tripoli in 1289, Acre and Tyre in 1291.

Right down to the fifteenth century, the idea of crusading to varying degrees inspired a number of Christian princes and ordinary individuals. The constitution of the Ottoman Empire following the capture of Constantinople by the Turks in 1453 changed the bases of the relations of European Christians with Jerusalem. But Alphonse Dupront has shown how the myth of Jerusalem has persisted, through a number of transformations, right down to the present day, when, in the very different context of confrontation between Americans and Muslim fundamentalists, crusading fervor is unfortunately again on the rise.

In the long term, judgment passed on the historical record of the Crusades has varied widely. Until quite recently, Western historians regarded the crusades above all as the expression of a ferment of European union and a sign of the vitality of the medieval West. But that view is increasingly undermined. Jean Flori has clearly identified what he calls "the paradoxes of the crusades":

1   "They were conducted by Christians in the name of a religion that originally claimed to be pacifist toward the Muslim faithful of another religion which, in contrast, had from the very start incorporated the *jihad* into its doctrine even though, however, it practiced considerable tolerance in the lands that it conquered."

2   "The Crusades were the end result of a far too extensive movement of Christian reconquest which, right from its start, in Spain, began to take on aspects of a Holy War. These were magnified once the object of the reconquest became Jerusalem and the Holy Sepulchre. In the West, the reconquest was totally successful, but in the Near East it was a failure that prompted a Muslim counterattack, which led to the capture of Constantinople in 1453 and extended the threat of Ottoman power over the whole of eastern Europe."

3   "Initially, the aim of the Crusades was to come to the aid of the Christians of the East, which had been the cradle of Christianity, and to help the Byzantine Empire to reconquer the lands overrun by Muslims, with a view to unifying the Christian churches. But in the event the Crusades accentuated and set the seal on their separation."

4 "The Crusades, as preached by Urban II, were presented as a war to
liberate Palestine and also as a pilgrimage to the Holy Sepulchre. However, that struggle was deflected so as to win many other battles for the
Church, or rather for the papacy, battles waged against not only external enemies but also internal ones: heretics, schismatics, and political
rivals."

It is my belief that the crusades did far more than simply aggravate the
relations between Christian Europe and both Islam and Byzantium. Today,
Muslims, who certainly do not lag behind the Christians when it comes to
Holy Warfare, are digging up old historical scores against the Christians, in
the shape of memories of the aggression represented by the Crusades. It
seems to me that, quite apart from this recent conflict, the Crusades marked
the end of a European Christian illusion: namely, the idea that Jerusalem
was the capital of Christendom. In this respect at least, the failure of the
Crusades proved very favorable to European unity. It set the seal on the
identification between Europe and Christendom for many years to come.
But as for Byzantium, the Crusades undeniably widened the gap between
the western and the eastern Europes, the Latin and the Greek Europes,
particularly after 1204, when the fourth crusade deviated from its course
to Palestine in order to conquer and sack Constantinople and set up an
ephemeral Latin empire there. It seems to me that, overall, the effect of the
Crusades was just as negative for Europe itself, that is to say for the West.
Far from promoting the union of Christian states, the Crusades sharpened
their rivalry. So much is clear from the relations that obtained between
England and France. It is also clear that the vital forces of Europe, such as
the Italian and Catalan merchants, took no more than a marginal role in the
Crusades, pursuing alongside and beyond them dealings with the East that
were to their own economic advantage. Meanwhile the Crusades, for their
part, were depleting both the manpower and the resources of Europe. Many
years ago I remarked that, in my opinion, the apricot was the only advantage for the West gained by the Crusades. I still believe that to be true.

Were the Crusades the Earliest Manifestation of
European Colonialism?

In the long-term perspective that this book has adopted, one other important question must be tackled. Did the creation, mediated by the Crusades, of
Latin states, in particular a Latin kingdom of Jerusalem in the Near East,
constitute the first manifestation of what, from the sixteenth century on, can

unquestionably be called European colonialism? A number of excellent historians, including the Israeli Joshua Prawer, have thought so. I do not agree. The Latin states of Palestine were not colonies of economic exploitation and settlement, except in a most limited sense. The economic power of Christian Mediterranean towns stemmed not from the Crusades but, in most cases, rather from a relatively peaceful takeover of Byzantine and Muslim riches. Christian immigration to the Near East was very limited. Furthermore, while, in the modern colonial period, the links between colonies and their mother country have in many cases loosened or even been shattered, no such links ever even existed between states in the Holy Land and the Christian states of Europe. The ephemeral foundations of the Crusades were strictly medieval phenomena.

5

The "Fine" Europe of Towns and Universities (Thirteenth Century)

The Successes of Thirteenth-Century Europe

The thirteenth century is regarded as the high point of the medieval West. Without altogether succumbing to the notion of high points and declines, it seems fair to say that it certainly was in the thirteenth century that the character and new strength of Christendom, forged over the preceding centuries, were confirmed. It was also the time when a model that may, taking a long-term view, be described as European became established, with all its attendant successes and problems. Its successes appeared in four main domains. The first was constituted by a surge in the creation of towns. We have noted how a rural Europe emerged in the Early Middle Ages. Now, in the thirteenth century, the most striking development took the form of the construction of an urban Europe. Europe was to be embodied principally in its towns. It was here that an intermingling of populations took place, that new institutions were established and that new economic and intellectual centers appeared. The second success was the revival of trade and the rise of the merchants, despite all the problems posed by the use and diffusion of money in the economy and society generally. The third success was in the domain of learning. Growing numbers of Christians were affected by the creation of urban schools corresponding to what we would call the primary and secondary levels of education. The scale of educational activity varied according to regions and towns, but in many towns it involved 60 percent or even more of the children. In some, Reims for example, even girls were affected. More important still, in the context of the present study, was the creation and success of centers of what may be called higher education, namely universities. They attracted many students and called upon the services of teachers many of whom were well known, even famous. It was here that the new learning emerged, the end result of the intellectual explorations of the twelfth century: scholasticism. Finally, the fourth success, which supported and fueled the other three, was the creation and extraordinary diffusion, within the space of 30 years or so, of new religious figures who lived in the towns and were mainly active there: these were the members of the mendicant orders. They shaped a new society and profoundly remodeled the Christianity that it professed.

1   URBAN SUCCESS: A EUROPE OF TOWN-DWELLERS

As we have seen, medieval towns, even those built on the sites of ancient towns, changed very much in their appearance and even in their functions. In a medieval town, the military function was only of secondary importance, warfare being linked mainly with the seigneurial castles. In antiquity, towns had been far less important economically, for apart from Rome and a number of eastern cities, they had many fewer inhabitants. Ancient towns were by no means the large centers of consumption that they were in the Middle Ages, when they also became trading centers, once markets and fairs moved to the towns. A medieval town was organized around a number of centers, but the market was generally the most visible and the most important of them. Another change was that the workshops of the great estates of antiquity were now superseded by craftsmen's shops in the towns. This gave the medieval town an important productive role. In the towns of today, the persistence of old street names such as Tannery Street, Draper Street, and so on calls to mind all that medieval urban activity. At the same time, medieval towns tended to preserve or even reinforce urban attitudes that were very much part of their historical pasts and power. The town/country opposition, more or less equivalent to the civilized/barbarian one, was already strong in the Roman world. It became even stronger in the Middle Ages when, as we know, the peasant masses were made up of people called, throughout Christendom, "villeins," and for a long time they were relegated to a nonfree status, first as slaves, later as serfs. Freedom was an attribute that coincided with the status of a townsman. As a medieval German proverb declared "the air of the town makes one free" (*Stadtluft macht frei*).

Christianity had meanwhile taken over and strengthened a concept of the town handed down by Aristotle and Cicero. For them, what defined and constituted a town were not its walls but its people, its inhabitants. This view was widely shared in the Middle Ages, thanks to encouragement from influential minds such as first Saint Augustine and later Isidore of Seville. It is reflected in the astonishing series of sermons preached by the Dominican Albert the Great in Augsberg in the mid-thirteenth century. These sermons, delivered in both Latin and German, proposed a kind of urban theology and presented a description of the spiritual life of a town in which dark and narrow streets were assimilated to Hell, open squares to Paradise. Clearly the thirteenth-century urban mentality incorporated an urbanistic ideal.

It is true that medieval roads had lost the solidity that the roads of antiquity had possessed and had become simply "places to go along," but from the twelfth century on, towns developed a concern for cleanliness, laid down more and more paving stones, organized the disposal of rubbish and waste water, and adorned themselves with monuments whose purpose was not solely to impose images of the power of the high and mighty, but was also to introduce an element of beauty. In the Middle Ages, the town was one of the main places where the notion of beauty was developed. This was a modern beauty, different from the ancient kind, which had more or less disappeared as aesthetic sensibility declined. Umberto Eco has drawn attention to the emergence of the medieval beauty that was embodied in monuments and theorized by urban scholasticism.

It seems appropriate that the European town of the Middle Ages, more than any earlier towns, should be described by the Italian-American Roberto Lopez as "a state of mind." This is perhaps the point at which also to mention an image of the town that reflected both material realities and mental representations: the image of town walls. Antiquity had bequeathed to medieval towns walls many of which had been built, as in Rome, in the third century, as a defense against barbarian invaders. By now most were in ruins. The people of the Middle Ages repaired them or, more often, built new ones, not just to protect themselves but because the symbol par excellence of a town was its ramparts. A proper town had to be surrounded by walls. Once towns came to possess a legal standing and to use seals, these would often bear a representation of the town's own walls. The importance attributed to town walls led to the particular attention devoted to town gates. People, beasts, and goods all had to pass through them, and this set up a dialectic between inside and outside that was fundamental for a medieval Christian, and that profoundly marked the whole of Europe. What was internal territorially, socially, and spiritually was valued more highly than what was external. "Internalization" became a European tradition, a European value.

Episcopal towns

The first type of town to become established in medieval Europe was the episcopal town. In fact, the presence of a bishop became the distinguishing sign of a town, for every human group of a certain size had to have a bishop as its leader, and he would be in charge of the ceremonies of the new religion, which were performed essentially in town churches. This establishment of urban Christian populations of the faithful found particularly revolutionary and spectacular expression in the urbanization of the dead. A corpse was no longer an object of horror, as it had been for the ancients, so Christianity brought cemeteries back into the towns, and also founded new ones there. Towns of the dead were situated inside the towns of the living.

"Big" towns

The mid-thirteenth century witnessed not only the creation of many new small and medium-sized towns but also the extension of a few big ones. We should not imagine the towns of Latin Europe in the Middle Ages on the model of modern metropolises or the great towns of the Byzantine or Muslim East. In the West, a town of any importance would have comprised between ten and twenty thousand inhabitants. Palermo and Barcelona were exceptional, with about 50,000 inhabitants. London, Ghent, Genoa, and, in Muslim territory, Córdoba had about 60,000, Bologna probably between 60,000 and 70,000, Milan 75,000. Only Florence and Venice had 100,000 or more inhabitants. The largest town of all was unquestionably Paris, which has been shown to have had probably 200,000 inhabitants in about 1300.

Urban literature

The success and prestige enjoyed by towns fueled a flow of literary works which, within the limits of what was possible in the circulation of manuscripts, also enjoyed great success. These works were in the main urban chronicles, or else were written in praise of particular towns. At a time when mountains and sea coasts evoked no admiration and even the notion of landscape did not exist, what geography offered to the admiration of the Europeans of the Middle Ages were towns. Admiration for a town would take into account the size of its population, the scale of its economic activities, the beauty of its monuments, the diversity of its trades and professions, the diffusion of its culture, the number and beauty of its churches, the fertility of its territory (for a town would be the dominating center of the surrounding countryside), and finally, the memories of its past. In many cases that past would be legendary, consisting of foundation myths and tales of founding heroes like those of antiquity which, in this case, the Middle Ages was content to revive. It was partly through the towns that a sense of history and European historiography began to develop. Towns, along with abbeys, were the principal subjects of a hesitant historiography. The most remarkable and exemplary of these works in praise of towns was probably the treatise (in Latin) entitled "Marvels (*magnalia*: great things) of the town of Milan," by the Milanese teacher Bonvesin della Riva (1288).

Capitals

The hierarchy of towns was classified not only according to size but also by politics. Two types of towns with political importance emerged. The first type were capitals, the seat of the supreme political authority. Very few medieval towns attained the status of a capital. Besides, the notion of a capital was different from that of modern times. Take the case of London. The subtitle of G. A. Williams's excellent book *Medieval London* (1963) is *From commune to capital*. But what people of the Middle Ages regarded as the seat of their capital was no more than the City of Westminster. The case of Rome is different and more surprising. It is true that Rome was the normal seat of the papacy, even if the Romans often ejected the pope from it, and that the papacy's seat in Rome was the Vatican and the walled city built in the ninth century by Leo IV. Nevertheless, Rome was only known as the *caput mundi*, the capital, because the imperial chancellery took the view that Rome, where the emperor had to be crowned, remained the capital of the empire and even of Christendom. As a capital, the greatest success was Paris. But it owed that success to the patient efforts of the Capet dynasty ever since 987, and above all, to the propaganda of the royal abbey of Saint-Denis, the burial place of the kings of France. Furthermore, the chronicles of Saint-Denis, the mainspring of French national feeling, ascribed the title of capital to Saint-Denis as much as to Paris. In truth, the capital was constituted by the combination of Paris and Saint-Denis. Very few of the present capitals of Europe were capitals in the Middle Ages; and Christendom itself had no real capital at all, not even Rome.

State-towns

The other type of developed town was one that had grown into a state. Most such towns were in Italy. Yves Renouard has distinguished three phases in the evolution of the Italian towns of the tenth to the fourteenth centuries. The first phase saw the establishment of an aristocratic commune that seized power from the local count and bishop. Next, faced with the conflicts that developed between the various factions of the aristocracy in power (the most famous opposition was between the Guelphs and the Ghibellines, in Florence), the town would turn to an outsider whom it would endow with limited powers, as a *podestà*. Eventually, government would be taken over by the trades and corporations of elite groups of merchants and craftsmen, the "well-to-do," who would then come increasingly into conflict with the common people. Everywhere, particularly in Genoa, Milan, Florence, Venice, and even Rome, power took the form of an unending struggle between great family clans. The policies of these great families and the councils that they dominated led, in particular, to a transformation of the land surrounding the town, which now fell under its domination. This was the first step in the evolution by which towns became states. The finest examples were Venice, Milan, and Florence. However, in the medieval Europe of towns urban Italy was an extreme case and an exception. For example, in Italy the nobles actually resided in the towns, whereas in the rest of Europe they lived in their castles in the countryside, even if the richest of them, at least, possessed secondary residences in town.

Towns and feudalism

The medieval urban phenomenon has often been set in opposition to the feudal phenomenon, and the medieval town has been considered to have had a destructive effect upon feudalism, acting as an outside, hostile force. However, Rodney Hilton, among others, has shown how, in the cases of England and France, the medieval towns not only came to terms with feudal structures in general, but were even part of them. We should recognize that, although in France the feudal system was by and large ruined by the French Revolution, in truth the Middle Ages bequeathed to Europe an economy and society founded on the medieval relationship between town and countryside, in which what predominated was not cultural antagonism but rather a complementarity in which the towns benefited from the countryside. The towns grew thanks to the immigration of peasants. The inhabitants of medieval towns were more or less recent peasants. The development and craftsmanlike and economic activities of the towns were fueled by agricultural surpluses. The government of the towns evolved from being of a seigneurial nature into new forms that became integrated into feudal structures.

The Character of a European Town

What characterized a medieval town, and was still to be a feature in modern Europe, was above all the constitution of a type of society and government which, while coming to terms with feudal structures, at the same time manifested remarkable differences and proceeded to evolve in its own particular way. This evolution began in the eleventh century and it eventually led to the end, or at least the considerable limitation, of the domination exerted over towns by bishops who had acquired civil functions and by the counts who had more or less been installed there by their emperors. Indeed, in many cases the bishops themselves officially performed the functions of those counts. In most towns revolts against this state of affairs took a peaceful form, but in a few cases they turned to violence, as in Laon in 1116, where the rebellious townsfolk assassinated their bishop-count. Usually what happened was that the lords granted the townsfolk privileges in the form of certain customs and rights. In many cases what the townsfolk wanted, but did not always obtain, was a form of self-government described as communal. Traditional historiography has encouraged the myth of a communal movement, but in fact, except in Italy, townsfolk seldom obtained such quasi-independence. On the other hand, the "customs" of Lorris, granted in 1155, served as models for many towns in the French royal domain. The count of Toulouse granted "liberties" to the people of Toulouse in 1147, and in 1198 agreed to the election of consuls by the people of Nîmes. The archbishop of Arles accepted a consulate and a municipal constitution in the town in 1142 and 1155. In England, Henry I granted "customs" to Newcastle-upon-Tyne between 1100 and 1135. Henry II gave royal privileges to London in 1155, and a charter to Dublin in 1171 and 1172. In Italy, Frederick Barbarossa, when defeated by the towns of the Lombard League, was forced to recognize their liberties in the peace treaty signed in Constance in 1183. In 1232, the king of Aragon granted the inhabitants of Barcelona exemption from all taxes on merchandise.

This self-government by town-dwellers profoundly marked European towns in the long term, in at least two respects. The first was the tendency of towns to resort to *jurists*, men of the law most of whom had little legal training (this would, however, become available later, in the universities), but had received both theoretical and practical instruction in urban schools that were very familiar with the daily problems of the townsfolk. Admit-. tedly, this was to engender a Europe of chicanery and bureaucracy. How- ever, in general it did encourage the acceptance of the results of the great legal movements of the twelfth and thirteenth centuries which stirred up the law in Christendom in a number of ways: by their revival of Roman law, their elaboration of canon law (which reserved the important fields of usury and marriage for the clergy), and their practice of setting down oral, feudal customs in writing.

The second way in which self-government by town-dwellers left its mark related to *taxes*. The men and women of the Middle Ages had a variety of dues to pay. Peasants were burdened with dues of a particular kind, feudal taxes. Soon, but hardly at all in the thirteenth century, further taxes were to be levied by monarchies in the process of becoming modern states; and these royal taxes, which we should today call state taxes, elicited from town- dwellers a fierce resentment that is still evident today. Finally, the main layer of taxes consisted of the dues instituted and levied by the towns themselves, chief among them the *tolls*. It was essentially in the towns that a Europe of taxes took shape. Town taxes were designed to finance projects of what we would term public utility, inspired in the thirteenth century by scholastic doctrines that preached of furthering the common good. Sad to say, this world of taxes soon also became a world of inequality and injustice.

The time when equality prevailed between town-dwellers linked by an oath sworn between equals – precisely what should have been a communal oath – if such a time ever existed, was short-lived. Greater and lesser degrees of inequality rapidly came to mark this more or less autonomous urban society, and urban elite groups of "notables" soon appeared. The members of these elite groups were increasingly distinguished by their wealth. This consisted of both movable chattels and buildings and land, of ready money, or else, as in the case of the Church, it was invested in artifacts made of precious metals. An urban hierarchy would also take into account the age and fame of families. This was a matter not of seigneurial lineages but of bourgeois genealogies and of relatively poor town-dwellers descended from some ancestor who had won a name and fame for himself. Such people did have a chance of being accepted as members of those elite groups. Finally, certain professions, quite apart from the income they could bring to those who practiced them, earned the latter respect and consideration. Apart from the money earned by a man's business ventures, the honor of his profession could be the basis of his distinction in urban society. In particular, such social status might stem from a knowledge of the law and the offices through which it could be placed at the service of the town and its bourgeois inhabitants. In this world where professions were founded on craftsmanlike or commercial skills or on legal competence, the ancient system by which occupations were evaluated underwent significant changes. The number of professions regarded as illicit and therefore condemned by the Church diminished. Thus, the calling of an innkeeper, considered lowly ever since antiquity, was rehabilitated. Eventually, only usury and prostitution continued to be condemned absolutely; and as we shall see, even usury was soon reduced to a limited number of practices of secondary importance, such as consumer loans, which were essentially the province of the Jews. Even prostitution came to be tolerated, if not encouraged.

The Church accepted prostitution as an inevitable consequence of original sin and the weakness of human flesh. Besides, what Georges Duby has called the "male Middle Ages" constituted a society that was less shocked than certain others by a practice that functioned for the benefit of men and to the detriment of women. In the thirteenth century, the strict and pious Saint Louis wanted to banish prostitution from his kingdom, and in particular his capital, Paris. His entourage, which included the bishop of Paris, made him see that it would be not only a futile enterprise, but contrary to social order. Prostitution was a means of controlling the excesses of a world in which there were many unmarried men, either clergy or simply young men without wives. The Church nevertheless did make attempts to humanize and convert the world of aging or repentant prostitutes. From the twelfth century on, marrying a prostitute was considered a meritorious action. The Church founded the feminine order of Mary-Magdalene, the convents of which took in prostitutes. Attitudes toward prostitution in northern and southern Europe seem to have differed. Towns in the north appear to have treated "girls" and pimps with considerable tolerance, although in some towns the girls were required to wear special clothing and were not allowed to wear the same kinds of belts and jewels as respectable bourgeois women. In southern Christendom, tolerance was even greater, for municipalities themselves ran brothels and benefited from their rents, a cut of their profits, and fines. With the rise of the artisan class, increasing numbers of poor female "workers" turned to prostitution. Some professions, although not officially illegal, were considered dubious, in particular working in bathhouses. These catered for medieval people's growing taste for cleanliness, but also employed women who, like the present-day masseuses in certain countries, were also prostitutes. This movement of tolerance that was linked with the evolution of urban societies encouraged some authorities of canon law to legalize prostitution in certain circumstances. It had to be practiced only as a last resort as an escape from poverty and as a means of existence, and not for pleasure. And the girls were not to resort to deception, for example by wearing excessive cosmetics. Prostitution increasingly became subject to the regulations that were customary in any profession. It was the beginning of a Europe of prostitution that still raises questions today.

The Hierarchy of Urban Professions and Trades

Inequality within urban society was particularly noticeable in the domain of the professions and trades from which power in the towns gradually came to stem. In Italy, where the organization of trades was strongest, a definite gulf separated the "major arts" from the "minor arts" (the Latin *ars* being the word for a skill or craft). In Florence, which boasted the most elaborate discriminatory system, distinctions were not only drawn between on the one hand the 11 major arts of the rich merchants, and on the other, the more numerous minor arts of the craftsmen. Even within those 11 major arts, preeminence was reserved for the five that included only the businessmen who operated on an international scale. Those five were the arts of Calimala (that is importers-exporters and dealers in woolen cloth), of Por Santa Maria (the silk trade), and of doctors, grocers, and small-ware merchants, all three of which were lumped together in the single "art" of trading in all the products that were known as "spices" (a handbook of the time lists 288 different kinds of spices). The urban elite groups formed what is sometimes, if controversially, called the "patriciate." There can be no doubt that the most wealthy and most powerful of these "notables" dominated the medieval towns and that they were merchants. However, it should not be forgotten that originally the fortunes of medieval towns depended upon, not trade, but industry. That phenomenon appeared most clearly in the other region of Europe where, as in northern and central Italy, medieval urban development was exceptional, namely Flanders. Pondering the question of whether trade or industry came first – or "Were they merchants or weavers?" – the Belgian historian Charles Verlinden has correctly concluded, "Industry was the initial cause of the demographic transformation that resulted in the birth and the development of the Flemish towns. It was trade that was born from industry, not the other way around."

Industry meant textiles. A Europe of textiles brought forth a Europe of merchants. But before moving on to consider those merchants, we must continue with our assessment of the medieval town, for this was the principal actor in the dynamics of Europe.

The European Town: Jerusalem or Babylon?

Imaginary representations taking symbolic forms played a crucial role throughout the Middle Ages and it was thus that the twelfth-century battle for and against the town took place within the framework of the biblical imaginary. That battle may be summed up in two significant declarations. When the world of teachers and students (to which we shall be returning) drew increasing numbers to Paris, Saint Bernard, the champion of monastic culture pursued in solitude, went there to warn the teachers and students of the Montagne Sainte-Geneviève: "Flee from the midst of Babylon, flee and save your souls, take flight, all of you, flee to the towns of refuge, that is to say the monasteries." A few decades later, in contrast, the abbot Philippe de Harvengt wrote as follows to a young disciple: "Impelled by a love for science, here you are in Paris, where you have found the Jerusalem desired by so many." In the thirteenth century, Jerusalem triumphed over Babylon, even if defects in the urban system were to appear at the end of the Middle Ages.

Towns and Democracy?

Social inequality was one of the most obvious of those defects. The "well-to-do," the merchants and the members of the major arts, stood in opposition to the "humble folk." The "well-to-do" made up the councils that governed the town, which were led by consuls in southern Europe and by municipal magistrates in northern Europe. But a medieval town was not just a center of economic stimulus which, through its crafts, its markets, and its money-changers (soon to become bankers) fueled the economic boom in Europe. Despite the ever growing presence within the town of humble folk, many of them poor, from a social point of view it could be seen as a rough model of democracy. Roberto Lopez has drawn a comparison between, on the one hand, the European medieval town and, on the other, the Byzantine town, the heir to the town of antiquity, the Muslim town, which never managed to unite in the face of the *umma* (the community of the faithful outside the town), and the Chinese town, without a center, without character, and without autonomy. He concludes as follows: "In Europe the urban experience was, all in all, more intense, more diversified, more revolutionary and (dare I say it?) more democratic than anywhere else." Throughout Europe, the town was a sign of historical progress. Towns emerged and developed from urban clusters linked either to seigneurial strongholds (*bourgs*, in France) or with a primitive form of commercial activity (the model of which is the *grod* in Poland and Slavic countries), and they spread throughout European Christendom, characterizing it and bringing it to life. That was true of the Celtic, the Germanic, the Scandinavian, the Hungarian, and the Slavic lands. The impact of those territories, which were little by little integrated into Europe, depended chiefly on the impact made by their towns. In eastern and northern Europe, urbanization was less developed and large towns were fewer, but this general phenomenon of growth and power took place everywhere. Only Iceland and Frisia remained untouched by this blossoming of towns.

Defining the Towns and Townsfolk of Medieval Europe

To define the medieval town and the medieval town-dweller, let me draw on two other French historians. According to Jacques Rossiaud:

> A medieval town was primarily a bustling society, concentrated in a small space surrounded by vast, sparsely inhabited expanses. It was a center of production and trade in which craftsmanship and trade were both fueled by a monetary economy. It was the center of a particular system of values that favored hard, creative work, a taste for business and money, a leaning toward luxury, and a sense of beauty. It was a system of organizing a space enclosed by walls which one entered through gates and within which one passed along streets and through squares featuring a forest of towers. But it was also a social and political organization based on proximity, in which the wealthiest formed not a hierarchy but a group of equals – sitting side by side – governing a mass united by solidarity. In the face of traditional time, framed and marked off by the regular sound of church bells, this secular, modern society imposed its will on community time, in which secular bells at irregular intervals sounded summons to revolt, to defend the town, or to come to someone's aid.

(I should add that, rather than focus on urbanism, I myself would be happier speaking of a medieval urban aesthetic and of the construction of a town as a work of art.)

This image of the medieval town is no doubt somewhat idealized in respect of its vision of an egalitarian society. As has been noted, a dominant elite group introduced injustice, particularly in the domain of taxation, a crushing burden for the more numerous poor masses; for this was also a

Europe of urban poverty. But it is fair to say that ideally the bourgeois model was egalitarian, or at the very least aimed for a horizontal hierarchy rather than a vertical one, as in rural and feudal society. In the medieval world, the myth of the Round Table alone inspired the idea of equals seated around a table, without any hierarchy at all, except for one leader, King Arthur. But that was a dream of aristocratic equality. Bourgeois equality was a principle that was always violated in reality, but it did provide the theoretical basis for a kind of equality that might possibly balance the only egalitarian model that did exist: the monastic community in which every monk belonging to the chapter had an equal vote, one that was expressed by the presentation of either a white or a black bean, the former indicating a "yes," the latter a "no."

For a portrait of a town-dweller I have turned again to Jacques Rossiaud and also to Maurice Lombard. If there ever was such a thing as "medieval man," one of his principal types was a town-dweller. Rossiaud ponders the problem as follows:

> What is shared in common by the beggar and the bourgeois, the canon and the prostitute, all of them town-dwellers? What is shared in common by an inhabitant of Florence and one of Montbrison? By those who had only recently become town-dwellers in the earliest settlements and their fifteenth-century descendants? Their living conditions and their attitudes may have been different, but the canon would inevitably encounter the prostitute, as the beggar would the bourgeois. They could not ignore one another, for all belonged to the same, small, densely inhabited world, which imposed forms of sociability unknown in the village, a specific way of life, the daily use of deniers (small monetary coins) and, in some cases, unavoidable contact with the outside world.

Maurice Lombard also sees this medieval merchant-townsman as

> a man in a network, linking different centers together, a man open to the outside world, receptive to the influences that arrive by way of the roads that lead to his town and come from others, a man who, thanks to this openness and this continuous stream of new factors, develops psychologically and, in a sense, by confronting new challenges, himself becomes more self-aware.

A town-dweller benefited from a community culture forged by the school, the public square, the tavern, the preaching, and the theatre (which was first revived in the monasteries and churches, then, from the thirteenth century on, began to flourish in town squares: Adam de La Halle's *Le Jeu de la feuillée* [Play among the foliage] was performed in Arras in 1288).

Town life also helped to give couples and individuals more freedom. The structure of the family evolved thanks to the introduction of dowries, which, in towns, would consist essentially of movable chattels and money. A town had a personality, formed by the individuals that it shaped. Modern urban Europe still retains many of the medieval town's fundamental features.

2 COMMERCIAL SUCCESS: A EUROPE OF MERCHANTS

The thirteenth century was not only an age of towns, but also a time of commercial revival and expansion that was closely linked with the rise of the towns.

Italian and Hanseatic merchants

The revival and development of large-scale trading in the twelfth and thirteenth centuries took place within the context of what, not without exaggeration, has been described as a "commercial revolution." Christendom was relatively peaceful and within it, in the background to the military episode of the Crusades, which was no more than a superficial epic external to Europe, peaceful trading intensified. Three great commercial centers emerged. The two poles of international trade were the Mediterranean and the North, so it was on the edges of Europe, out toward those two centers of attraction (Muslim in the south, Slavo-Scandinavian in the north) that two fringes of powerful commercial cities sprang up: in Italy and, to a lesser extent, Provence and Spain, and in northern Germany. Hence the predominance of two groups of merchants, the one Italian, the other Hanseatic. But between those two regions a zone of contacts developed, the outstanding feature of which was that, as well as facilitating exchanges between the other two commercial areas, it very early on became a center of industrial productivity. This area consisted of northwestern Europe: it incorporated southeastern England, Normandy, Flanders, Champagne, the Meuse region, and the lower Rhineland. This was the great center for the production of textiles and, apart from northern and central Italy, was the only region in Europe where one can reasonably speak of "industry."

Itinerant European merchants

A medieval merchant was first and foremost a merchant on the move. He was handicapped by the poor state of the roads, the defects of the means of transport for his merchandise, the insecurity of travel, and perhaps above all, the taxes, dues and tolls of all kinds levied by countless lords, cities, and communities for the privilege of using their bridges and fords, or even for passing through their territories. The only significant trading improvement in the twelfth and thirteenth centuries was the construction of many bridges spanning rivers. One particularly important achievement was the construction, in 1237, of the first suspension bridge, which opened up the shortest route between Germany and Italy, by way of the Saint Gothard pass. However, the commercial routes that most traders preferred were those that passed by way of the rivers or the sea. The two most important river routes were those of the Po and its tributaries and the Rhône, by which the Moselle and the Meuse could be reached. Finally, the tangle of Flemish rivers, extended from the twelfth century on by a whole network of artificial canals, or *vaarten*, and dams and locks, or *overdraghes*, produced a thirteenth-century commercial revolution comparable to the eighteenth-century industrial revolution triggered by the construction of canals in England. However, the primary kind of medieval transport was transport by sea, despite the great fear that the ocean inspired in medieval people, who regarded it as a world of biblical monsters and shipwrecks (Saint Paul was famous for the shipwrecks that he endured) and a symbol of danger and tribulations (the ship of the Church was often imagined and represented as a vessel tossed this way and that by the waves). Notwithstanding such fears, a Europe of the sea made its appearance in the Middle Ages. Progress in this domain was slow but decisive. The capacity of ships was increased: in the Italian, above all the Venetian, fleets, a capacity of one thousand tons was achieved. The progress made in the thirteenth century was mainly due to the diffusion of the stern-post rudder, the lateen sail, the compass, and cartography. Trading by sea remained slow notwithstanding, but its chief merit was that it cost infinitely less than overland trading.

The fairs of Champagne

At the end of the twelfth century and in the thirteenth, a great commercial event, which testified to the progress and European character of the merchant revolution, was the establishment of the fairs of Champagne. They were held at Lagny, Bar-sur-Aube, Provins, and Troyes, one after another throughout the year: in Lagny in January–February, in Bar in March–April, in Provins, where the May Fair took place in May and June, in Troyes, where the Saint John's Fair was held in July–August, then in Provins again, where the Fair of Saint-Ayoul spanned September and November. Finally, in Troyes again, the Fair of Saint-Rémy took place in November–December. Champagne thus provided a quasi-permanent market for the goods of the Western world. The merchants and inhabitants of the towns in which the fairs were held enjoyed important privileges, and the success of the fairs was closely linked with the growing power of the counts of Champagne and their liberal policies. They favored safe-conduct passes, exemptions from taxes, communal dues, and the institution of a police force to oversee the legality and honesty of the fair's transactions and guarantee the viability of its commercial and financial operations generally. Initially, most of the special officials, the Fair Guards, who performed these public functions were themselves merchants, but from 1284 on their tasks were taken over by royal officials. It is sometimes said that these fairs played "the role of an embryonic clearing-house," for it became customary for people to meet at the fairs to clear their debts. This example shows that the economy needed the aid of public authorities and their supervision in order to develop. In the twelfth and thirteenth centuries, commercial activity was organized around contracts and business partnerships, but those partnerships were usually only valid for a limited series of contracts and for a limited period of time. Only at the end of the thirteenth century did proper commercial companies appear.

Monetary Problems

International trading such as this required a monetary medium that was stronger and more general than the many feudal currencies. The Byzantine besant played this role up until the twelfth century, but once European trade took off it was no longer satisfactory. The West now reverted to the minting of gold coins that Charlemagne had abandoned. From 1266 on, France was minting gold écus, but it was the great Italian commercial towns that took the lead here. From 1252 on, Genoa was regularly minting gold deniers and Florence was producing its florins. In 1284 Venice began minting its gold ducats. But despite the prestige and wide use of florins and ducats, the multiplicity of currencies remained one of the hindrances that held back the medieval economy. The feudal system had been characterized by fragmentation. This affected the circulation of money; and the fact that there was no single currency and not even a smaller, more manageable number of currencies for international use limited the prosperity of medieval commercial Europe.

A Europe of Merchants

Itinerant merchants were increasingly being replaced by sedentary ones who ran their businesses through the intermediary of a team of accountants, commissioners, representatives, and employees, all known as *factors*. These would be placed abroad, where they would receive and execute the orders sent by their bosses at home. The merchant class thus became increasingly diversified. In a study of Bruges, Raymond de Roover has picked out many kinds of factors: moneylenders, often known as Lombards (that is to say Italians) or Cahorsins (for Italy and the town of Cahors were the earliest centers famous for arranging international loans), who lent money against security and were considered superior to the Jewish moneylenders who provided consumption loans; the second group was that of the money-changers, who provided what must have been the most frequent financial operation needed in the Middle Ages, given so many different currencies; finally, there were cambists, who were merchant-bankers. These had started out as exchange brokers but had then branched out from their functions in that capacity in order to accept deposits and reinvestments using loans. Banking Europe was born.

As we have seen, the world of merchants was essentially an urban one. However, even though merchants belonged, particularly in Italy, to what was called the "people," they could be divided into two levels of wealth and power. Such social distinctions were perfectly clear-cut and counted for more than legal ones. Although the status of a member of the bourgeoisie was accompanied by certain privileges and was more exclusive, it counted for less in a town's economic, social, and political matters than did differences of wealth and economic and political roles. As Yves Renouard observes, "What the political domination of businessmen established was really a class regime." The domination of the merchants manifested itself in many ways. They profited from the fact that salaried jobs were widespread among craftsmen and industrial workers, and because they fixed those salaries, they controlled the job market. They also dominated the house market, for they not only provided jobs but also owned real estate. Furthermore, they maintained their own power and, along with it, social inequality, through the inequality of what we would call taxation, the chief tax being the "toll," which was fixed by the councils they dominated. In a famous text of the second half of the thirteenth century, an account of Beauvais customs, the jurist Beaumanoir provides a clear explanation for the roots of this urban Europe of inequality: "In communal towns, many complaints are made about the toll, for it often happens that the rich men who govern town affairs declare less than they should, they and their family, and they allow other rich people to benefit from the same advantages so that the whole weight of taxation falls upon the body of poor people." Tax evasion was such that scandals sometimes erupted, as in Arras, where the famous Crespin banking family "forgot" to declare 20,000 livres worth of profits. The Europe of tax evasion was off to a good start.

The Justification of Money

At first, and still in the twelfth century, every merchant was more or less a usurer and so was condemned by the Church, but when usury became practically confined to the Jews and the power of the merchants increased, the Church gradually came to justify the profits made by merchants and drew a somewhat vague distinction between profits that were allowable and profits that were not. Some of the justifications put forward were linked to the actual techniques of commerce. The Church allowed the merchants to charge for compensation when they had suffered from delay or damage in the course of their deals. The work of merchants introduced into European attitudes and ethics the notions of chance, risk, and uncertainty. Most importantly, as we shall see, the justification of merchants' profits was based on recognition of the fact that the profit was remuneration for some kind of work. Better still, the diffusion, through scholasticism and preaching, of the idea of the common good and general utility came to be applied to the situation of merchants. Thus, in the thirteenth century the canonist Burchard of Strasburg declared: "Merchants work for the good of one and all and their work of carrying merchandise to and from the fairs is of public utility."

As early as the beginning of the thirteenth century, the English Thomas of Cobham, in his handbook of confession, observed, "There would be great hardship in many localities if merchants did not bring what is plentiful in one place to another place where that commodity is lacking. So they have a perfect right to be paid for their work. Large-scale international trade is now a necessity willed by God; it is part of the scheme of Providence."

The prestige and growing power of the merchants brought about great changes in European attitudes. As Michel Mollat has observed, thanks to the merchants money became "the basis of a society." However, merchants did not systematically oppose feudal values. By living like nobles, they tried to pass themselves off as nobles, and sometimes succeeded. Seeking to acquire the fundamental basis of medieval power, namely land, they bought landed property and derived income from exploiting both it and its peasants.

New religious practices, about which there will be more to say below, provided other justifications for the activities of merchants. They involved themselves in many charitable works (as the Church called them), in particular the distribution of alms. They were largely responsible for the creation of the first urban hospitals, such as the hospital of Santa Maria della Scala in Siena. At a different level, the Church now introduced prayers for the souls in purgatory and encouraged belief in this antechamber to paradise, where it was possible to purge sins that had not been washed away by confession. These innovations offered merchants hope of the salvation that, until the thirteenth century, the Church had denied to all usurers. A text from the German Cistercian Cesaire of Heisterbach tells the story of a usurer from Liège who was conveyed first to purgatory, then on to paradise, thanks to the prayers of his widow.

The patronage dispensed by most merchants from the thirteenth century onward is particularly interesting. They showed their commitment to the towns where they established themselves by funding the construction of churches and, above all, paying artists to adorn them. (In about 1300, Giotto, the first "modern" artist, was handsomely remunerated by the great Florentine bourgeois who had commissioned his services.) Merchants also seem to have been well to the fore among the men of the Middle Ages who first acquired a taste for beauty and were the most moved by it: an unexpected alliance between money and beauty.

Finally, the evolution of commercial techniques and, in particular, the increasing importance of written records in the profession of merchant-bankers encouraged the development of what is sometimes called an intellectual merchant culture. The merchants' need for such a culture led to the creation of urban secondary schools such as were to be found in Ghent as early as 1179. It prompted the development of a secularization of culture through the promotion and diffusion of writing, arithmetic, geography, and living languages. At the end of the thirteenth century, a Genoese was advising one merchant, "You must always remember to write down all that you do. Write it down immediately, before it slips your mind." In the following century a Florentine was observing, "One must never be lazy about writing." In the field of arithmetic a work that is particularly exemplary is the treatise on the abacus (*Liber abaci*) published in 1202 by Leonardo Fibonacci. He was a Pisan whose father was a customs officer for the Republic of Venice, working in Tunis in northern Africa. It was in the Christian-Muslim world of commerce in Tunisia, Egypt, Syria, and Sicily, where Leonardo Fibonacci traveled on business, that he learned of the mathematics that the Arabs had taken over from the Hindus. He introduced the use of Arabic figures, the zero (an innovation of capital importance for the place-value system), operations using fractions, and proportional calculations.

By the end of the thirteenth century, the merchants had acquired two fundamental gains, one material, the other spiritual, which until then had been incompatible. Previously, they had earned money, but by doing so were damned, as is illustrated by a Roman sculpture in which the purse carried by a merchant round his neck drags him down to hell. Now he could keep his money and, after spending a more or less lengthy time in purgatory, could proceed to rise up to paradise. He could have his purse *and* everlasting life.

Italians and Hanseatics

The thirteenth-century world of commerce was dominated by two groups of people, the Italians in the south, in the Mediterranean area, and the Germans in the north, across the board from the British Isles and Flanders to the Baltic Sea. The Italians were impressive by reason of their presence in the Byzantine world and on the fringes of the Muslim world, and also their increasing activity in Flanders. However, the most impressive expansion of all was that of the Hanseatic merchants. These were the successors to the merchants of the Early Middle Ages, first the Frisians, then the Flemish. However, they possessed not only greater dynamism but also a far greater quantity of merchandise. In the twelfth century, Tiel, on the Rhine delta, had been superseded as the main center by Utrecht, which was frequented not only by the Flemish and the Frisians but also by Rhinelanders, Saxons, Danes, and Norwegians. Bruges had become the foremost commercial center of the Netherlands. These merchants imported and reexported Rhineland wines, the great rivals of French wines in Europe, metal articles, precious stones, luxury textiles from as far afield as Constantinople, and weaponry from Mainz. The most spectacular success was that of the merchants of Cologne, who exported their goods westward both to Britain and to Denmark. They were particularly successful in England, where, in 1130 at the latest, they obtained the right to reside in London, where they acquired a house on the banks of the Thames, upstream from London Bridge. It was known as the Guildhall, and they made it their business center. In 1157, King Henry II granted the merchants of Cologne his special protection. In the northeast, Baltic trade was in the hands of the sailor-peasants of Gotland, and this brought success to Novgorod in Russia.

Russian merchants also made their mark elsewhere in the Baltic and in Denmark, where they encountered more Prussians and Estonians than Germans. As the towns developed, the whole commercial scene was transformed. The origin and development of the Germanic Hanseatic League were closely linked with the urban movement.

Philippe Dollinger has described the process which, pushed forward by the merchants, confirmed the status of the Hanseatic towns in the thirteenth century. He summarizes it as follows:

> The populations of a number of favourably situated settlements were increased by the immigration of rural craftsmen and by the permanent establishment of merchants; within such fortified precincts, both a merchant quarter – called a *Wiek* in northern Germany – and also an older administrative center, either ecclesiastical or secular, would become established; a uniform legal system, peculiar to that town, would be developed, paying particular attention to commercial and real estate matters; a community of bourgeois would be set up, in many cases involving some kind of oath; the predominant influence in this community would be that of the merchants, who would in some cases form a guild; the wealthiest families would take over the leadership of the city; the town would become increasingly independent of the local lord; and finally administrative organs run by the bourgeois would develop.

Right at the end of the twelfth century, the Council (*Rat*) became the ruling assembly of the town as it was constituted from now on. In this process, the creation of an urban legal system played a particularly important part, with most of its laws essentially dating from the thirteenth century on. Among the legal models that were the most influential were the law of Dortmund, which remained the "higher court" for appeals and jurisprudence for the towns of Westphalia, the law of Goslar in Saxony, and above all, the law of Magdeburg, which became known as "German law" throughout eastern Europe, Poland and the Slavic countries included.

An event of major importance was the 1159 foundation of the town of Lübeck by the count of Holstein, Adolph II of Schauenburg, a vassal of Henry the Lion, Duke of Saxony. Adolph II entrusted the construction and government of the town to what Fritz Rörig calls "a consortium of entrepreneurs." Lübeck was to become the head of the urban and merchant empire known as the Hanseatic League. Up until the mid-thirteenth century, the German merchants of Lübeck competed in prosperity with the merchants of Gotland, where many of them established themselves. The glory of Visby, the leading town of Gotland, was brilliant but ephemeral. In the mid-thirteenth century it was surrounded by a stone wall 11,200 feet long, enclosing a space at least as large as that of Lübeck. The ruins of 18 medieval churches, the largest of which, Saint-Mary-of-the-Germans, built between 1190 and 1225, was the parish church of the German community, still testify today to the importance of that northern commercial Europe of which Visby was briefly the capital. But Lübeck soon superseded and outdid Visby in this role. Lübeck organized the building of many merchant ships capable of rivaling the galleys used by the Italians. Its ships were *Koggen*, with greater tonnage capacity. Lübeck dominated a powerful maritime and commercial network that was dependent on new towns such as Rostock, Stralsund, Stettin-on-the-Oder (a Slavic town enlarged by a number of German quarters), Danzig (Gdansk) on the Vistula, and Elbing in Prussia (now Elblag in Poland), whose town seal in the early thirteenth century bore the oldest known representation of a stern-post rudder. Lübeck coordinated its commercial activities with the efforts at conversion and conquest of a new German military order, the Teutonic Knights, then active in Prussia.

The people of Lübeck, and more generally the German merchants of the north, were in favor of the foundation, in Sweden, of Kalmar, and even more so, in about 1250, that of Stockholm, and Bergen in Norway. The commercial expansion of the people of Lübeck and the Hanseatic League also extended westward. They and other merchants from further east began to frequent the ports of England: Yarmouth, King's Lynn, Hull, Boston, and eventually London. King Henry III of England granted to the merchants of Hamburg, in 1266, and to those of Lübeck in 1267, the right to form an association or *Hanse*, modeled on the *Hanse* of the people of Cologne. This was when the term first appeared.

In 1252 and 1253, the German merchants also obtained a series of privileges from the countess of Flanders. The success of Hanseatic trade increased without pause right down to 1356, which was the date of the first Diet of the Hanseatic League and the definitive formation of the *Hanse* or federation of its towns.

As the rise of the Hanseatic towns progressed, so too did the prosperity of Bruges which, as Philippe Dollinger puts it, "was on the way to becoming the world market of the West." Bruges welcomed merchants of all nationalities: English, Scottish, and Irish, bringing wool for the textile industry, Dutch and Frisian selling their cattle, and also merchants from the Anglo-French Atlantic coast between La Rochelle and Bayonne, bringing their wine. The Spaniards and Portuguese also brought their wool and southern fruits to Bruges.

More or less abandoning the Champagne fairs, the Italians now also established themselves in Bruges, which thus became the foremost financial center of northern Europe. From the late thirteenth century on, Genoese galleys, then Venetian ones, traveling in convoy, also regularly brought their cargoes of spices to the Zwin (the waterway linking Bruges to the sea). Through maritime trading, a European world economy developed, extending from Italy all the way to Flanders and to the Baltic.

3   THE SUCCESS OF SCHOOLS AND UNIVERSITIES

The European thirteenth century of towns and trade was also the European century of schools and universities, and these too were centered on the towns. As we have seen, encouraged by the bourgeoisie, schools had been multiplying in towns ever since the twelfth century. These "primary and secondary" schools provided the essential basis of learning in Europe, but the most spectacular creation was that of the "advanced schools" known as universities, which inaugurated a tradition that is still very much alive today. At the end of the twelfth century an advanced school was referred to as a *studium generale*, a general school, an expression that indicated both its superior status and the encyclopedic type of instruction that it dispensed. These schools evolved within the great movement that was organizing trades and professions in the towns, so they set themselves up as corporations like any other trade. They adopted the term "university," which meant corporation, and which was first used in Paris in 1221 to designate the whole Parisian community of masters and students (*universitas magistrorum et scolarium*).

We should immediately note a distinction that history did not perpetuate. The university corporations of the Middle Ages followed two models. In the Paris model, the teachers and the students formed a single community. In the Bologna model, legally the *universitas* was constituted solely by the students. Only the Paris model has survived to the present day. The emergence of the university teacher in the thirteenth century occurred in parallel to the emergence of the merchant. The merchant was at first accused of selling time that belonged to God alone (the profit from interest came to him even as he slept); but in the thirteenth century he was justified because he worked hard and was useful. He thus forms a kind of pair with the university teacher, who was also accused of selling something that belonged solely to God, namely knowledge, but was later justified by the work that he undertook when he taught students, who accordingly should rightly be expected to pay for the lessons. A Europe of intellectual work thus emerged alongside the Europe of commercial work.

A university teacher combined with his teaching work that involved reflection and writing, what we nowadays call research. In the case of many university teachers, their reputation and their contributions to social and political discussions (on, for example, mendicancy on the part of priests and monks, royal powers, and pontifical taxation) gave them a third role, one that has been recognized to belong to intellectuals since the nineteenth century. That is why I have called these university teachers "the intellectuals of the Middle Ages."

The universities were directed by rectors, who were elected by the masters and supervised by a chancellor, generally appointed by the local bishop. However, as the universities gradually acquired almost total autonomy, the importance of the bishop lapsed. Generally, universities also managed to foil interference and attempts at domination on the part of the temporal authorities, both those of the towns and those of the monarchy. On the other hand, given that the universities were Church institutions, they were obliged to accept pontifical interventions. However, in general these were both distant and slight. In certain cases the local bishop would use his theoretical power to interfere forcefully in the affairs of the university and impose a kind of censorship. The most spectacular case of this kind was the condemnation by Étienne Tempier, the bishop of Paris, first in 1270, then again in 1277, of propositions drawn from the teaching of certain Parisian teachers, one of whom was Thomas Aquinas. The condemnations were directed above all against real or supposed borrowings that Parisian teachers had taken from Averroës, an Arabic commentator on Aristotle. Averroës taught what was known as the theory of double truth, according to which, as well as dogmatic truth (for Christians, the truth of the Bible and the teaching of the Church), truth according to reason was also considered legitimate, and this could be taught even if it was contrary to the truth of the Church.

For thirteenth-century universities, Aristotle was, in a way, *the* great man, particularly for the university of Paris. His logical works had long been available in Latin translations, but not until the thirteenth century were Latin translations of metaphysical, ethical, and political treatises available. These works, which attracted the eager curiosity and longing of students, had at first been banned from university teaching, but now they could be read in universities. It is even fair to speak of a medieval Latin Aristotelianism that became fashionable and that, between 1260 and 1270, made its way into virtually all university teaching. The Dominican Thomas Aquinas, also a fashionable figure, was one of the greatest teachers who introduced Aristotelianism into the universities. But after about 1270, the vogue for Aristotelianism waned as a result of, on the one hand, the condemnations of traditionalists such as Étienne Tempier, on the other, attacks by more "modern" masters who set in opposition to Aristotelianism ideas that were more mystical and less rational. Some, such as John Duns Scotus

(1266–1308) and William of Ockham (who died in 1347), were Franciscans. Another was the Dominican Master Eckhart (about 1260–1328). Aristotle's intellectualism was now considered an obstacle to knowledge, which was becoming more experimental and open to free discussion.

The universities were organized into faculties, according to disciplines. There were four faculties and in theory all universities were composed of all four. In practice, however, that was not necessarily the case. Very often one faculty predominated, even if the others did exist. Thus, Bologna was primarily a university for law, Paris a university for theology, Montpellier for medicine. There was a hierarchy of faculties, according to the subject's place in the curriculum and its reputation. Thus the first three faculties, mentioned above, rated more highly than the faculty of preliminary education, in which the arts of the *trivium* (grammar, rhetoric, and above all dialectic) and the arts of the *quadrivium* (arithmetic, geometry, astronomy, and music) were taught. This faculty of arts was frequently overshadowed by disciplines that would nowadays be termed scientific. From a social point of view, moreover, this was the faculty filled by the youngest, rowdiest, least wealthy students, only a minority of whom moved on to pursue their studies in a higher faculty. There were two specializations above the faculty of arts by which those students might be attracted: either in the faculty of law, where both kinds of law, civil and canon, were taught, or in the faculty of medicine, where the instruction would be more bookish and theoretical than practical and experimental. At the top of the hierarchy, the supreme faculty of theology crowned them all.

The first university was that of Bologna. Although it did not receive its statutes from the pope until 1252, as early as 1154 Emperor Frederick Barbarossa had granted privileges to the masters and students of Bologna. Similarly, the masters and students of Paris received privileges from Pope Celestine III in 1174 and from the king of France, Philip Augustus, in 1200. However, it received its statute from the pontifical legate Robert of Courson only in 1215, and from a very important papal bull issued by Gregory IX in 1231 (*Parens scientiarum*). This contained a famous passage in praise of the university as an institution and of theology, this theology which had become in the university a "science," as M. D. Chenu puts it. The universities of Oxford, Cambridge, and Montpellier were founded in the early years of the thirteenth century. The university of Naples was founded by Emperor Frederick II in 1224. In 1288 the university of Lisbon was founded and also the *Studium* of the pontifical curia, which acquired the role of a veritable university where, as Agostino Paravicini Bagliani has shown, optics and the sciences were particularly favored. The history of the stages in the foundation of the university of Salamanca is revealing. It was founded as a royal institution by King Alfonso IX of León in 1218–19, and was created an institution of higher education by the *carta magna* of Alfonso X the Wise, the king of Castile, in 1254. Pope Alexander III conferred upon it the *licentia ubique docendi* in 1255. The historian of the university Antonio Garcia y Garcia has described the special privileges granted to Salamanca by Alfonso X in 1254:

> The *carta magna* created one chair of civil law, three of canon law (one by decree and two by general edict), two of logic, two of grammar, two of physics (medicine), a post for a librarian, to provide the masters and students with the necessary books, one for a master organist, and one for an apothecary. As time passed, the number of chairs increased. The professors' salaries were mainly funded by one-third of the tithes of the diocese of Salamanca. Professors and students also received many ecclesiastical grants.

The case of the university of Toulouse was exceptional. This was imposed by the papacy during its struggle against Catharism, as a foundation instituted by the Treaty of Paris, which brought the Albigensian crusade to an end in 1229. An extensive publicity campaign was launched to recruit students and a recommendation penned by John of Garland, the great English professor at the university of Paris, was circulated throughout Christendom. It praised the climate of Toulouse and all the town's attractions, including those of its women. The university was much resented by the people of southern France, who regarded it as an instrument of domination in the hands of northerners. The teaching of theology did not take off there, and it was not until the second half of the thirteenth century that the university began to thrive, particularly in the field of law.

One of the long-lived innovations that the new universities bequeathed to Europe in the thirteenth century was the practice of strikes. The longest and most famous strike was that of the Parisian masters and students that lasted from 1229 to 1231 and overcame the hostility of both the bishop and Queen Blanche of Castile (it was said that this was the first time Louis IX stood up to his mother, for he supported the university and managed to wrest the *Parens scientiarum* bull from the pope). Another innovation was the insertion of a month of summer holidays into the program setting out the calendar of university courses. These holidays insinuated themselves into Europe as a quasi-liturgical ritual.

Thanks to the activities of the Church, thirteenth-century Christendom was well accustomed to internationalism. But the universities were remarkable for the way that they turned both masters and students into wandering scholars who were prepared to seek knowledge in foreign countries and to move from one to another according to the fashion or reputation of particular universities and particular teachers. The most famous Parisian teachers of the thirteenth century were the German Dominican Albert the Great, the Italian Dominican Thomas Aquinas, and the Italian Franciscan Bonaventure.

What ensured the success of the universities in the Middle Ages and afterward was their right to confer degrees that were valid throughout Christendom. This constituted one of the new bases of the future Europe. If they possessed sufficient ability and enough financial resources, students could obtain a series of diplomas, the most prized of which was a master's degree in theology, for which 11 years of study were required. The first stage was the baccalaureate, a kind of initiation comparable to that which a young noble, a bachelor, passed through before becoming a knight. Next came the key diploma, the *licentia ubique docendi*, permission to teach anywhere, which has become the French *licence* (similar to an English Bachelor of Arts degree). Only the pope could grant universities the right to bestow this title and the privilege that stemmed from it. The third and topmost degree was the doctorate, which made those who earned it *masters*. In this way a Europe of professors was born. A university master's degree was accessible to non-nobles and nobles alike. We know of university masters who were the sons of peasants. Robert de Sorbon, famous in his time, the thirteenth century, as the founder (thanks to the grace and generosity of his friend Saint Louis, the king of France) of the Sorbonne, the most famous of the Parisian colleges, came from a very modest background, as a companion of his, the sire de Joinville, never failed to remind him. However, a university education was costly, mainly because the students had to support themselves for years on end in towns where the cost of rooms and food was constantly increasing. As a result, students who could afford to pursue more than one or two years of study at university were in the minority.

To make it possible for gifted and hardworking students to overcome the handicap of their social origins, a number of benefactors founded or funded houses where students with what we would call scholarships could lodge and eat free of charge. These were the university colleges, the most famous of which were in Paris. After the Sorbonne, the most famous were the Collège d'Harcourt and the Collège de Navarre, both founded right at the beginning of the fourteenth century. A college would often take in students from one particular geographical region or those specializing in one particular discipline. Thus, in the thirteenth century, the Sorbonne welcomed above all poor students studying theology; and in Oxford, Merton College was mostly reserved for students of mathematics. From the thirteenth century on, the universities, and in particular the colleges, thus trained a class of, as it were, administrators, who soon took over most of the principal posts of authority in both the Church and also among the secular authorities. As many of them had been trained as lawyers, by the end of the thirteenth century, in France, under Philip IV the Fair, for example, they constituted a government of *legalists*. A Europe of Christian mandarins was in the making.

A Civilization of Books

The thirteenth century prolonged the twelfth-century renaissance and ensured the decisive rise of the book. Books had enjoyed an early success between the fourth and the seventh centuries, when the *volumen* of antiquity, a scroll that was not very handy to consult, was replaced by the *codex*, which was revolutionized by the introduction of pages in manuscripts which, apart from liturgical texts, were mostly of quite modest dimensions and therefore easy to carry about and consult. The diffusion of the *codex* book was hindered by two factors. The first was of a socio-intellectual nature. The only people who could read were monks trained in monasteries, for the only libraries of the time were to be found in monastery *scriptoria*. Secondly, the *codex* book manuscript was written on parchment; and the number of calfskins or, more usually, lambskins needed to make a book was very high. Consequently, books were extremely expensive. The demand for books increased as urban schools and above all universities multiplied.

Ivan Illitch has declared: "In about 1140, in the civilization of books, the last monastic page was turned, to reveal the first scholastic one." The great initiator of the art of reading was Hugh of Saint-Victor, the theologian and scholar of the suburban monastery of Saint-Victor, near Paris. It was in the thirteenth century that new materials and techniques definitively established a new look for books and new uses for them. Punctuation was improved, titles and subtitles were introduced into manuscripts, books were divided into chapters, and indices of the contents were arranged in alphabetical order. Even more revolutionary was the abandonment of reading aloud, except before chosen audiences, and its replacement by silent, private reading. A Europe of reading individuals was born. Quite apart from the expansion of schools and universities, the appearance of new professions specializing in the use of writing, such as jurists, and the spread of literacy among the nobility, merchants, and craftsmen all furthered the use of books. As Daniel Baloup has remarked, "Books became, all at once, tools for secular studies, for work, for leisure, and for private piety." As the form of books evolved, so did their contents, which became more diversified. Books were now more adapted to the tastes and interests of readers, especially when they were written in vernacular languages. In university books, pages were set out with wide margins that could accommodate a reader's comments. Jobs connected with books multiplied, particularly within university frameworks. Bookshops appeared. There was an increasing call for parchment-makers, copyists, and bookbinders. The blockage caused by the prohibitive cost of parchment was only slowly removed by the gradual introduction of paper, which did not come into general use until the fifteenth century. Paper was then 13 times cheaper than parchment.

Another new technique that affected books was introduced and developed in the thirteenth century, namely the technique of the *pecia*. Before the invention of the printing press, the reproduction of manuscripts obviously presented a serious problem. Manuscripts were often immobilized for several months before a single copy could be obtained. In the late twelfth century in Bologna, and above all in the thirteenth century in Paris, a new system for reproducing texts was invented, using a different type of model, the *exemplar*. Louis-Jacques Bataillon has described the *pecia* technique as follows: "The copyist would hire a text written in numbered notebooks, each formed of two double pages, called *pecie*. The scribe would borrow these items one by one, leaving the rest of the notebooks free for other scribes to use. In this way, several copyists could work on the same text simultaneously, and this allowed many more copies of the work to be made available more rapidly." Two centuries before the introduction of printing, there was thus a thriving Europe of copyists. However, this technique, much used in Bologna, Padua, Paris, Montpellier, Naples, and Avignon, was never adopted in England nor in Germanic and Slavic countries, and was abandoned in Paris in 1350. Not until the second half of the fifteenth century was a Europe of Books really to take off.

All the same, the twelfth and thirteenth centuries did represent a new era for books, as many new categories of readers emerged. As well as teachers and students, a growing number of laymen were entering the world of reading. As most of these new readers were ordinary lay people, this may be seen as a secularization of Christendom through the evolution of books. To be sure, religious matter and prayers continued to fill many manuscripts. But in the thirteenth century a type of devotional book designed especially for women began to be produced. So books, along with schools, played their part in the promotion of women. This category consisted of books of hours. A book of hours was a psalter to which were added prayers addressed to the Virgin (which explains the large number of women readers), a calendar (signs of the zodiac and the seasonal tasks of each month), psalms of penitence, litanies and intercessory prayers to the saints, and prayers for the dead that were inspired by religious concern for the dead and the belief in purgatory. The books of hours were works destined for the rich and powerful, for their brilliant illustrations made them particularly costly at a time when "fine books" adorned with miniature paintings were going out of fashion. Books for universities and the growing number of books for utilitarian purposes were gradually superseding books produced as fine art objects.

Encyclopedias

Another type of book became very successful in the twelfth and particularly the thirteenth century and further helped to divert learning toward profane knowledge and secular culture. These were encyclopedias. Their proliferation was a response to the needs of new categories of readers and the spread of general knowledge that was one of the characteristic features of the twelfth-century renaissance. These encyclopedias offered information about everything to do with nature and society.

Encyclopedias increasingly included information about secular philosophical learning as well as theology. Alongside supernatural and metaphysical matters, they provided a whole compendium of information about nature and the physical world in general.

Hugh of Saint-Victor may be considered the initiator of the production of encyclopedias. In his *Didascalion* in particular, Hugh recorded a mixture of sacred and profane knowledge, distinguishing between a lower level of the arts and philosophy and a higher one of hermeneutics, and intermingling sacred and profane history. Those distinctions were carried over into the encyclopedias of the late twelfth and the thirteenth centuries. Even as early as the *De philosophia mundi* of William of Conches (ca. 1090–ca. 1154), a clear distinction was drawn between philosophy and "physics," understood as a science of nature that was more wide-ranging than medicine.

Alexander Neckam's *De naturis rerum* took the form of a decidedly Aristotelian encyclopedia. Another of the most popular encyclopedias of the thirteenth century was that of Bartholomew the Englishman, who combined Isidore of Seville and Aristotle (between 1230 and 1240). A *De proprietatibus rerum* was translated into Italian, French, Provençal, English, Spanish, and Flemish. In 1372 King Charles V of France had this retranslated into French by his chaplain. Thomas of Cantimpré, in his *Liber de natura rerum* (also between 1230 and 1240), produced a synthesis of the knowledge of natural history of his time, intending to use it as an introduction to theology. However, since his work was criticized for being too profane, he instead devoted the last years of his life to spiritual matters, particularly in his essay entitled *Bonum universale de apibus* (On the universal good of bees), which turned Book IX of the *De natura rerum* into a lengthy comparison of human society to a large beehive. Most of the encyclopedists were members of the mendicant orders, about which there will be more to say below. The third most famous of them (after Bartholomew and Thomas) was Vincent of Beauvais. In the 1230s this Dominican, who died in 1264, was required by his order to assemble within a "Book of books" all the knowledge needed for the education of brothers who had not studied at universities. Vincent of Beauvais, who worked for much of the time in the Benedictine abbey of Royaumont, made use of a whole team of helpers, who collected texts for him – a very modern kind of operation. To this end, he produced a *Speculum majus* (Great mirror) in three parts, *Speculum naturale*, *Speculum doctrinale*, and *Speculum historiale*. His reputation was such that after his death an apocryphal *Speculum morale* was attributed to him.

A number of works of greater intellectual quality were also produced, as separate treatises offering an overall encyclopedic view. Their authors included the German Dominican Albert the Great (ca. 1200–1280), the English Franciscan Roger Bacon (ca. 1214-1292) and the Catalan Raimon Lull (1232–1316). Lull was a lay writer, the author of theological, philosophical, pedagogical, legal, political, and "physical" works and also of poems and novels. In Majorca, he initiated the teaching of ancient and modern languages. He traveled widely in the Mediterranean region and in Christendom and was indefatigably involved in converting Jews and Muslims. Like most of these great encyclopedists, Lull insisted that faith and reason were indissolubly linked, using his extraordinary and most unusual talents of persuasion to support this view.

Scholasticism

The most important thirteenth-century inheritance for intellectual activity, particularly in the universities, consisted of the collection of methods and works that are classified as scholastic, meaning intellectual products linked, from the thirteenth century on, with schools, and more especially the thirteenth-century universities. Scholasticism emerged from the development of dialectic, one of the *trivium* disciplines. Dialectic was "the art of arguing by means of questions and answers in the situation of a dialogue."

The father of scholasticism was Anselm of Canterbury (ca. 1033–1109), for whom dialectic was the fundamental method for ideological thought. The aim of dialectic was "an understanding of faith," *fides quaerens intellectum*, an expression that has remained famous ever since the Middle Ages. Dialectic implied the use of reason, and Anselm elaborated his doctrine by suggesting that free will and grace were compatible. Scholasticism can be regarded as the establishment and justification of concord between God and man. Anselm also provided scholasticism with a basis: rational proofs of the existence of God. Twelfth-century experimentation with a new method of thinking and teaching had prepared the way for the so-called scholastic method of the universities. It was a matter of first constructing a problem, then introducing a *quaestio*. This *quaestio* was then discussed (this was called the *disputatio*) between master and students. Eventually, after this discussion, the master produced the solution (the *determinatio*). The program of thirteenth-century universities included a twice-yearly session of exercises in which the masters could manifest their intellectual brilliance. The exercises consisted of questions *quod libeta* in which the students could ask the master a question to do with any problem that they chose. The reputations of masters frequently depended upon their ability to think on their feet and answer those questions.

University teaching was expected to lead to publications, which is why the universities played such an important part in the diffusion and promotion of books. In the twelfth century, the main type of scholarly publication was the *Florilegium*. This was not simply a collection of quotations from the Bible, from the Church Fathers, and from ancient masters, for each quotation that appeared in it was accompanied by a commentary by a contemporary master. Gradually, a *florilegium* thus developed into a scholastic summary. An intermediary stage that was essential to this development involved the production of another type of book, a collection of "sentence commentaries." These "sentences" constituted an elaboration of fundamental texts intended for scholastic discussion. The principal elaborator of such sentences was the bishop of Paris, the Italian Peter the Lombard, who died in 1160. His *Book of Sentences* (probably composed about 1155–7) became the basic thirteenth-century textbook used in university theological faculties.

Thirteenth-century scholastic works took two principal forms. One was that of the *commentary*. Along with the *disputatio*, the commentary constituted the essential stimulus in the development of thirteenth-century knowledge. A commentary was a means of elaborating new knowledge that masters derived from contemporary preoccupations, continuing to rely on tradition yet at the same time getting it to evolve. The Europe of commentaries ushered in a Europe of intellectual progress which, however, managed not to break with tradition. As Alain de Libera has remarked, "The history of the commentary is a history of the progressive liberation of philosophical thought from the precepts of tradition." The other important product of thirteenth-century scholasticism was the *summa*. The very word conveys the desire of thirteenth-century intellectuals to provide a well-documented and well-argued synthesis of a philosophy that had not yet separated from theology. It is perhaps worth remembering that M. D. Chenu has stressed the fact that theology was presented as a "science."

The thirteenth century produced many famous and exemplary scholastics the greatest of whom certainly deserve a mention. The first great *summa* to emerge from the universities was that of the English Franciscan, Alexander of Hales, in the 1230s. The Dominican Albert the Great, who in 1248 was the first German to obtain the title of Master of Theology from the university of Paris, expanded knowledge by extending his works to cover areas of the arts and sciences not taught at university. He made considerable use of the Arabic philosophers al-Farabi, Avicenna, and Averroës. Albert the Great's oeuvre was not only encyclopedic but also testified to his great efforts to reconcile philosophy and theology. He was, furthermore, the master of Thomas Aquinas in Cologne, his own native town.

Thomas Aquinas was the scholastic whose influence made the greatest impact on European thought, continuing down to the present day. This Italian, from the lower nobility, who spent several periods in Paris, first as a student, then as a professor, but also studied in Orvieto, Rome, and Naples, was a fashionable teacher who attracted students and fired them with enthusiasm. At the same time, however, as a bold thinker, he also aroused the hostility of many colleagues and also a number of influential prelates. He was the kind of attractive and controversial European intellectual who could not fail at once to illuminate and also to trouble intellectual and religious circles. From his immense oeuvre, let me mention but two *summae*: the *Summa against the Gentiles* (1259–62) and the *Theological Summa*, his main work, left unfinished when he died in 1274, at the age of 50. Although he did insist on the superiority of theology, Aquinas at the same time manifested "an astonishing confidence in the power of reason" (as Étienne Gilson put it). The *Summa* reconciles what is sometimes called "a lower theology," which expresses all that reason allows man to know of God and the world, and "a higher theology," which shows how divine truth descends to man through revelation, bypassing the intellect. As Ruedi Imbach has observed, according to Aquinas, man is determined by three relationships: his relationships to reason, to God, and to his fellows.

As Aquinas saw it, man is a total human being, not simply one of God's creatures that is a rational animal, but also "a social and political animal" who, to manifest his individuality, makes use of an essential God-given gift, language. Scholastics in general paid great attention to language and certainly earned their place in the European history of linguistics.

I must cite one more scholastic master, another famous and controversial figure who deserves to be included in the long list of European intellectuals that stretches from the Middle Ages down to the present day: the Franciscan Roger Bacon (ca. 214–ca. 1282). He published a *summa* in three parts, the *Opus majus*, the *Opus minus*, and the *Opus tertium*, which he composed at the request of his friend and protector Pope Clement IV (pope 1265–8). He worked in the university of Oxford. He was both a philosopher and a theologian and was at once aggressive and prophetic, making numerous enemies, including the Dominican Albert the Great, against whom he launched a violent attack. Bacon ascribed a particular importance to a kind of astronomy that was really astrology, and he dreamed up all sorts of prophetic techniques and inventions that make him, as it were, a thirteenth-century Leonardo da Vinci.

In conclusion, let me mention the three essential contributions that scholasticism made to European intellectual activity. Abélard who, in the twelfth century, was one of the foremost prescholastics, underlined a fundamental lesson learned from Aristotle: "The first key to wisdom is a ceaseless questioning. Aristotle said that to doubt everything is by no means useless. For whoever is led to seek and who does seek seizes on the truth." In his *Dialogue between a Philosopher, a Jew, and a Christian*, Abélard also observed: "Whatever the subject of a discussion, rational demonstration carries more weight than citations from many authorities." Abélard's doubt, which the scholastics took over, thus holds a decisive place amid the new forms of the critical thinking elaborated by the Greeks which, right down to the present day, have defined the European critical thinking which Gramsci, in the twentieth century, considered to be embodied in the critical intellectual.

Secondly, as Alain de Libera rightly points out, scholasticism brought with it great "intellectual freedom." It thus inserted into the European intellectual tradition the idea that knowledge is liberating.

Finally, through its desire to set ideas in order and to expound knowledge and thought as clearly as possible, medieval scholasticism reinforced, if it did not create, the taste for order and clarity customarily attributed to Descartes, who has all too often been presented as the chief actor in a modern revolution of European thought. Descartes had predecessors, and those predecessors were the scholastic masters. Descartes himself was a brilliant child of medieval scholasticism.

Linguistic Europe: Latin and the Vernacular Languages

Latin had remained the language of learning, and its prestige was strengthened by the fact that the Christian liturgy was also expressed in Latin. However, during the last centuries of the Roman Empire, between the first and the fourth centuries AD, Latin had evolved to a point where specialists speak of "low Latin." Furthermore, as schools had declined, the lay masses had gradually taken to speaking languages that eventually were not Latin at all. Historians have pondered the question of when it was that people ceased to speak Latin and began to speak so-called "vernacular" languages. Of course, the peoples who had been Christianized and had only then become subjects of Christian kingdoms spoke other languages, mostly Germanic ones, for only the clergy and elite groups had learnt Latin. The general view is that by the ninth century the language spoken by lay people was no longer Latin; and the birth of vulgar tongues is often dated to a famous text, the *Strasbourg Oaths* of 841, sworn by the two sons of Emperor Louis the Pious. One swore the oaths in a language that was on the way to becoming French, the other used a language that was on the way to becoming German. The political organization of Christian Europe was effected by the constitution of national structures beneath those of the community of Christendom as a whole. The Church recognized the legitimacy of these new languages. The Church Fathers had distinguished three main languages: Hebrew, Greek, and Latin. But Augustine had stressed that no one language was superior to the rest and that this was the message of Whitsun, when the Holy Ghost, with no discrimination and paying no attention to any hierarchy, had bestowed upon the apostles the gift of tongues. The retreat of Latin obliged the religious and political leaders of the Early Middle Ages to come to some important decisions regarding languages. In 794, the synod of Frankfurt declared, following Augustine: "Let no one believe that God may be worshipped in three languages only. God is worshipped in all languages and people's prayers are answered if they just." But the most important decision was that reached by the Council of Tours in 813. It invited preachers to deliver their sermons in vernacular languages: "Let every preacher take care to translate his homily clearly into a vulgar Romance or Germanic language so that everyone may more easily understand what is said." This text has been hailed as "the birth certificate of national languages." In the thirteenth century these vernacular languages evolved further and continued to do so throughout the late Middle Ages. Above all, in time they were not just spoken but also written; and once they became written languages they gave birth to literature written in the vernacular. In many cases masterpieces were produced, such as the *chansons de geste*, courtly novels, and *fabliaux*. How would this linguistic and literary Tower of Babel manage to become integrated into a European community? Even the Latin spoken by scholastics was neither classical Latin nor a Latin that was spoken generally. Scholastic Latin was an artificial language. However, as it continued for centuries to be used for all university purposes, both in theology and philosophy and to express other ideas, it was one of the bases of European thought – the thought of an elitist Europe, however.

The evolution of the so-called "vernacular" languages was slow (the word *verna* meant slave in antiquity, so originally these were languages spoken by individuals who were considered socially and intellectually inferior). A crucial turning point came with their written use in legal works and with the development of literature in vulgar languages. Here again, the twelfth and thirteenth centuries were of essential importance. The promotion of these languages was linked with the development of states, during a period that lasted from the twelfth to the sixteenth centuries and in which the thirteenth was particularly crucial.

After the year 1000, the vernacular languages came to form a small number of linguistic groups, according to their origins. First, let us distinguish the languages that derived from Latin and that remained relatively close to it. These were the *Romance* languages, primarily French, the Iberian languages, and Italian.

French emerged as an alloy of Latin and the Germanic language of the Franks. A merging of the dialects spoken in Gaul led to the emergence of two languages, the *langue d'oc* in southern France and the *langue d'oïl*, which was spoken in the court of the kings of France, who were both political and cultural leaders, and this prevailed in northern France. Subsequently, following the northerners' victories, conquests, and interventions in the south, it also prevailed over the *langue d'oc*.

The case of England was unusual, for up until the fifteenth century three languages were spoken there. Following the Norman conquest in 1066, alongside the old English spoken by the Anglo-Saxons, French became established, in the form of an Anglo-Norman dialect. Latin was, of course, the third language. English gained ground, spreading upward from the lower social strata, and eventually acquired a prenational character (Edward I (ruled 1272–1307) was the first English king to speak it). However, right down to the fifteenth century French remained the language of power, of aristocrats, and of fashion. The great noble families sent their children to study in Normandy, to learn to speak good French there.

The unification of German was even more problematic. The very notion of German was of late date and the word *deutsch* made a timid appearance only in the ninth century. Linguistically, Germany remained territorially split between Low German, Middle German, High German, and Frisian, plus a small enclave of Swabian-Slavic.

The political and ethnic situation of the Iberian peninsula also produced an unusual situation. There, the principal dialects or languages spoken were often linked to the prevailing political situation. Mozarabic was a mixture of Christian dialects and Arabic ("Mozarabic" comes from the word *musta'rab* or *musta'rib*, meaning "that is Arabized," a term that appeared in the eleventh century). Following the disappearance of Mozarabic, by the thirteenth century Castilian had eliminated most of the other dialects spoken in the peninsula, such as the language of León and Galician (although the latter remained the poetic language everywhere). Only Catalan and Portuguese survived. The unification of Spain strengthened Castilian even further.

Throughout Europe, more or less generally, the upper strata of society were bilingual and could more or less cope with Latin. But increasingly the social and political elite found it necessary to know and use vernacular languages.

In the thirteenth century, under the twofold influence of the royal administration and the university of Paris and despite the obligatory use of Latin there, Francien unified the d'oïl dialects. In truth, although the university Latin was neither the classic Latin of antiquity nor the vulgar Latin that was spoken here and there, but was a new, artificial language, it nevertheless played an important role in the intellectual unification of Europe, for it was "the technical language of abstract thought" (to borrow Christiane Mohrmann's expression).

As Philippe Wolff has noted, the 1246 statutes of Bologna ruled that candidates aiming to become notaries had to show that they were capable of reading out documents, which they had penned in Latin, in the vulgar tongue, for the benefit of their clients.

It was in Italy that the linguistic situation was the most uncertain – so much so that many linguists hesitate to speak of thirteenth-century Italian at all. In the mid-thirteenth century, the Franciscan Salimbene of Parma reckoned that the languages of Tuscany and Lombardy were languages in their own right, on a par with French. At the end of the century, linguistic knowledge was dominated by Dante. In his treatise *De vulgari eloquentia*, written in about 1303 (in Latin!), he distinguished 14 groups of dialects in Italy and relegated them all to an inferior level, even those regarded as proper languages, such as Roman, Milanese, Sardinian, Sicilian, Bolognese, and even Tuscan. What he recommended in their stead was a vulgar language that he called the *volgare illustre* which, according to him, transcended all the dialects but appropriated elements from each. Dante truly was the father of Italian, in a country that was not politically united until the nineteenth century and whose cultural unification is still far from complete.

The people of the Middle Ages themselves certainly realized that a multiplicity of languages constituted an obstacle to communication in a Europe where, particularly in the economic domain, Latin could no longer play a unifying role. They therefore worked toward a simplification of multilingualism, chiefly by constructing states that would later turn into nations. The language problem remains one of the greatest difficulties in the construction of present-day Europe. However, the medieval example does show that limited multilingualism can function perfectly well in a European community, and also that such linguistic multiplicity is preferable by far to a single language that would not be rooted in any long cultural and political tradition, as would be the case if English or any other European language were to become the language of Europe.

If the future of Europe became clearer in the thirteenth century, that is largely thanks to the evolution of various literatures. Europe represents a variegated bouquet of literary genres and works. Great literary works confirmed and supported the success of national languages.

Great Literatures and Masterpieces

The French language made its mark from the late eleventh century on, with the genre constituted by the *chansons de geste* and, in particular the *Chanson de Roland*. It was also very influential thanks to its courtly romances, the greatest of whose authors was Chrétien de Troyes. Many *chansons de geste*, in particular, were translated or imitated in the Germanic language. Arthurian literature, centered on the partly legendary Celtic hero Arthur, inspired the creation of a genre that was destined to enjoy a prodigious success in Europe that continues even today. This was the novel, with two main branches, the one historical, the other romantic, the former about heroic individuals, the latter about couples: stories over which, in many cases, a horizon of death loomed. The Europe of Eros and Thanatos had emerged.

Castilian made its mark in the mid-eleventh century with the *Cantar del mio Cid*. The Cid was a noble Christian adventurer who, in 1094, set up the first Christian state in Islamic territory, in the Valencia region. He was a real "frontier adventurer" and served now the Christian, now the Muslim rulers. He was known as El Cid, a name derived from the Arabic *Sayyid*, "lord."

The Diffusion of Prose

In the thirteenth century something happened in the realm of literature that was to affect the European literary world right down to the present day. The *chansons de geste* were written in verse. The first literary monument of Scandinavia, the Edda, was also written in verse. The Edda was a collection of 30 or so mythological and heroic poems composed between the ninth and the twelfth centuries in Scandinavia. It was preserved in an Icelandic manuscript dating from the last third of the thirteenth century. The thirteenth century replaced poetry by prose, which then became the principal form of literary writing. The intention was to replace the artifices of rhyme by more realistic writing. In the thirteenth century courtly poetry was thus recast in prose, as was the Edda, which was reworked by the great Icelandic Snorri Sturluson (1179–1241).

Historical literature also appeared in the thirteenth century. But at that time history was neither a subject that was taught (not until the nineteenth century would it figure on the curriculum of either schools or universities), nor was there a recognized historical genre of literature (this was before the enjoyable accounts of the chronicles of the fourteenth and fifteenth centuries had made their appearance). Nevertheless, the authority and attraction of the past and its strong ideological value ensured that memoirs, if not history, had an important place in literature.

The literary genres that would nowadays be classified as historical consisted, in medieval Europe, of several different types of works. One type was the universal chronicle, which had been inaugurated by Eusebius of Caesarea in the fourth century and which reflected a globalization of knowledge in a Europe that knew nothing of the continent of the Americas and very little about most of Africa and Asia. Another genre that became very popular was biography. This took the form of Lives of the saints, or hagiography. In the thirteenth century, such hagiography reached an exceptionally high standard in the *Golden Legend* composed by Jacobus de Voragine, the Dominican archbishop of Genoa.

In England, a number of successful works such as those by William of Malmesbury (1095–1143) and, in particular, a *History of the Kings of Britain* by Geoffrey of Monmouth (who died in 1155) purveyed a historical image that established a continuity between Britain's Celtic, Anglo-Saxon, and Norman kings. Above all, a series of works dominated by a character called Brut (the first king of Great Britain, according to Geoffrey of Monmouth) spread the popularity of King Arthur and promoted the idea of a

Trojan origin of the English monarchy. A series of chronicles entitled *Brut* was extremely popular in the thirteenth century.

In parallel, a myth of the Trojan origins of the Franks had been developing in France ever since the Early Middle Ages. This was particularly encouraged by the monks of the royal abbey of Saint-Denis, with a view to promoting the Capetian dynasty. In 1274, the senior monk of Saint-Denis presented King Philip III with a synthesis commissioned by Philip III's father, Saint Louis. This became the source for the great chronicles of France. It was known as the *roman aux rois* (*roman* being a reference to the language in which it was written, not to the literary genre). These legendary histories testify to a European desire, in the face of the Greeks of antiquity, to be connected with some other origin. In the *Aeneid*, Virgil had already portrayed the Romans as descendants of the Trojan heroes who survived the Trojan War and found refuge in Europe. The Italians of the Middle Ages welcomed this tradition. The Middle Ages furthermore enriched this myth of Trojan origins by producing a story about fugitive Trojans who, before reaching western and southern Europe, spent several centuries in central Europe on the site of the ancient Roman town of Aquincum (Budapest). This was an episode in the myth that the Hungarian monarchy was quick to exploit in the Middle Ages.

4   THE SUCCESS OF THE MENDICANT FRIARS

The thirteenth century of towns, merchants, universities, and vernacular literatures was also affected by clerics of a new type, whose activities marked European society for many years to come. They belonged to the Mendicant Orders, the chief of which were the Order of the Friars Preachers (Dominicans, also known as the Black Friars) and the Order of the Friars Minor (Franciscans). These orders were not made up of monks living in the collective solitude of isolated monasteries. Instead, their members lived out in the community amid ordinary town-dwellers. It was this new urban society that they influenced through their preaching and liturgical activities, spreading a new Christianity that took much more interest in secular society and manifested a great concern to involve clergy and lay people alike in the expansion of European Christianity. The influence of these mendicant friars was strong and most effective.

The Church was faced with a number of serious problems. The Gregorian reform was not yet completed, heresies were spreading rapidly, the Church had failed to adapt to a society in which money circulated and wealth had become a value, and the monastic culture linked with a rural society was no longer capable of satisfying the demands of many Christians. Response to these problems came from a number of figures – some from the clergy, others secular – who set up orders of a new type. They were not monastic and were accepted by the papacy only with difficulty. They were called Mendicant Orders because their most striking feature was their commitment to humility and poverty. The order founded by Francis of Assisi was, equally suitably, known as the Order of the Friars Minor. These orders were so successful that by the beginning of the thirteenth century they were multiplying fast. However, in 1274 the second Council of Lyon reduced their number to four: the Preachers or Dominicans, the Minors or Franciscans, the Hermits of Saint Augustine, and the Carmelites. To these, the papacy, in the early fourteenth century, added the Servants of Mary, founded by a group of penitent Florentine merchants who had committed themselves to working in a hospice dedicated to the Virgin Mary and had retired from the town to take up a life of poverty in this community. Their success was confined to Italy, chiefly northern Italy. Many of them later became reintegrated into cities, for example Rome, where they were presented with the Church of San Marcello. For others, study was the chief priority, and these attended the university of Paris. However, historiography tends not to include them in the group of Mendicant Orders.

The great prestige of the Dominicans and Franciscans stemmed to a large degree from the personalities of their founders. Dominic, born in Caleruega in Castile in about 1170, became the canon of the chapter of Osma in 1196. Traveling through Languedoc in the course of his mission, he was horrified by the number of heretics he came across. He decided to fight them on their own ground, living in poverty and devoting himself to preaching. He established bases at Prouille and Fanjeaux, between Carcassonne and Toulouse, and gathered together a fraternity of clerics. The success of the group was such that, in 1215, it was recognized by Pope Innocent III. In that same year, the Fourth Lateran Council prohibited the creation of new orders. However, as Dominic's group followed the rule of Saint Augustine, as was customary in canonical circles, he gained authorization to form an order which, in a pontifical bull of 1217, was named "the Order of the Friars Preachers." Dominic sent his brothers forth into a number of urban centers, preferably quite large ones, in particular Paris and Bologna, for they were keen that their preaching be founded upon serious scholarship. (The Dominicans usually established themselves in large towns, unlike the Franciscans, who were more attracted to medium-sized and small ones.) Toward the end of his life Dominic himself preached above all in northern Italy, and he died in the monastery of Bologna in 1221. He was canonized in 1234.

Francis of Assisi was quite different. He was the son of a textile merchant in the little town of Assisi and was at first tempted by a knightly style of life. In about 1206 he decided, in spectacular fashion, to renounce this life and not to follow in his father's footsteps as expected. He abandoned all his fine clothes in the public square, denounced money and trade, and called upon his fellow citizens to join him in a life of poverty devoted to the service of Christ. With a few companions, he formed an itinerant group with bases at two modest churches in the vicinity of Assisi, San Damiano and the "Portiuncula." Following difficult negotiations with Pope Innocent III, Francis's fraternity, composed of both clerics and laymen, gained recognition as a new order, for which he composed his own rule. He was obliged to rewrite this at the bidding of Pope Honorius II, who finally approved it in 1223, once Francis had deleted the most provocative passages relating to poverty and community life. Before rapidly considering the early days of the Franciscan Order, which, unlike those of the Dominicans, were extremely troubled, let us note what was new about these two new orders.

The most striking novelty was no doubt their implantation in urban surroundings and the fact that towns were the main centers targeted by the preaching and activity of both the Dominicans and the Franciscans. But they also pursued their activities on the roads along which they passed and by organizing retreats in mountain hermitages. Furthermore, the way in which they lived was radically different from the lifestyle of the monks. They owned no property, neither land nor income. They lived off alms. Some alms took the form of gifts that enabled them, contravening the instructions of their founders, to construct churches, increasingly large ones as time passed, although these did preserve a degree of moderation in their decoration. The Mendicant Orders truly did place Christ and the New Testament at the center not only of their own piety but also that of lay people. Francis of Assisi went to extreme lengths to identify with Jesus. In the mountainous solitude of Mount Alverna in central Italy, a seraphim appeared to him and imprinted upon his body the stigmata, that is to say the scars of the wounds that Christ had received on the cross. Through their intense preaching, the Mendicant Orders also taught the people, particularly those of the towns, new religious practices. They brought forth a Europe of speech, of sermons, which, when secularized, would become the Europe of political speeches and of the hustings, the Europe of militant speech.

Francis, fascinated by God's divine work, that is to say the whole of creation, sang its praises in the famous *Canticle of Brother Sun*, also known as the *Canticle of God's Creatures*, to which some scholars have traced the origin of the European sense of nature. Originally the Mendicant Orders, placing their apostolate at the service of the Church, had devoted themselves to pastoral activities. However, the papacy soon diverted their energies into new missions. Faced as it was with so many heretics, the Church, at the risk of warping their vocation, propelled the mendicants beyond preaching and toward inquisition. Soon the papacy withdrew the direction of inquisitorial courts from the bishops and entrusted it, instead, to the Mendicant Orders. As a result, their reputation in thirteenth-century European society was extremely mixed. On the one hand they were admired, honored, and followed. In 1233, a campaign to pacify the conflicts tearing apart the towns of northern Italy, known as the "Alleluia movement," for a short time enjoyed a spectacular success. On the other hand, in some quarters they were attacked and became the objects of hostility or even hatred. An exemplary case is that of the Dominican inquisitor (Saint) Peter the Martyr, a virulent inquisitor in northern Italy, who in 1252 was assassinated on the road leading from Como to Milan. Representations of him show a saint with a knife cleaving his skull. His case illustrates the distance that was beginning to separate the Church and the Mendicant Orders on the one hand from the majority of the faithful, on the other, where attitudes toward the Inquisition were concerned.

Both orders found themselves the butt of searing criticism from laymen on the subject of teaching and knowledge, above all in the university of Paris. Secular masters, chief among them William of Saint-Amour and poets such as Rutebeuf and Jean de Meung, strongly attacked the Mendicant Orders, primarily with regard to the very principle of begging and poverty. Should not men, including clerics, live by the product of their own labors and not off alms that enabled them to live in idleness? As we shall see below, such feelings were fueled by the emergence of a Europe of work and the promotion of the very idea of work. Were the mendicant brothers true beggars? Should one not prefer to bestow one's alms upon real beggars who were condemned to mendicancy by their poverty, not by their own choice? The mendicants' takeover of functions belonging to the secular clergy (i.e. nonmonastic clergy), such as the bestowal of the sacraments and the administration of churches, which drew attention to the money to be earned from religion, shocked a number of the faithful and above all stirred up many of the secular clergy against the Mendicants. Another factor that fueled, rather than calmed, the conflict was the papacy's tendency, from the mid-thirteenth century on, to select bishops from among mendicant friars, thereby blurring the distinction between regular clergy (i.e. those belonging to orders with rules) and secular clergy.

The Dominicans had right away declared their interest in study, and the Franciscans had followed suit, despite Francis of Assisi's doubts about an activity that would eventually lead to the purchase of books. But in the universities, particularly in Paris, the Mendicants had from the start been viewed askance because, at the time of the great strike of 1229–31, they had made the most of the attitude of the secular university teachers in order to get university chairs created for themselves. They were perceived by the university world as strike-breakers, "scabs." In the course of the thirteenth century, the conflict between Mendicants and secular scholars repeatedly poisoned the atmosphere of the university of Paris. When the papacy intervened it usually took the side of the Mendicants and its interventions aggravated, rather than calmed down the quarrel, in which Bonaventure and Thomas Aquinas both played a leading role in the defense of the legitimacy and merit of voluntary poverty. With the appearance of the Mendicants, the thirteenth century thus constituted a key moment in the long history of poverty in Europe, which sadly has still by no means come to an end.

Other forms of dissent, in this case internal, also troubled the Franciscan Order in the thirteenth century. Even in the lifetime of Saint Francis, a strict, ascetic attitude had clashed with a tendency to compromise with the necessities of life in society. Francis seems usually to have taken the part of the more rigorous party, but he always avoided disobedience to the Church and the Holy See. Many of the conflicts that disturbed the order after his death arose in connection with his own image and his memory. The first clash was occasioned by the construction of the Basilica of Assisi by Francis's successor, Brother Eli, despite the fact that the latter had been personally designated by Francis. The dimensions and splendor of the Basilica seemed in contradiction to the spirituality of Francis. Later, conflict continued to erupt chiefly in connection with the biographical texts that were devoted to Francis. This was the beginning of what the great nineteenth-century modern biographer of Francis, the Protestant Paul Sabatier, called "the Franciscan question." As Sabatier saw it, this question arose in particular out of an event that ought to have resolved the problem then and there, in the late thirteenth century. In 1260, the general chapter of the order decided that the Minister General, Bonaventure, should produce an official Life of Saint Francis, to take the place of all those written earlier, and it moreover decided (incredibly) that all those previous Lives should be destroyed. If the condemnations of Bishop Tempier in Paris are also taken into consideration, it cannot, unfortunately, be denied that the thirteenth century saw the birth not only of the Inquisition but also of a Europe of censorship.

A Europe of Charity

Through their preaching, the Mendicants shaped a Europe of speech. They also brought to life a Europe of charity, and were thus the ancestors of a Europe of social security. The system that they set in place in the thirteenth century was known as "works of mercy." These were founded on a New Testament text, Matthew 25, which states that on Judgment Day, the son of God will separate human beings into two groups and tell those placed on his right that they are to enter the kingdom of God as a reward for the acts of kindness they performed for him in his earthly life. Good works consisted of visiting the sick, bringing water to the thirsty, feeding the hungry, ransoming captives (in the thirteenth century, mostly prisoners of the Muslim pirates of the Mediterranean), clothing the naked, welcoming strangers, and founding religious services in memory of the dead. The Mendicant Brothers were more active than anyone in preaching and performing such works of mercy. They were also active in hospitals, more and more of which were appearing in the towns. A Europe of hospitals was born.

The Third Orders: In-between the Clergy and Laymen

The last feature of the Mendicant Orders to note was a fruit of their concern for secular townsfolk. They founded the Third Orders, groups of lay people from a variety of walks of life, many of whom were quite well off, who, while remaining with their families and continuing to practice their respective professions, at the same time endeavored to lead a life as close as possible to that of the friars. In accordance with the wishes of their founders, the Mendicant Orders consisted of three kinds: one for men, one for women (the Franciscan Clare Sisters and the female Dominicans), and also a Third Order. The latter considerably extended their influence in urban society, which thus found itself supported on all sides by these three orders. However, the Mendicant Orders were always dominated by the first of the three, that of the friars, the males, and by the papacy. It was not very long before this first order became clericalized, as a result of which, as Father Desbonnets has shown in the case of the Franciscans, the Mendicant Orders passed rapidly from "intuition to institution." Despite the progress made by laymen as members of the Church, the thirteenth century failed to form a Europe of laymen.

OTHER ASPECTS OF THE "FINE" THIRTEENTH CENTURY IN
EUROPE

Gothic Europe

The thirteenth century was a great period for art, particularly architecture. Art generally and architecture in particular constituted one of the great manifestations of European unity and one of the elements that cemented Christendom together. Although they shared common features, the various literatures were separated by the differences of their respective languages; but the language of art was more or less universal. Already the Romanesque style which, as its name suggests, to a certain extent represented a return to ancient Roman art, had spread throughout Europe, developing individual features peculiar to particular peoples and regions. Gothic art, sometimes known as French art, for its part flooded the whole of Christian Europe, spreading out from northern France and in particular from the heart of what was known in the thirteenth century as "France in the strict sense" and later came to be called the Île-de-France. This new art, very different from the Romanesque style, constituted a response to both a great demographic surge forward that called for larger churches and also to a profound change in taste. Quite apart from its greater dimensions, the Gothic style was characterized by an attraction to verticality, light, and even color. Large towns (for this, far more than Romanesque art, was an urban phenomenon) competed in boldness and in beauty as they constructed Gothic edifices, the most famous of which were cathedrals. Georges Duby has called this period "the time of cathedrals." It produced a Europe of gigantic edifices and excess. The watchword of Gothic architects seems to have been "higher, ever higher." After a first generation of cathedrals produced between 1140 and 1190, of which those of Sens, Noyon, and Laon are outstanding examples, the thirteenth century became the great age of cathedrals, starting with Notre-Dame in Paris. The frantic quest for length and height found expression above all in the cathedral of Amiens, built between 1220 and 1270, that is to say during almost the whole of the reign of Saint Louis. It was here, in its choir, already completed in 1256, that Saint Louis pronounced his famous Declaration of Amiens, arbitrating between the king of England and England's barons. Amiens cathedral was 145 meters long and 42.50 meters high. That record height was equaled and exceeded by the choir of Beauvais Cathedral which in 1272 reached 47 meters but then, in 1284, collapsed.

A spiritual notion of light inspired the construction of the tall windows of Gothic churches. The theory behind such architecture had been expounded as early as the twelfth century by Suger, the abbot of Saint-Denis, who initiated the reconstruction of this abbey's church, in accordance with the new theological and aesthetic principles. Unlike the windows of Romanesque buildings, which were generally of transparent or opaque glass, Gothic windowpanes bloomed with color, thanks to the progress made in the cultivation of dye-producing plants such as woad, and technical improvements in methods of staining glass. The effects of the colors of stained-glass windows in combination with the many colors of painted sculptures have been celebrated by Alain Erlande-Brandeburg in his work entitled *Quand les cathédrales étaient peintes* (When cathedrals were painted). Gothic architecture was indeed accompanied by a flowering of sculpture, mostly for the ornamentation of cathedrals. The development of the sculpted porches of cathedrals provided a spectacular setting for sculptures, in particular representations of the Last Judgment, which would fill those who saw them with a mixture of awe and hope, just as the vertical sweep of the building and the brilliance of its windows did.

The Europe of stained glass is particularly well represented by the cathedral of Chartres, where the blues used in the windows are famous. The great French cathedrals were often imitated in other countries. Most imitations were modeled on the type with three aisles, but some followed the five-aisled example set, for instance, by Bourges. The finest copies were built in Spain. The cathedral of Burgos is outstanding and León and Toledo are also impressive. In England, a particular type of Gothic spread from Normandy, one of the earliest expressions of what, in the fourteenth and fifteenth centuries, would be called flamboyant Gothic. In Italy Gothic art was somewhat "squeezed out" by on the one hand the persistence of Romanesque art, on the other the earliest examples of Renaissance art. Thanks to the Mendicant Orders, however, the Gothic style did enjoy a limited diffusion, as in Assisi. In the Germanic and above all the Hanseatic region, a particular type of Gothic church developed under the influence of the merchants. These churches were constructed around a single nave and were known as hall-churches. In an inaugural lecture delivered at the Collège de France on March 14, 2002, Roland Recht recently drew attention to the longevity of the Gothic tradition, the influence of which can still be detected today:

> If we look carefully at distinguished twentieth-century buildings, we can see that in many cases they prolong, enrich, and bring up to date a whole series of techniques developed between 1140 and 1350 in north-western Europe. Many modern architects owe much of their architectural culture to those developments: figures such as Poelzig, Bruno Taut, Mies van der Rohe, Gropius,

Niemeyer, Gaudí, but also others such as Nervi, Gaudin, Gehry, and so on. Liberating itself from the classical ideal, the architecture of the modern movement has made it possible to draw inspiration from all that that ideal had blocked: the redefinition of the wall in terms of placing and aesthetics, the establishment of freestanding structures, the prefabrication of standardized elements, and above all, clear readability of the function through the form.

A digression to take in all the different forms of Gothic would lead us too far afield. But we should not forget that the Gothic Europe of the thirteenth century was a Europe not only of architecture but also of sculpture, ranging from cathedral porches to the sculpted pulpits of Pisa and statues of angels, virgins, and princesses. It was also a Europe of paintings, ranging from frescoes to miniatures. The Gothic thirteenth century wonderfully enriched our Europe of images.

Courtly Europe

During the Middle Ages, manuscript copies were made of the third-century *Disticha Catonis*, written in verse, and the thirteenth century witnessed the consolidation of a Europe of good manners. Modern historians and sociologists call these aspects of civilization, but the Christians of the thirteenth century spoke, rather, of courtliness. Later, the words "urbanity" and "politeness," associated with the urban space, also came to be used to designate a refinement of sensibilities and modes of behavior. The first comprehensive study of this development was produced in 1939 by the German sociologist Norbert Elias. His innovative work was entitled *Über den Prozess der Zivilisation* (published in English as *The Civilizing Process*). The people of the Middle Ages called this development "courtliness." The very etymology of the word indicates that this movement, which dates from the Middle Ages and in particular the thirteenth century, had two social origins, the court and the town. In the twelfth and thirteenth centuries the combination of noble and bourgeois *mores* inspired a number of handbooks on courtliness, some written in Latin, others in the vernacular. They included, in England, the *Liber Urbani* and the *Facetus*, in German *Der wälche Gast* (*Wälche* was a medieval German term for "foreigner") by Thomasin de Zerklaere and a Poem by Tannhäuser, and also a *Treatise on Courtliness* by the Milanese educator Bonvesin della Riva. The advice on good manners offered in these works mainly concerned table manners, natural functions, sexual relations, and the campaign against aggressive behavior. Bonvesin, for instance, declares:

One must never drink from the soup bowl but use a spoon, as is more fitting. Whoever leans over the soup-bowl and, in unseemly fashion, drools into it like a pig, would do well to go off and join the other beasts.

The use of the fork, which did not catch on when it was brought from Byzantium to Venice at an early date, only began to spread gradually in the fourteenth and fifteenth centuries.

The culmination of all this literature was the *De civitate morum puerilium* (On the civility of the manners of children), a treatise by Erasmus written in Latin and translated into several languages, which was to enjoy a great success in the sixteenth century. The Europe of good manners was born in the thirteenth century.

The Ambiguous Promotion of Work

The thirteenth century also witnessed an important change in attitudes and behavior in an essential area of human activity, in which medieval traditions are still perceptible, namely that of work. In the Middle Ages, the status of work was ambiguous, and was particularly problematic in the monastic world. Monastic rules, in the first instance those of Saint Benedict, established that monks should do two kinds of work: intellectual, that is to say the copying of manuscripts, and economically productive work, namely subsistence agriculture. For monks, obligatory work was an act of penitence. The Book of Genesis declared that God punished the original sin of Adam and Eve by condemning them to work. Monastic penitence, in the form of work, was thus also a kind of atonement. In this way, a notion of the value of work appeared. Given that in the early medieval society monks enjoyed great prestige, the very fact that they worked somewhat paradoxically conferred upon work a positive value. This was enhanced between the eleventh and the thirteenth centuries. The technological improvements to rural work, the development of craftsmanship in the towns, and the pursuit of wealth and high social status as the fruits of hard work also reflected well upon the image of work. As we have seen, merchants and university teachers were justified by their work. The friars of the Mendicant Orders were criticized for their refusal to work but defended themselves, claiming that their apostolic mission was itself a form of work. Some social classes claimed superiority on the grounds that they did not have to work: these included contemplatives and the clergy, and warriors, knights, and nobles. But they were forced to beat a retreat in the face of the promotion of work on both social and spiritual grounds. Warrior activity was now presented as useful work undertaken to protect the weak. Even before the defense put up by the Mendicants, the hard work involved in the apostolate of the clergy was also recognized and praised. Most under threat from the high value placed on work was the world of courtliness and chivalry. One adage that emerged at this time was "Labor is greater than prowess." Nevertheless, the image of work was still seriously disadvantaged. There was no precise word for it, so the very concept did not exist. On the one hand, *labor* suggested, above all, effort (but it did produce "laborer" and the English "Labour"). *Opera*, on the other hand, designated a product of work, an oeuvre (although it did give rise to the term for worker, *ouvrier*). So a distinction, in fact an opposition between manual labor, ever more despised, and other honorable and honored forms of works remained and was even reinforced. The poet Rutebeuf boasted proudly, "I am not a manual worker." Such was the birth of a Europe with ambiguous attitudes toward work, which was sometimes seen as dignified, sometimes as undignified. The fact that society, in particular the Church and the high and mighty, appeared to lavish their praises on work essentially in order to ensure that workers continued to be enslaved by their employers inevitably contributed to this ambiguity. The debate continues today. The fundamental transformations of work in our society constitute one of the major turning-points of our so-called "advanced" societies.

Europe, the Mongols, and the East

The thirteenth century witnessed the consolidation of a development that deeply affected the problem of the formation of Europe. As usually happens, a European identity took shape in reaction to enemies or "others." In antiquity the "others" were the Persians, then they were barbarians and pagans as a whole, eventually the Muslims. The final permutation of the "other" was added, in the thirteenth century, when "the other" was identified with the Mongols. The Mongol invasion of 1241, which advanced as far west as Silesia, but then pulled back eastward, produced severe shock and panic-stricken fear among the Christians. The king of France, Saint Louis, expected death to be martyrdom; and throughout his crusade in the East he was preoccupied, now positively, now negatively, by those strange Mongols who might prove to be terrible enemies but just might turn out to be allies in the fight against Islam. Fear of the Mongols fueled a change in attitudes that was already quite pronounced anyway and that led to the abandonment of the Crusades. The wave of fervor for the crusades had been smothered by the Christians' increasing preoccupation with their lands, their goods, and the affairs of the West. The Mongol threat cemented together all those strands of waning interest in the Holy Land.

In contrast to the slow construction of frontiers still represented by territorial zones rather than by lines that would later be fixed by national states, a new decisive factor of Christian Europe appeared in the east. The Christian countries that established this new view of Europe were first Hungary, then Poland. These two presented themselves as the ramparts of Christendom against the pagan barbarians, primarily Mongols, but also Cumans for Hungary, and Prussians and Lithuanians for Poland. The clearest expression of this new situation and these new views is to be found in a letter addressed to the pope by the king of Hungary, Bela IV, between 1247 and 1254. In it he declares that the Tartars (the traditional name for Mongols) are determinedly preparing shortly to launch their innumerable forces *against the whole of Europe* (*contra totam Europam*). He then goes on to say, "If, God forbid, the empire of Constantinople and the Christian regions overseas were to be lost, even that would not be such a great loss *to the inhabitants of Europe* as if the Tartars occupied our kingdom." In even clearer terms, at the second Council of Lyon in 1274, the bishop of Olomouc, in Moravia, declared that the Crusades were distracting Christians from the real frontier against pagans and infidels which he, like Bela IV, located at the Danube. This politico-geographical concept of a Europe that discounted the Carpathians, let alone the Urals, as frontiers to Europe reflected not so much an identification between Europe and Christendom, but rather a completely new territorial concept of Europe.

This was a "new Europe." It was a product of the great progress made in Christendom between roughly the eleventh and the mid-thirteenth centuries. I believe it possible to detect, between approximately the mid-twelfth and the mid-thirteenth centuries (for the great movements of history can seldom be pinpointed precisely) a profound mutation in a fundamental collection of values within European Christian society. This turning-point seems to me to have been produced by many men and women of this period becoming aware of the great progress that Christendom had made, and the principal consequences that stemmed from this. As we have seen, that progress had been manifested with varying degrees of intensity, and at different times in different places and different social circles, in all the domains that contribute to social life: technological, economic, social, intellectual, artistic, religious, and political. The new values pertained to all these domains, interacting in a complex fashion, with one domain then another playing a particularly stimulating role. The stimulus would come now from the growth of the towns, now from the agricultural revolution, now from demographic expansion, now from the appearance of scholastic methods or Mendicant Orders, now from the birth of new states, now from the evolving peasantry, now from the emergence of new urban categories such as the bourgeoisie. The constant interaction of all these elements combined to produce this mutation.

Heavenly Values Coming Down to Earth

I define this period when people became aware of the great surge forward of the Middle Ages and of a mutation of values as the time when heavenly values came down to earth. I think that of all the possible responses to the challenge that this progress constituted in the face of the values of the Early Middle Ages, Latin Christendom – without totally rejecting the doctrine of contempt for the world (*contemptus mundi*) that would survive for a long time to come – chose to convert to the earthly world insofar as this was compatible with the Christian faith. Thitherto, the innovations that the great surge forward had introduced had had to be camouflaged behind respect for the ancient tradition, whether pagan or Christian. The famous remark of Bernard of Chartres comes to mind: "We are dwarves standing on the shoulders of giants." The first sign of a change in values in the thirteenth century was the abandonment of the traditional condemnation of all that was new. For example, the Life of Saint Dominic, written in the first half of the thirteenth century, exalted Dominic as a *new* man and his Order of the Friars Preachers as a *new* order. To be sure, the people of the Early Middle Ages had also worked and struggled for life on earth and for earthly power, but the values in the name of which they lived and fought were supernatural ones: God, the City of God, Paradise, Eternity, contempt for the world, conversion, the example of Job, prostrate before the will of God. Those people's ideological and existential cultural horizon was heaven.

In the thirteenth century and after, people were still Christians deeply concerned for their salvation. But now that salvation could be obtained by investing in the earth as well as in heaven. Legitimate earthly values that could lead to salvation emerged, such as those now attached to work, which were no longer negative and penitential, but positive in that they collaborated with God's creative oeuvre: heavenly values came down to earth. Innovation and technical and intellectual progress were no longer sinful; and the joy and beauty of paradise could at least begin to be realized here on earth. Mindful of the fact that man was created in the image of God, people now believed that man could create here on earth not only negative conditions but also the positive conditions for salvation. Emphasis was laid on the way that Jesus saved Adam and Eve from Hell when he descended into Limbo. History no longer mapped a decline toward the end of the world but rather an ascent to the point at which time would have run its course. The prophetic ideas of the Joachimists, which inspired a minority with millenarian aspirations, filled most people with a positive sense of history. Amid the new values, new *authentica* appeared: the new kinds of authority held by university masters, the *magistralia*. The idea of progress in the economic domain would not develop until the late seventeenth century. However, what did emerge was the idea of growth. The more intensive use of mills and the development of new applications for them (there were iron mills, water mills, beer mills, fulling mills, and so on), the replacement of the vertical weaving loom by a horizontal one, and the thirteenth-century invention of the camshaft, which could convert continuous movement into alternating movements, all drew attention to a new value: productivity. Like manna from heaven, abundance was showered upon the earth. In the agricultural domain, wherever the soil, the climate and the farming systems permitted, the gradual switch from biennial to triennial rotations of crops increased the cultivated area of land by one-sixth and made it possible to diversify seasonal crops (spring wheat as well as autumn wheat, and other so-called "catch-crops"). The values of growth and yield thus made their appearance. Agricultural knowledge once again, as in late antiquity, became a subject worth writing about, and a number of handbooks on agriculture appeared. One was Walter of Henley's work entitled *Housebondrie*, another the *Ruralium commodorum opus* by Pietro of Crescenza, which the king of France, Charles V, had translated into French in the mid-fourteenth century. These mutations should certainly not be exaggerated, but they did constitute signs that people were being converted to the world. The notion of shameful profit (*turpe lucrum*), which condemned profit and the practice of charging interest, was increasingly avoided, thanks to the economic casuistry at which the Mendicant Orders excelled. More and more these justified the activities of merchants, on the grounds that they made available to increasing numbers of human beings goods that heaven had at first confined to just a few parts of the earth. The diffusion of new values was facilitated by a greater use of reason and calculation (the Latin word for both is *ratio*). The rationalization of rural farming and the collection of revenues led to an extraordinary undertaking, well ahead of its time, initiated by the new king of England, the Norman William the Conqueror. In 1085, he produced a full inventory of all Crown property and all the income obtained from it. This was commonly known as the Domesday Book (the Book of the Last Judgment) and the name stuck. There could be no better illustration of the idea advanced above of a switch of emphasis from heaven to earth. In 1187, the count of Flanders, following suit, arranged for a detailed estimate of *his* revenues to be drawn up; it was known as the "Gros Brief" of Flanders. King Philip-Augustus of France (ruled 1185–1223) likewise made sure that regular accounts of the royal domain were kept; a fragment relating to 1202–3 has been preserved. Albeit in a modest fashion, a Europe of budgets was thus born. Alexander Murray has shown that around the same time, in about 1200, western Europe was seized by a veritable "craze for arithmetic." Everything had to be counted, even the years spent in purgatory. Jacques Chiffoleau refers to this neatly as "accountancy in the Beyond."

The fact is that the men and women of the thirteenth century, mostly clergy but also lay people, took to encroaching on God's territory. A desire to establish more control over the time of daily life resulted in the introduction of mechanical clocks throughout thirteenth-century Europe. From their university Chairs, professors lectured on some of the knowledge that only God used to purvey. Knowledge of God itself became a part of human learning: in the twelfth century, Abélard had invented the word theology and, as M. D. Chenu has shown, in the thirteenth century this became a branch of learning in the universities. Finally, the invention of purgatory in the late twelfth century made it possible for the Church and Christians generally to appropriate some of God's power over the dead, by instituting a system for delivering souls from purgatory by means of the intercessory prayers that human beings offered up to God. People's intellectual and mental equipment evolved, allowing them to establish greater control, thanks to the development of means of acquiring knowledge. More books now took the form of useful handbooks rather than artistic artifacts or religious tomes. Writing invaded the world of merchants and jurists, and it was learned in schools. It was desacralized, or rather its heavenly power was now inscribed on earth. The human body became an object to be cared for, not just repressed. At the end of the thirteenth century, Pope Boniface VIII forbade the dismemberment of corpses to which, for example, the body of Saint Louis was subjected as late as 1270. Gluttony, previously a very serious capital sin closely connected with lechery, was now justified by the progress of culinary and nutritional refinement. According to the Polish historian Maria Dembinska, the earliest known medieval cookbook was written in about 1200 for the Danish archbishop Absalon, who probably employed a French cook. By the end of the thirteenth century, a Europe of gastronomy had emerged.

In the Early Middle Ages, in accordance with monastic rigor, laughter had been severely condemned. But in the early thirteenth century it became a positive feature in the spirituality of Francis of Assisi and his first Franciscan followers. There developed a general tendency to delay for as long as possible the departure of people's bodies, to await the Last Judgment. Agostino Paravicini Bagliani has revealed the passionate interest that both the Franciscan Roger Bacon and the thirteenth-century pontifical curia took in the hope of prolonging human life on earth. Knowledge of the world also became a subject of cartographical research that produced maps considerably more accurate than the essentially ideological ones of the Early Middle Ages, which had showed scant concern for scientific accuracy. In the mid-twelfth century, Bishop Otto of Freising, the uncle of Frederick Barbarossa, had reckoned that the Christianization of the earth had been completed and the City of God, which heralded the end of history, had been realized. Now, however, under pressure from the monarchical endeavors of England and France, the *Reconquista* in Spain and the great councils of Rome, not forgetting the influence of Joachimist ideas, Europe was rediscovering its sense of history.

The twelfth and thirteenth centuries witnessed the emergence of two kinds of human ideal, both of which set their sights on success essentially here on earth, even if that success was supposed also to prepare for salvation. The first ideal was *courtliness*, inspired by courtly manners and diffused in the noble and chivalric classes. As we have seen, in the thirteenth century this became synonymous with politeness and even with civilized behavior in the modern sense.

The other ideal was probity, an ideal of wisdom and moderation, a combination of courage and modesty, prowess and reason. This too was essentially a secular ideal. Those two ideals were embodied by the two principal figures in one of the most successful books of the twelfth and thirteenth centuries, the *Chanson de Roland*. Roland was a champion, but Oliver was wise. The king of France, Saint Louis, for his part, was as much a man of probity as a saint. Salvation could now be won on earth just as in heaven.

Finally, although they did not turn their backs on collective ideals, such as membership of a lineage, a brotherhood, or a corporation, the men and women of the thirteenth century, or at least a minority among them, attempted to promote the individual. At the end of one's earthly road, an individual Beyond, purgatory, awaited, before the collective Beyond of the Last Judgment. Michel Zink has studied the way in which the "I" made a breakthrough in literature, and literary subjectivity triumphed in thirteenth-century Europe.

6

The Autumn of the Middle Ages or the Spring of a New Age?

I have borrowed the above title from a stimulating book by Philippe Wolff (1986), who himself took it over from a famous work by the Dutch historian Johan Huizinga, *The Autumn of the Middle Ages*. The fourteenth to fifteenth centuries are traditionally considered as the end of the Middle Ages. They are also represented as a period of crisis following the relative stability and prosperity of thirteenth-century Europe. Guy Bois has recently proposed that we should revise this view and has produced a more positive analysis of what, according to him, was no more than a passing crisis in feudalism. His demonstration of this thesis is largely confined to Normandy and this limits the scope of his hypothesis. The trials and tribulations of the fourteenth and fifteenth centuries preceded a new renaissance which, this time, was to turn into the great Renaissance, and I, for my part, like most medievalists, believe that they reflected both a crisis in the general structures and growth of European society and also the catastrophic appearance of new misfortunes. The men and women of the fourteenth century were frequently in thrall to apocalyptic visions that seemed to fall upon the earth from heaven, and for them many of the catastrophes that they had to face seemed to be expressed by the image of the three horsemen of the Apocalypse: famine, war, and disease. None of these phenomena were unknown in the earlier phases of the medieval period, but their very intensity and certain new aspects to them made them appear unprecedented.

Famine and War

The famine was particularly dire. Historians of the climate such as Emmanuel Le Roy Ladurie and Pierre Alexandre diagnose a worsening of the climate, particularly in northern Europe. Long periods of extreme cold and successive waves of torrential rain caused a return of famine on an unprecedented scale. It lasted from 1315 to 1322.

Throughout the Middle Ages, warfare had been more or less endemic. But action to promote peace taken by the Church and monarchs such as Saint Louis, the quest for conditions favorable to prosperity, and the condemnation of feudal warfare expressed by the newly developing monarchies had all combined to limit bellicosity. When warfare erupted virtually everywhere in the fourteenth century, what must have struck people at the time was the fact that it took new forms. The slow formation of national states, which had at first favored the pacification of feudal quarrels, little by little engendered "national" forms of warfare. A good example is provided by the interminable Hundred Years' War, which revived the ancient Anglo-French hostilities of the twelfth and thirteenth centuries in more modern forms. Slow but spectacular technological progress also transformed warfare. Its most visible sign was the appearance of cannons and gunpowder, but siege techniques also improved and the combination of such changes led to the gradual eclipse of the feudal fortified castle and the introduction of two new types of noble country residences: on the one hand, the aristocratic castle, essentially a residence and a place of ostentatious pleasure, and on the other, the fortress, usually the property of the king or prince, which was designed to survive cannon fire. Furthermore, warfare now became diluted and a matter for professionals. The economic and social crisis swelled the numbers of vagabonds who, if they found a leader, would form armed bands whose looting and destruction were even more horrendous than those of more regular armies. In Italy, warlords or *condottieri*, many of them prestigious, hired out their services to towns or states, and in some cases themselves became political leaders. Finally, monarchies, particularly the French monarchy, raised armies of permanent soldiers who received regular pay (in cash); and meanwhile mercenaries, in a more permanent and organized manner than in the past, hired themselves out to towns and princes. The Swiss, in particular, became famous in this role.

William Chester Jordan has produced a brilliant analysis of the great famine of the early fourteenth century. He describes how this calamity was regarded as "unprecedented" by the people who experienced it and how, as they saw it, both natural and divine causes had combined to produce it. The climate, the rains, warfare, and the wrath of God were the causes that contemporaries detected. They resulted in an abrupt decline in cereal harvests and in epizootic diseases. Prices soared, swelling the numbers of the poverty-stricken and increasing their distress; and the expansion of the still limited sector of wage-earners did nothing to compensate for the spiraling price increases. The inadequate organizational powers of the monarchies and the towns and the deficient means for transporting supplies and storing them all aggravated the consequences of the great famine, or at least made it impossible to take effective action to redress them. It was not yet possible to construct a Europe that could face problems of the countryside and food production in a united fashion.

Philippe Contamine has produced an excellent description of the new military scene that became established in Europe between the early fourteenth and the late fifteenth centuries. At a time when treatises on agriculture and the economy were making their appearance, the progress and changes in the military art led to the production and diffusion of didactic treatises devoted to the art of warfare, military discipline, and army organization. The treatise composed in about 1327 by Theodore Palaeologus, the second son of the Byzantine emperor Andronicus II, was translated first into Latin, then, at the end of the fourteenth century, into French, for Philip the Bold, the duke of Burgundy. The Benedictine Honoré Bovet composed *L'Arbre des batailles* (The battle tree), based on the *De bello* (On warfare) of the Italian jurist Giovanni di Legnano, and dedicated it to the young king of France, Charles VI. In 1410, the Italian Christine de Pisan, then living in Charles VI's court, wrote *Le Livre des faits d'armes et de chevalerie* (A book on the facts of weaponry and chivalry). In 1449, the Italian Mariano di Jacopo Taccola produced a *De machinis* (On machines) devoted to war machines. Collections of military ordinances multiplied and spread throughout Europe: in 1369 those of Florence, in 1374 the grand ordinances of Charles V of France, in 1385 the statutes and ordinances of Richard II of England, in 1419 those of Henry V of England, and most notably, in 1473, the military ordinances of Charles the Rash and the whole body of campaign regulations concerning the military forces deployed by the Swiss cantons.

Abundant archaeological evidence complements the written documentation. Philippe Contamine notes the discovery, at Aljubarrota, in Portugal, of holes arranged in lines or in a checkerboard pattern, probably dug in 1385 by the English archers of Ghent, in which to insert stakes to block the charges of the Castilian cavalry. Excavations of the pits into which the dead were thrown after the battle of Visby, on the island of Gotland, in 1361, have made possible a scientific study of their entire defensive weaponry. Studies have also been made of the precincts of towns, castles, fortified churches, and fortified houses built or restored at the end of the Middle Ages: at Avignon, York, Rothenburg, Nördlingen, and the castles of Vincennes, Fougères, Salses, Karlsteyn, and Tarascon. A large number of European museums help us to learn about the military Europe of the fourteenth and fifteenth centuries: in London the Armoury of the Tower of London and the Wallace Collection, in Brussels the museum of the Porte de Hal, in Paris the Musée de l'Armée, in Rome the Castello Sant'Angelo, in Florence the Stibbert Museum, in Turin the Armeria Reale, in Madrid the Real Armeria, in the Tyrol the collection housed in the castle of Ambras, and so on.

Philippe Contamine has also pointed out that the last two centuries of the Middle Ages witnessed the deployment of both regular and irregular warriors throughout Europe: large companies of soldiers in France and Spain, companies of adventurers in Italy, Écorcheurs in France and the western part of the Germanic world. Among the wars were the Hundred Years' War, the wars of succession in Brittany, the wars over the constitution and the division of the state of Burgundy, the Spanish Wars, the Church's military expeditions to reconquer the papal state, maritime wars between Genoa and Venice, between Hanseatic Germany, Denmark and England, wars against the Czech Hussites, conflicts between the Teutonic Order and its neighbors, the Wars of the Roses in England, the collapse of the kingdom of Granada in Spain, and the Turks' advance into the Balkans.

Iconography and archaeology also show that in Europe this period definitely became the age of horses, war-horses now, rather than horses for hunting. The infantry underwent changes too. Between the mid-fourteenth and the mid-fifteenth centuries it declined both in numbers and in quality. But then, in the mid-fifteenth century, essentially with the appearance of German mercenaries, Lansquenets, and Swiss mercenaries, it recovered its importance and prestige. More striking still was the appearance of artillery. Gunpowder and cannons from China arrived in Italy by way of the Muslim world, and between 1329 and 1345 they spread throughout Europe. "This bellicose or diabolical instrument commonly called the cannon," as John Mirfield put it in 1390, revolutionized the military art only slowly. It did so essentially in two ways: through the role of cannons on the battlefield, and through their efficacy in breaching the walls of castles and towns. The competition to produce ever bigger cannons was prompted by a desire for prestige and the power to terrify as much as by a concern for efficacy. At the end of the fourteenth century, a Europe of bombardment emerged. Throughout the second half of the fifteenth century, towns and states poured more and more of their resources into their artillery budgets. By the end of the century the metallurgical military industry was booming, particularly in Milan and the rest of northern Italy, while, as the Italian wars were to show, in both quantity and quality the production of French artillery was second to none.

The militarization of Europe was completed by profound changes in the organization of military service. In the fourteenth century in Engand, feudal service was replaced by the establishment of national and voluntary militias. In the kingdom of France, contracts of commitment to military service were introduced generally from the mid-fourteenth century on. In the fifteenth century, every community and parish in the realm had to supply independent archers and crossbow-men whenever the monarchy called for them. Italy, where the urban ruling classes turned away from the military function, depended essentially on mercenaries, who were used in the *condotta* system. However, almost everywhere in Europe, the nobility continued to provide most of the cavalry units, for it continued to honor its warrior traditions.

In the fifteenth century virtually all the European powers set up permanent armies. Feudal warfare had been intermittent and dependent on the temporary requisitioning of warriors, usually in the spring and for a limited period. Wartime in feudal Europe was full of gaps. The military fabric of modern Europe gradually became uniform. Even the Italians found that they needed to be able to call directly upon permanent armies in their service. As early as 1421, the Senate of Venice declared: "It is always our policy to have men of valor available in times of peace just as in times of war."

All the same, this Europe of generalized warrior violence had not forgotten the aspiration to peace that had been the deep-seated ideal of society, the Church, and the political authorities of the Middle Ages. The Benedictine Honoré Bovet, the author of "The Battle Tree," lamented, "I see all of holy Christendom so riven by wars and hatred, and pillage and strife that one is hard pressed to find any small country, any duchy or county at all that is truly at peace." In the fifteenth century, George of Podiebrad, the king of Bohemia, wrote a Latin *Treatise on the peace to be made throughout Christendom*. He produced this work in the hope that

> such wars, pillage, disturbances, conflagration, and murders which, as we report, alas, with great sorrow, have assailed Christendom itself from every quarter, leaving the countryside devastated, towns looted, provinces rent asunder, kingdoms and principalities crushed beneath countless disasters – in the hope that all this should end and be completely wiped out so that we can return to a seemly state of mutual charity and fraternity by entering into a praiseworthy union.

This fifteenth-century king probably put forward the very finest plan and justification for the European union that is still struggling, painfully, to become established six centuries later: a plan for a peaceful Europe.

The Black Death

In the mid-fourteenth century, one of the most catastrophic events of medieval Europe occurred: the Black Death. The name stemmed from the fact that, of the two forms of the disease, the one respiratory, the other affecting the groin, the latter was by far the more common. It was characterized by the appearance of swellings, known as buboes, in the groin. These were filled with black blood, from which the disease and the epidemic took their name. Already in the sixth century, at the time of Justinian, bubonic plague had ravaged both the East and the West. It then totally disappeared from the West. But in central Asia and probably also in the Horn of East Africa, it remained endemic. In 1347–8 it revived and returned to afflict Europe. Its point of origin can be fixed and dated. The Genoese colony of Caffa, in the Crimea, was besieged by Asiatics who used as weapons the corpses of plague victims, which they tossed over the town walls. The bacillus was carried by the fleas of rats that arrived in the West aboard ships sailing from Caffa. In the course of 1348 it spread throughout practically the whole of Europe. The Black Death was a catastrophic phenomenon that did not die out in the West until 1720, when the last great outbreak occurred in Marseille, again brought in from the East.

The whole epidemic was catastrophic because it attacked so rapidly. Men and women contaminated by the bacillus were struck down after a very short incubation period by a fever that in most cases resulted in death within 24 or 36 hours. The second reason for the panic was the westerners' realization that it was contagious. People had, to be sure, thought (wrongly) that leprosy was contagious; but when the plague arrived, the contagion was undeniable. Finally, the plague was accompanied by terrifying physiological and social phenomena. Those infected suffered from dramatic nervous symptoms; and the inability of their families, communities, and the public authorities to do anything at all to help them made this affliction seem to be of a diabolical nature. The consequences of the epidemic were particularly spectacular because of the contagion within groups of people who lived in close communities. As a result, the group structure that was fundamental to medieval society was undermined or, in many cases, altogether destroyed by the epidemic. Families, extended families, monasteries, and parishes were no longer able to ensure that the dead were given decent, individual burials. Many plague victims could not be offered the sacrament of extreme unction or even prayers and blessings as they were buried in the communal pits. We do not possess documents on which to base precise estimates of the mortality rate in this epidemic. It varied from one region to another. In all probability it was nowhere lower than one-third of the population, but a more likely calculation would be between a half and two-thirds of the population of Christendom. In England, the population fell by 70 percent; by 1400 it had dropped from 7 to about 2 million inhabitants. The catastrophic effects of the plague were furthermore increased by more or less regular and more or less severe recurrences of the epidemic. In 1360–2, there was an outbreak that claimed above all children as its victims. There were further repeats in 1366–9, 1374–5, 1400, 1407, 1414–17, 1424, 1427, 1432–5, 1438–9, 1445, 1464 . . . The sense of terror was amplified by the combination of the plague with other diseases such as diphtheria, measles, mumps, scarlet fever, typhoid, smallpox, influenza, and whooping cough, and the tendency for people to associate together that apocalyptic trio: death, warfare, and famine.

The fourteenth-century doctors were unable to discover the natural causes of the epidemic, but they were sure that such causes existed and that it was above all contagion that they should fight against. Their certainty did to some extent counterbalance the explanation constituted by divine wrath, which, however, was the one most frequently given and most strongly believed.

In the absence of any appropriate medical knowledge, at least some precise and effective measures were taken. For example, gatherings around the beds of the dying and the dead were forbidden, as were funeral gatherings and the use of the clothes of plague victims. In general, the battle against contagion was fiercely waged. Possibly the most effective measure was to flee from the cataclysm and find refuge far from the densely populated towns, in the sparsely populated countryside. One famous work in particular evokes such a situation: Boccaccio's *Decameron*, which describes the flight of a group of wealthy Florentines who take refuge in a country house. Of course, such a response to the problem of the plague was only within the means of elite groups. The plague aggravated social conflicts and all the misfortunes of the poor and was certainly a factor in the wave of social violence, about which more will be said below.

Public authorities, particularly in the towns and above all in Italian towns, also introduced a number of measures primarily designed to promote cleanliness, and notable progress was made in the field of hygiene. They also passed measures to deter ostentatious displays of luxury on the part of the rich, as such luxury seemed a provocation that led to divine wrath and punishment. The plague also gave rise to new forms of Christian piety, in particular the promotion of saints characterized by special features. These became great names throughout Europe: Saint Sebastian, for example, pierced by arrows that were interpreted as the scourges of the fourteenth century, and, in western and southern Europe, Saint Rocco.

Death, Corpses, and the Macabre Dance of Death

The plague also fueled a new kind of sensibility and religiosity. In the past, when faced with death, what men and women feared most was essentially the risk of hell. Now that fear was absorbed into a prior preoccupation: death itself, the visible horrors of which, manifested by the plague, seemed just as horrendous as the torments of hell. To be sure, as the iconography of the period testifies, hell continued to be feared well beyond the mid-fourteenth century, although, as Jean Delumeau has shown, there was a growing tendency to offset the horrors of Hell by the delights of Paradise. All the same, the principal beneficiary, so to speak, of the new sensibility to death was the corpse.

In the mid-fourteenth century, confrontations with corpses constituted an iconographic theme that enjoyed considerable success. Such images show three living men confronted by three dead ones. The three living, who are young, handsome, happy, and carefree, find themselves face to face with three corpses, generally lying in their coffins, in a cemetery. A theme already very popular throughout Christian Europe now assumed an exceptional importance: the theme of the *Memento mori*, "Remember that you will die," now became the basis of piety and of a whole style of life and reflection. Many illustrated treatises on the art of dying appeared: the *artes moriendi*. They are the subject of an excellent study by Alberto Tenenti. Reflection on the theme of the *Memento mori* led, in the sixteenth century, to Montaigne's declaration, "To philosophize is to learn how to die." The whole of Europe was swept by this iconographic theme, which reflected a particular feeling and philosophy centered on the macabre. One of its most spectacular manifestations was the representation of a corpse on the tombs of the great. This figure was known, in French, as *le transi* (literally, the "stiff"). The most famous example was that of Cardinal Legrange, sculpted in about 1400. Seventy-five such fifteenth-century figures are known.

Another iconographic theme favored by fourteenth-century Italy was that of the triumph of death. A dramatic example was to be found in the Campo Santo of Pisa in 1350, two years after the Black Death struck. Two other themes enjoyed an even greater success. One was that of Vanity, a representation of a skull. It continued to be popular throughout the Renaissance and even into the Baroque period. The other was the dance of death, very typical of the art and sensibility of the fifteenth century.

The dance of death was remarkable for the wide social range of the figures it involved and the manner in which they were portrayed. If the corpse was essentially an individual image of death, the dance of death was a representation of the whole of society, with all the social and political categories of which it was composed. Led by the pope and the emperor, the dance swept along the whole of the human race, from the king, the noble and the bourgeois right down to the peasant, and including women. The other remarkable aspect of this theme was the dancing itself. The Church had firmly condemned dancing, which it considered to be frivolous or even pagan, and unseemly. It had been forced to make concessions with regard to the dances of the court which, however, did not triumph totally until the sixteenth century; but it certainly discouraged peasant dances such as "carols." The dance of death brought together secular culture and the clerical view. Its message was that dancing was a pernicious distraction and that society was dancing to its perdition and was capable of doing so even without Satan as its dancing master. The Europe fixated on the macabre was a Europe of madness. The history of Europe now incorporated a recurrent thread of madness.

The walls of fifteenth-century Christian Europe were covered by images of the dance of death. The first masterpiece in this category appeared on the cemetery wall of the church of Les Saints Innocents, in Paris, in 1425. By 1440 it was matched by the fresco of the Holy Innocents on the cemetery wall of Saint Paul's, in London. The great painter Konrad Witz painted one in the cemetery of the Dominicans in Basel; another was painted in Ulm; a large painted canvas represented a dance of death in the Marienkirche of Lübeck, and in 1470 a similar painting was produced in La Chaise-Dieu. What is surprising is that dances of death are also to be found in the little churches of small towns and even villages: for example, in the transept of Kernescleden (Brittany, second half of the fifteenth century), in Saint Nicholas (Tallinn, late fifteenth century), in Beram (Istria, 1474), in Norre Alslev (Denmark, ca. 1480s), in Santa Maria in Silvis (Pisogna, near Ferrara, 1490), in Hrastovlje (Slovenia, 1490), in Kermaria (Brittany, 1490), and in Meslay-le-Grenet (Eure-et-Loir, late fifteenth–early sixteenth century).

A Europe of Violence

As well as the major outbreaks of violence caused by the plague, famine, and warfare, other events and developments gave rise to conflicts and violence in fourteenth- and fifteenth-century Europe, and these contributed to the image of crises and struggles that characterizes the late Middle Ages and that seems to have posed a threat to the constitution of Europe.

A variety of hypotheses have been offered to explain these phenomena. The Czech historian Frantisek Graus has studied the pogroms which, in the 1320s, accompanied the accusations leveled at the Jews, who were said have poisoned the wells, and also the massive pogroms that marked the 1348 plague, above all in central Europe. He has put forward two explanations. One (which others too have suggested) rests upon a general hostility toward Jews, seen as scapegoats; Graus's second, more important suggestion resituates these pogroms within an overall analysis of, as he puts it, "the fourteenth century as a time of crisis." He underlines the structural dangers to the European economy, ever threatened by crisis in the form of conflicts between peasants and their overlords, and between craftsmen and merchants. He suggests that these may, in the long term, shed light upon the internal hazards to which Europe is still vulnerable. Furthermore, the relative weakness of political authorities – monarchies undermined by dynastic conflicts, threatened by popular revolts, and unable to rely upon the necessary fiscal resources – is indicative of political deficiencies that may continue to weaken Europe even today. In his fine book entitled *"De grace especial." Crime, État et Société en France à la fin du Moyen Age* ("Special grace and mercy": crime, state and society in France at the end of the Middle Ages), Claude Gauvard has suggested another explanation for the violence of fourteenth- and fifteenth-century France: the appearance of a new type of punishable behavior, namely *crime*, which was quite different from the feudal types of violence. This was accompanied by the expansion of a monarchal police force. He believes that this kind of crime might be explained as a reaction against the construction of the modern state, at a time when repression of such criminality involved a massive increase in documentation. The archives that enable us to trace instances of this violence may give the impression that violence was on the increase, whereas, in truth, it may simply have been repression and documentation that were making progress. Perhaps a similar interpretation could be applied to the incidence of violence in present-day Europe. However, as Claude Gauvard's remarkable analysis shows, what was peculiar to medieval society was that the principal value recognized generally by the social components of those medieval populations was a sense of honor. But possibly the most important feature of all these long-term phenomena that are still at work in present-day Europe is that political authorities, that is to say the monarchies of yesterday and the states of today, are expected not only to punish but also to pardon. In the fourteenth and fifteenth centuries in France, that pardon took the form of "letters of remission," which some of those convicted received. Such a manifestation of mercy was the supreme form of a political authority to which certain elements of divine power had been transferred. A Europe characterized by both repression and mercy was emerging.

The above explanations, in particular the one representing the pogroms as punishment of a scapegoat, have recently been questioned by the American medievalist David Nirenberg, in a study of the violence in Spain in the first half of the fourteenth century, in particular in the kingdom of Aragon. Nirenberg studies the persecution and, above all, the violence suffered by minorities: Jews and Muslims above all, but also women. In his view, "violence is a central and systemic aspect of the coexistence of majorities and minorities." He himself focuses on the coexistence of a majority and minorities in the Iberian peninsula, but in much of the rest of Europe too, it would appear, that was the source of the violence that seems to have threatened the cohesion of Europe at the end of the Middle Ages. However that may be, two points should be made about that late fifteenth-century cohesion. First, it makes no sense to speak of tolerance and intolerance in the Europe of those times, for the very concept is anachronistic. The day had not yet come for the Europe of tolerance that is now making some progress but has still not really emerged. The second point is that in both western and southern Europe, the Jews were ejected: from England by the end of the thirteenth century, from France at the end of the fourteenth century, and from the Iberian peninsula in 1492. And what is worse, in that last case it was not a religious argument, anti-Judaism, that was put forward, but a racist one, *limpieza del sangre* (blood purity). In central and eastern Europe, two other solutions were adopted. One was tolerance (even if that is not what it was called), which meant, for example, that in its treatment of Jews, as well as witches, sixteenth-century Poland acted as "a state without execution pyres." The other solution, which was adopted in Italy and much of Germany, was confinement which, however, offered protection: the ghetto. All the same, the Europe of the end of the Middle Ages was a Europe that expelled its Jews.

The persecution of witches

Another form of violence developed in the fourteenth century and, above all, in the fifteenth: the repression of witchcraft. The Church had always attacked magic beliefs and practices and those who indulged in them, namely sorcerers and witches. But when it was confronted by heresy that struggle against witchcraft became secondary. As we have seen, the Inquisition, which was founded at the beginning of the thirteenth century, essentially targeted heresy. However, witchcraft did become another of its targets, and eventually, when the Waldensian and Cathar heresies began to die out, witchcraft became the chief object of inquisitorial repression. This is clear from the fourteenth-century handbooks for the guidance of inquisitors, for example the one by Bernard Gui, the Dominican inquisitor for Languedoc, and in particular the *Directory of Inquisitors* by the Catalan Dominican Nicholas Emerich, which appeared in 1376 and circulated widely. As Norman Cohn has shown, in the fifteenth century witches replaced heretics as the major prey of the Inquisition. Michelet, albeit on the basis of a text that turned out to be apocryphal, intuitively detected that it was in the fourteenth century that witchcraft became a mainly feminine preserve. At that point, witches took center-stage in Europe and continued to do so right down to the seventeenth century. Many were burnt at the stake. The book that orchestrated the hunt for witches was the *Malleus Maleficarum* (The hammer of the witches) by the two Dominican inquisitors for the Rhine Valley and Alsace, Jacques Sprenger and Henry Institoris. It appeared in print in 1486. The two authors set the battle against witches in the dramatic and panic-stricken context of their age. As they saw it, this was afflicted by disorders of every kind, in particular those of a sexual nature, and was the prey of uncontrollable devilry. "The Hammer of the Witches" was certainly both a product and an instrument of what Jean Delumeau has called "a Christianity of fear." In the context of this new intolerance, a terrorized belief that witches engaged in a hallucinatory practice, the sabbath, introduced a note that was the more spectacularly dramatic in that it tended to inspire many iconographic representations. A Europe of witch hunts and the witches' sabbath had come into existence.

Peasant movements

Outstanding among the incidents of violence at the end of the Middle Ages were workers' revolts involving peasants and also urban workers and craftsmen. Robert Fossier has spoken of "the new intensification of class conflicts," and Marxist interpretations such as those of the British historian Rodney Hilton may seem justified. Economic development resulted in the impoverishment of increasing numbers of peasants but at the same time enriched others. Peasant revolts, traditionally called *jacqueries* in French, since in France a peasant was traditionally referred to as a "jacques," were nevertheless, in the main, demonstrations made not by poor peasants but, on the contrary, by well-to-do, privileged ones who felt that those privileges were threatened. Jacquerie found expression in the richly silt-laden territories of the Beauvais and Valois regions and regions around London and in Sussex, but the chief centers were large towns such as those of Catalonia and Flanders and in the zones of intense circulation along the Rhine and the Elbe. In France the principal incident of Jacquerie broke out in May 1358 in the Beauvais region, quickly spreading to the regions of Soissons, Valois, and Brie. It took the form of pillage and arson among the local chateaux, but produced no similar unrest in the towns, nor any influential leaders or clearly expressed doctrines. The repression instigated by the feudal lords was extremely savage.

In 1378, the general impoverishment in Languedoc and the appearance of groups of bandits also gave rise to an endemic jacquerie, known as the jacquerie of the *Tuchins*, an old word for bandits and looters who holed up in the forests. This movement was also repressed. It is worth noting that in Italy such peasant revolts were rare. There, the weight of the towns' domination over the countryside made resistance impossible. So, generally speaking, there was no "peasant problem" in fourteenth- and fifteenth-century Europe. The only great, organized peasant movement arose in Germany at the beginning of the sixteenth century. That was the "Peasant War."

Urban revolts

On the other hand, there certainly was an urban problem. After 1260, the extraordinary urban boom weakened and was replaced by crisis. Unemployment, fluctuating wages, and the increasing numbers of poverty-stricken and marginal people gave rise to virtually incessant bouts of rioting and revolts. The violence of the lower urban strata, when not vented upon the Jews, increasingly targeted the representatives of royal power, whose fiscal greed and repressive policing proved more and more unendurable. The fact that the concentrated groups of craftsmen were so dominated by the corporation masters sparked revolts among ordinary craftsmen and the poor. These did try to organize themselves. In 1285, the French jurist Beaumanoir wrote: "When certain people commit themselves or agree to withdraw their labor unless their wages are increased, they form an alliance against the common profit." Already in 1255, in Figeac, craftsmen formed a *collegatio*, which could be translated as a trade union. These urban rebels spelled out their claims and their plans. They demanded shorter working hours. In 1337, the Ghent fullers revolted, with cries of "work and liberty." Unlike in the countryside, in the towns the rebels found leaders. Robert

Fossier has named a few of them: Berenguer Oller in Barcelona, Jean Cabos in Caen, Peter Deconinck in Bruges, Michele di Lando in Florence, Simon Caboche in Paris, Honoré Cotquin in Amiens, Bernard Porquier in Béziers. Only one of these leaders appears to have possessed exceptional stature: Henri de Dinant of Liège, who controlled the town for four years, from 1353 to 1356, with dreams of a classless society. Apart from Liège, three towns were the scenes of urban revolts of a truly revolutionary nature, in the fourteenth and early fifteenth centuries. They were Paris, London, and Florence.

In Paris, reaction to the defeat of the king of France, John the Good, at Poitiers, and the intrigues of Charles the Bad, the count of Evreux and king of Navarre, produced an uprising of a large section of the Parisian population, which found a leader in the person of an eminent bourgeois, Étienne Marcel, the provost of the merchants. He was not a revolutionary, but he did wish to curb the powers of a monarchy that was turning out to be more and more absolute. After a number of successes and failures, in particular his attempt to gain support among the peasants, Étienne Marcel was assassinated on 31 July 1358 and the Parisian revolt was crushed.

A short-lived but violent movement of rebellion occurred in 1382, when the monarchy restored the taxes that Charles V had imprudently abolished on his deathbed. The rebels seized the maces (*maillets*) stacked in front of the Hôtel de Ville, to serve in the event of an attack by the English, and used them to attack the authorities. This was known as the revolt of the *Maillotins*.

Another flareup occurred in the context of a clash between the people of Armagnac and those of Burgundy, both of which wished to seize the power of the authorities surrounding the mad king, Charles VI. The Burgundians supported a group of rebels led by a butcher named Caboche, who persuaded Parliament to vote for a reform law in May 1413. However, the Armagnac faction's return to power swept that aside. In France and elsewhere too this pattern of abortive reforms and urban revolts continued right down to the French Revolution.

In London, a great revolt broke out when workers rose up against the reinforcement of a statute designed to repress them and the imposition of a new tax, the "poll tax." What made these rebellious movements exceptional was the combination of a revolt of urban craftsmen and workers and a peasant uprising. This particular revolt found leaders. One was Wat Tyler, who was demanding the abrogation of the statute and the emancipation of villeins, the other a poor priest, John Bull, who coined the striking expression, "When Adam delved and Eve span, who was then the gentleman?" For a short period the rioters controlled London, but they were eventually overcome and once again brutal repression followed.

In Florence, events took a rather different turn. The town was dominated by the important textile industry and the great power of the leaders of the rich corporations of textile producers and merchants. It was the textile workers who led the revolt against the rich families. These *Ciompi* secured control of the town for three years, from 1378 to 1382. The movement even spread beyond Florence, to Siena for example. But the subsequent return of the wealthy families reestablished their power over a long period. The fifteenth century was the age of the Medicis.

Other movements, mostly instigated by unemployed and marginal inhabitants of towns in which there were "dangerous quarters," erupted almost everywhere. They had been prefigured already in the 1280 to 1310 period, at Douai, Ypres, Bruges, Tournai, Saint-Omer, Amiens and Liège; also in Languedoc, at Béziers and Toulouse; in Champagne, at Reims; in Normandy, at Caen; in Paris and northern Italy – in Lombardy, at Bologna in 1289, at Viterbo and Florence in Tuscany. A second period of disturbances extended from 1360 to 1410, when a "modern" form of worker violence made its appearance: the destruction of machines. The towns most affected were those of northwestern Europe and the empire: the Rhine valley (Strasburg, Cologne, and Frankfurt) and central Germany (Basel, Nuremberg, Ratisbonne).

A final period, shorter and less violent, lasted from 1440 to 1460, involving Germany (Vienna, Cologne, and Nuremberg), Flanders (Ghent), and as ever, Paris, in 1455. Pierre Monnet has analyzed the particular character of the conflicts that, on no fewer than 250 occasions, rocked over a hundred German towns between 1300 and 1350. These resulted in neither the establishment of Italian-type tyrannies nor in any democratization of trades. The return to peace was organized by elite groups that had managed to preserve their power.

Conflicts in northern Europe

In Scandinavian Europe, social conflicts were complicated by clashes between Hanseatic merchants and Scandinavian craftsmen and peasants, and rivalry between the nordic kingdoms. In 1397, in Kalmar, the three kingdoms of Denmark, Norway, and Sweden declared a perpetual dynastic union. However, by 1434 the Swedish nobles and peasants were rebelling. One example of urban violence in this sector is provided by the 1455 uprising of the population of Bergen, instigated by the Hanseatic League. It was directed against the royal power, the bishop and about 60 other figures, who were put to death. The Scandinavian world, which was both divided and also deeply hostile to the German and Dutch merchants of the Hanseatic League, was a particularly unstable sector of Europe. Elsewhere, in 1478 the grand prince of Moscovy seized Novgorod, and by 1494 Hanseatic traders had ceased to operate there. The emergence of incipient Russian power called into question relations that had earlier united Russia with Europe.

The Shattering of the Unity of the Church: The Great Schism

Another event that contributed to the disarray of the Christians in the fourteenth century involved the papacy. It was sparked off by the ceaseless conflicts that wracked the population of Rome following the 1300 Jubilee. To escape from these troubles, the French pope Clement V, archbishop of Bordeaux, who was elected in 1305 and crowned in Lyon, did not then proceed to Rome. He convened a council, to take place in 1312 in Vienne, on the Rhône, and in 1309 installed himself in Avignon, hoping for a pacification that would allow him to move on to Rome. However, Clement V's immediate successors never did move on from Avignon. They had built a superb pontifical palace there and set up an efficient administration for Christendom, thanks to institutions largely financed by heavy taxation. It boasted an Apostolic Chamber, a Treasury, and a Chancellery. A variety of papal audience chambers and a penitentiary office combined to turn the Avignon papacy into the most successful monarchic government in four-teenth-century Europe. The geographical position of Avignon, roughly at the center of Christendom, had greatly favored these papal successes. Yet what was uppermost in the minds of most Europeans at this time was their attachment to all the symbolism represented by the town of Rome. Even today, Europe continues to be sensitive to the prestige of particular places and memories and what they symbolize. Throughout the fourteenth century most of the public opinion that was beginning to find expression not only within the Church but also among the laity clamored for the papacy's return to Rome. In 1367, Urban V, heeding this demand, did leave Avignon for Rome, but in 1370 the situation there caused him to return to Avignon. Eventually, in 1378, his successor Gregory XI did manage to return the papacy definitively to Rome.

Rome's internal conflicts had increased while the papacy was established in Avignon, fueled by the rivalry of the city's great aristocratic families and the presence of a populace ever ready to be won over by agitators. One exceptional episode in Rome at this time involved Cola di Rienzo, a modest but highly educated man, brought up on ancient literature. He was an inspired orator. Through his eloquence, a mixture of citations from antiquity and fashionable prophetic flights of fancy, he won the support of the masses and, with their aid, he gained control of the municipal headquarters of Rome, the Capitol. However, the hostility of the great Roman families, combined with that of the pope, who had sent in troops under the command of Cardinal Albornoz, forced Cola di Rienzo into exile. He later attempted a comeback in Rome, but was unable to regain power there and in 1354 was assassinated. This episode had deeply shaken not only Rome but the whole of Christendom, encouraging a renaissance of the Latin thought of antiquity. Gregory XI's return to Rome, far from reestablishing peace within the Church, sparked an even more serious crisis. His premature death led to a conclave that developed into a riot. The new pope, Urban VI, who was elected in this troubled situation, aroused fierce hostility. A majority in the conclave annulled his election and elected Clement VII in his place. But Urban VI refused to stand down. There were thus two popes simultaneously in office, the Italian Urban VI in Rome and the Genevese Clement VII in Avignon. Both rallied sections of Christendom, which was thus divided. The countries obedient to Avignon included France, Castile, Aragon, and Scotland. Those obedient to Rome included Italy, England, the Germanic empire and the peripheral kingdoms of eastern and northern Europe. Both popes were supported by cardinals who, when the popes died, formed their own separate conclaves. Urban VI was succeeded by Boniface IX (pope 1389–1404), Innocent VII (pope 1404–6), and Gregory XII (1406–9). In 1394 Clement was followed by Benedict XIII. It was remarkable that – as was to happen in the sixteenth century, in the context of the Reformation – all national Churches abided by the decisions made by their respective monarchs and political leaders. The situation scandalized and traumatized many Christians, clergy and lay people alike. From 1395 on, France pressed for a solution according to which both popes would cede their positions and retire simultaneously. Benedict XIII refused to do so. Nevertheless, in 1409 a council composed of cardinals drawn from both camps deposed both popes and in their place appointed Alexander V. Shortly after, Alexander was succeeded by John XXIII who, however, tradition has never recognized as a true pope, so his name does not appear in the official list of popes. As both Benedict XIII and Gregory XII persisted in clinging to their positions, there were now not just two popes, but three. John XXIII was then ejected from Rome and in 1415 was deposed by the Council of Constance. At this point Gregory XII abdicated; Benedict XIII, now isolated, was once again deposed, and at last, on November 11, 1417, the Council elected Martin V, a unifying pope of reconciliation. Another short and less serious period of schism developed between 1439 and 1449.

However, the Council of Florence and Pope Eugenius IV eventually brought this definitively to an end and, *in extremis*, even attempted a reconciliation between the Roman Latin Church and the Greek Orthodox one. However, this was to be wrecked in 1453, when Constantinople fell to the Turks.

The Great Schism put a great strain on Christian Europe. For many long years its unity was undone. On the positive side, the schism may have revealed the strength of Christians' attachment to the Roman Church, but on the other hand the latter's unifying power had been deeply undermined. National Churches had distanced themselves from Rome and monarchies were now preparing to switch to a system of bilateral treaties with the papacy. A Europe of concordats was emerging.

The New Heretics: Wycliffites and Hussites

In the fourteenth and fifteenth centuries, the great heresies of the previous period faded away. Little by little, the Cathars disappeared and the Waldenses survived only by dint of withdrawing into isolation, mostly in the Alpine valleys and a few isolated regions in northern Italy. But new heresies, generally considered to be "modern" and to constitute a direct prefiguration of the Protestant Reformation of the sixteenth century, now emerged. The two main ones were that of John Wycliffe and the Lollards, in fourteenth-century England, and that of Jan Hus and the Hussites, in Bohemia in the early fifteenth century. John Wycliffe (ca. 1335–1384) was a master of theology in Oxford. He resurrected the old idea that the validity of the sacraments depended not on the office of those who administered them, but on the latter being in a state of grace. Hence the nonvalidity of sacraments received from priests who were unworthy. Furthermore, the only components of the Christian religion that he considered valid were those to which the Bible referred. He therefore denied the validity of all Church decisions that did not originate in and correspond to the Holy Scriptures. On these grounds, he discredited the use of images, the practice of pilgrimages, and the provision of indulgences for the dead. At the end of his life he took to preaching his radical ideas on the Eucharist ritual, attacking transubstantiation and also the religious orders, which he regarded as "private" religions.

Wycliffe's ideas on the Eucharist were condemned in Oxford in 1380 and in London in 1382. Rumor had it that he had inspired, if not openly supported the workers' revolt of 1381. In the long term, his greatest influence probably stemmed from his English translation of the Bible. His ideas continued to be diffused after his death, above all in Oxford. They were an object of considerable controversy at the beginning of the fifteenth century and lived on here and there up until the Protestant Reformation of the sixteenth century, in which some of them were to be found.

By the end of the fourteenth century, Wycliffe's ideas had inspired disciples, the Lollards, who were referred to as *beghards*, a word synonymous to "beggars." This term was also pejoratively applied to others who subscribed to marginal religions, such as another group of Wycliffe's disciples, preachers from Oxford who were joined by a variety of other "poor priests." These gained considerable influence in important political and social circles, where they found a number of protectors, and they continued to diffuse Wycliffe's English translation of the Bible and to provide inspiration for a number of radical projects. One was a plan to secularize the property of the clergy: in 1410, Parliament was considering confiscating all episcopal and monastic property. The Lollards were subjected to violent persecution: in the first half of the fifteenth century they were being condemned to be burnt at the stake. However, their influence persisted well into the sixteenth century, when several of their ideas were taken up by the Protestant Reformation.

The other great, in the first instance semiheretical, then decidedly heretical movement was launched by Jan Hus (1370–1415) in Bohemia. Jan Hus, a student at the recently established university of Prague, became involved in increasingly violent clashes that set Czechs and Germans in opposition both professionally and ethnically. In 1409–10, he became rector of the university. Hus's teaching had transmitted ideas influenced by Wycliffe. The Germans favored a nominalist theology, but Hus professed a radical realism that affirmed the existence of universals in the divine intelligence, given that ideas were transcendent realities. His influence was by no means confined to university circles, for from 1402 on he preached, in Czech, in the Chapel of Bethlehem, in Prague. He called for a moral reform of the Church and strict obedience to God's word, and so found himself in conflict with the ecclesiastical hierarchy. Supported by his Czech colleagues, he had persuaded the king of Bohemia to pass the decree of Kutna Hora (1409), which forced all the German masters and students out of the university. These went off and founded the university of Leipzig. In 1410 the works of Wycliffe were burnt in public and Jan Hus was excommunicated. He left Prague and went into voluntary exile, where he devoted himself to preaching and writing polemical tracts. In his *De ecclesia*, for instance, he defined the Church as an assembly of the predestined and rejected the primacy of the pope. In 1414, he accepted an invitation to go and justify himself before the Council of Constance. But upon arrival, he was immediately thrown into prison and, despite all his denials of the charges brought against him in a public assembly, on July 5, 1415 he was condemned and burnt at the stake. His ashes were scattered in the Rhine.

Most Czechs rejected his condemnation and clung to his ideas. This constituted the first confessional division ever to affect Christendom. Prague now fell into the hands of the Hussites and revolted against the emperor, who was also the king of Bohemia. The insurrection took a graver turn when it adopted the ideas of the most radical group of Hussites, the Taborites. From a religious point of view, the Czechs split away from the Roman Church and extended communion in both kinds to the laity. From a national point of view, the movement confirmed its preference for the Czech language and values rather than foreign – and, in particular, German – ones. From a social point of view, the movement promoted the peasants to a position of prime importance and did away with the structures of feudalism. Between 1421 and 1431, the Church and the German Electors led four crusades against the Hussites. The Hussite forces, peasants fighting on foot from behind their carts, inspired by their religious faith, overcame the enemy cavalry and, in 1428–9, carried devastation and terror into Lusatia, Saxony, and Franconia. The Hussite movement was the first great European revolutionary movement and Europe was stupefied by it. Emperor Sigismund had to content himself with compromising with the Hussite moderates. These took George of Podiebrad as their leader and for many years he won victory after victory. As king of Bohemia, between 1458 and 1471, he took possession of the German strongholds in Bohemia.

The *devotio moderna*

Religion thus gave rise to many of the problems that rocked the Europe of the fourteenth and early fifteenth centuries; and those problems led to many more or less violent conflicts. However, this picture of violence needs to be offset by the mention of a peaceful development in Christian piety that probably affected European sensibility even more profoundly. This was the movement of what was known as *devotio moderna*. It stemmed from the experiences of the son of a textile merchant of Deventer, in the Netherlands. His name was Gerard Grote. He became a priest but in 1374 he abandoned his living and withdrew to the Charterhouse of Monnikhuizen. He then devoted himself to organizing religious communities in which priests, clergy, and lay brothers all lived together as the Brothers of a Common Life. Alongside, he set up a branch for women. Grote and his disciples preached reform, attacking simony, the accumulation of multiple livings, priests living with concubines, and nonobservance of vows of poverty. The impact of the *devotio moderna* movement was not as deep as the mystical inspiration that burgeoned in thirteenth- and, above all, fourteenth-century Europe, but it did address concrete problems and recommended a simple and practical kind of piety, modeled on the humanity of Christ. This produced *The Imitation of Jesus Christ*, attributed to Thomas à Kempis, who died in 1471. For centuries thereafter, this remained the devotional text constantly read by many pious people of both sexes in Europe. The *devotio moderna* may have proved of no more than marginal inspiration for the more radical wings of the Protestant Reformation, but it certainly provided Ignatius of Loyola with some of the ideas on which Jesuit piety was based.

The Birth of National Feeling

Some historians believe that the conflicts that erupted in fourteenth- and fifteenth-century Europe were fueled by a psychological phenomenon: national feeling. Others question the existence of any such thing at this period. Bernard Guenée reckons the question to be ill-formulated. A better way of putting it would be: "What, in any given state, would a European of the Late Middle Ages have understood by 'nation'? Would its inhabitants have seen themselves as a nation? What were the elements of the national feeling that inspired them, and how intense was it? What strength and what degree of cohesion would that state draw from such national feeling?" Guenée's reply is that the word "nation" acquired its modern meaning only in the eighteenth century. In the Late Middle Ages, the words used as synonyms for "nation" were "race," "country," and "kingdom." In the Late Middle Ages, the word "nation," in the modern sense, was applied only to realities with which it had no deep relationship: thus, in Germany, it was linked only with the idea of the empire – which was not to be confused with that of Germany or even any Germanic affiliation. In France, the birth of national feeling has been closely associated with the Hundred Years' War. Bernard Guenée does, however, declare that the distant origin of this feeling can be traced to the thirteenth century. It is perhaps in England, and especially in English historiography, that a phenomenon most closely resembling what we would call "national feeling" can first be detected. In a fine recent study, Olivier de Laborderie has shown how at the end of the thirteenth century and the beginning of the fourteenth, illustrious genealogies could only be understood in the perspective of English national feeling that went back to the twelfth century. He suggests that the success of Geoffrey of Monmouth's *Historia regnum Britanniae* (ca. 1136) was decisive in this respect. It had popularized *Brut* (King Brut, the legendary ancestor of the Breton kings) and the semihistorical King Arthur. All the same, even if the Hundred Years' War was not at the origin of true national feeling, it did bring about a change of capital importance that was to fuel its development among the English. French, which was now seen as the language of the enemy, was abandoned as the official language of England and was replaced by English, the language of the people. Linguistic coherence is not invariably linked to national feeling, but in England it certainly did strengthen the latter's development. Shakespeare, who is often seen as representing the point at which national feeling reached full development, was the first to give English nationalism magnificent expression, in a famous speech pronounced by the eponymous protagonist of *Richard II*.

Similarly, it is fair to underline the incidence of references to "France" in the works composed in the abbey of Saint-Denis which, from 1274 on, were known as *Les Grandes Chroniques de France*. In both cases, there certainly seems to be a connection between "national feeling" and monarchy. This link between country and monarchy is also evident in the episode of Joan of Arc. In that case, though, it may have involved a "popular" attitude. Even so, usually the evolution of national feeling seems to have involved only an elite minority and was far from possessing the rich set of associations that it was to acquire later on. It would perhaps make more sense to speak of a "patriotic spirit," for Ernest Kantorowicz has shown how widely the adage *Pro patria mori* (to die for one's country) was diffused by the end of the Middle Ages. At any rate, any assessment of the development of national feeling in fourteenth- and fifteenth-century Europe is a delicate matter, and clearly the formation of a nation is not just a matter of feelings and psychology.

So let us now consider uses of the term "nation" that played a part in the development of its modern meaning. In the fifteenth century the term "nation" was applied to two specific kinds of gatherings: universities and councils. In the interest of the smooth running of the institution, universities grouped their many students of different origins into nations. Such a division first appeared around 1180, in Bologna, where the university was organized into two groups, classified according to whether the students came from north or south of the Alps. The Cismontane students were divided into three subnations (Lombards, Tuscans, and Sicilians). The Ultramontane students formed 13 groups that more or less corresponded to the various other kingdoms and political units of Christendom. In Paris, a similar system appeared in 1222 but was limited to the Arts faculty, which was divided into four nations: Normandy, Picardy, France, and Anglo-Germany. This example shows that a medieval "university-nation" could certainly not be identified by any common nationality held by its members. For example, here the "French nation" encompassed the masters and students of other Mediterranean countries; and the "Anglo-German nation," which seems to us a veritable hybrid, was in fact very important in the fifteenth century and, according to medieval norms, it functioned perfectly well. In contrast, in Prague, as we have seen, the Czech and the German nations were divided according to strictly ethnic criteria, and this led to violent conflict, as a result of which the German nation was eliminated from the university.

The great councils of the early fifteenth century, above all the Council of Constance, also used and diffused such national divisions. Each "nation" taking part in the council represented several separate countries that were more or less related geographically, historically, or linguistically. The idea of a "nation," as then understood, was simply a way of organizing European space and society. Similarly, in the context of European expansion outside Europe, European merchants working abroad in trading posts or even in fairs would form "nations" composed of the natives of one particular town or region, and would represent and lend assistance to them.

Political Prophecy

Political prophecy was a phenomenon closely related to national feeling and it found forceful expression in the fourteenth and fifteenth centuries. Through their reading of the Old Testament and their meditation on it, the clergy of the Middle Ages became accustomed to ascribe great importance to prophets and to the political aspects of their prophecies. Colette Beaune reckons that "the fourteenth century was decisive" in the diffusion of such an attitude. Most European nations and large Italian towns fabricated prophecies of their own. In France, prophecy had it that a king named Charles, also the son of a Charles, would assume power at the age of 13, prevail over first a number of revolts, then the English, and go on to be crowned as emperor in both Rome and Jerusalem, before reconquering the Holy Land and dying in Jerusalem. In Spain, Ferdinand of Aragon was the hero of a prophecy that foresaw his definitive victory over the Moors and the foundation of a new world. Colette Beaune writes as follows: "By the end of the fifteenth century, prophecy was everywhere. It justified the Italian Wars and launched Christopher Columbus upon his maritime journey of discovery. In a medieval world that found it hard to conceive of the idea of progress, prophecy was one of the few means of conceiving of a future already set down." This prophetic Europe foresaw a Europe that would be victorious and dominant, a modern Europe. I do not agree with historians such as Mikhail Bakhtin, who associate a so-called medieval renaissance with carnival as opposed to Lent, laughter as opposed to tears. But the Middle Ages, the period when heavenly values came down to earth, did manage to offer men and women enjoyment even in this earthly life, as has been shown by the splendid recent collective work, *Le Moyen Age en lumière* (ed. Jacques Dalarun, Paris: Fayard, 2002).

Printing Presses

Meanwhile, as fifteenth-century Europe dreamed of a glorious future, it was at the same time opening up to a happier civilization, in the first instance actually down here on earth. The discovery of printing was to lead to a considerable spread of reading and a triumph for writing and books. The first means of printing in the western world probably took the form of wooden blocks bearing relief engravings. As early as 1400, these were used to reproduce texts called xylographs, on paper. However, this xylography was not widely diffused. It engendered fewer texts than the manual transcription of manuscripts which, at the beginning of the fifteenth century, was carried out in special studios where several dozen copyists would work under their master's dictation. The use of paper constituted the first breakthrough, but the definitive invention came in about 1450 with the systematic use of movable metal type. Whether the German Gutenberg invented, or simply perfected and diffused this method, it was he who, in Mainz, launched the first European printing press. By 1454, a printing works here was producing books exclusively by means of movable metal type produced with the aid of hollow copper moulds. In 1457 the Mainz printing works produced a colored psalter, featuring red and blue as well as black. By the end of the fifteenth century printing had spread throughout virtually the whole of Europe. In 1466 a chair was created for a professor of printing in the university of Paris and in 1470 the first printing works was set up in Paris. Two towns soon became the foremost centers of printing, Antwerp, already the primary economic centre of Europe, and Venice, where the artist Aldo Manuzio (ca. 1450–1515) became the leading printer. We are familiar with the name of *incunabula* for the books printed before 1500 that have come down to us. The printing revolution took a while to make an impact. Even apart from luxury volumes, printed books were extremely costly and in the late fifteenth century reading even suffered a slight decline. Furthermore, it was not until some time later, in the course of the sixteenth century, that the contents of books began to change. For many years printing presses turned out mostly bibles and medieval religious works, and the works were illustrated only by miniatures of a medieval nature. However, eventually printed books were to revolutionize not only learning but the very practice of reading. A Europe of new readers was in the offing.

A World-Economy

The fifteenth century was also a period of great expansion for the European economy. Its foremost historian is Fernand Braudel, who used the term "world-economy" to describe and explain it. World-economy implied the constitution of a space within which regular economic exchanges took place under the direction of one particular town or region. According to Braudel. in the fourteenth century regular relations were established between northern Europe, Flanders, the great Italian ports (Genoa, Venice) and the Asiatic world. Braudel suggests that it was this that created a European world-economy, the fifteenth-century center of which was Antwerp. The Roman "globalization" of antiquity was limited to the Mediterranean world, so this constituted the first great modern globalization. Like all globalizations, overall this enriched the towns, regions, social groups, and families that took part in it. But at the same time it impoverished the victims of those commercial exchanges. Many towns thus witnessed a growing pauperization and marginalization of a large section of their inhabitants. Fernand Braudel stresses that such globalization affects not only the economic sector but also the political and cultural sectors. From a political point of view this world-economy brought about what was to be called a European balance of power. This was the birth of a Europe of globalized economic exchanges, but also one in which social and political inequalities were aggravated.

An Expanding and Flowering Europe

This evolution of Europe, marked by growth and openness, bloomed into what is traditionally called the Renaissance, which blossomed in dazzling fashion in the fourteenth and fifteenth centuries. In my earlier work *Le Moyen Age en images* (The Middle Ages in pictures), I tried to show how this blossoming found expression in the iconography of the period. Let me briefly repeat myself. As Philippe Ariès has shown, in the past the child had been neglected, not in daily life, in which it was the object of the abiding love of its parents, but certainly as a positive value. But in the thirteenth century, children were propelled to the fore by the Infant Jesus, now affectionately discovered in the apocryphal accounts of his childhood that were multiplying and supported by the new cult that was devoted to him. Now children began to be seen as beautiful and enchanting creatures. Happily and mischievously at play, they invaded the world of the angels, in the form of plump little babies, *putti*. Along with this promotion of the child, women too came to take center-stage. As the cult of the Virgin Mary spread, images of the *pietà* of Mary , the Virgin of Mercy, were to be seen everywhere; and at the same time Eve, who had previously been relegated to the background as a dangerous woman, now came forward, embodying the carnal seduction of earthly woman. The beauty of her face even rivaled that of the Virgin.

The early fourteenth century saw the appearance of another novelty that was destined to enjoy an extraordinary success: the portrait. It was the product of the affirmation of the individual and of the new code of representation known as realism. Its subjects included both the living and the dead. The faces of corpses ceased to be conventional and became "real." The earliest portraits presented the countenances of the mighty – popes, kings, lords, and rich bourgeois; later, portraits became democratized. The invention of oil painting, in the fifteenth century, and the development of the use of the easel favored the portrait, but the latter also held a place of honor in frescoes. A Europe of portraits was born and was to endure right down to the nineteenth century, when it was partly taken over by the photograph.

In this blooming Europe, *gastronomy* introduced a new kind of luxury; and many more banquets were held. The Pheasant Banquet that the duke of Burgundy, Philip the Good, laid on in Lille in 1454 earned a quasi-mythical renown. Gambling now spread well beyond aristocratic circles and invaded every walk of life. In the early fifteenth century tarot cards supplemented dice. A card-playing Europe emerged, fueling an explosion of betting, particularly in England. This Europe seemed to be endeavoring to ward off plague by reverting everywhere to dreams of chivalry and to what the Dutch historian Johan Huizinga, in his famous book *The Autumn of the Middle Ages* (1919), calls "a fierce taste of life," "aspirations toward a finer life," "dreams of heroism and love," "dreams of an idyllic life." This was a Europe that threw itself into not only dances of death but also festive dances. These took place everywhere, to the accompaniment of music which, revived by the fourteenth-century *ars nova*, evolved to produce rhythmic sounds of great subtlety that exploited to the full all the resources of the singing voice and musical instruments. This was a time when a confident Europe asserted itself, dancing, singing, and playing music.

Florence, Perhaps the Finest Flower of Europe

The most brilliant expression of all this flowering was to be found in Florence. There, what was to become known as the Renaissance was already beginning to bloom. Fifteenth-century Florence became the most illustrious example of an Italian city-state developing into an enlightened tyranny. It was the creation of the great families of merchant-bankers there, foremost among them the Medicis. This was not the type of development that was to prevail politically in Europe, for the future favored states such as England, France, and Castile. However, the urban and despotic regimes of this period did encourage the development of the new Renaissance art, for the great families who governed these towns and city-states, above all in Italy, were great patrons of the arts.

Before considering Lorenzo the Magnificent, who was not only a patron but also a poet of distinction, we should note the essential role played by his grandfather Cosimo, who controlled Florence from 1434 to 1464. Cosimo collected antique statues, stones, coins, and medals, and founded a number of libraries, including one of his own that contained 400 volumes from all over Europe and the East, which he had ordered to be purchased or copied. It was Cosimo who discovered and supported Marsilio Ficino, the son of his own personal doctor. He paid for Marsilio's studies and welcomed him to his villa in Careggi, which became the headquarters of the neo-Platonic academy that Marsilio founded there. Cosimo was also the benefactor who befriended the master of rhetoric Cristoforo Landino, who is said to have persuaded the Humanists to switch from the use of Latin to that of vernacular languages. Cosimo was likewise responsible for the restoration of the monastery of the reformed Dominicans of San Marco and Brunelleschi's church of San Lorenzo. His own palace was designed by his favorite architect, Michelozzo. He had many villas built in the neighborhood of Florence, and also the abbey of Fiesole, palaces in Milan, the College of the Italians in Paris, and a hospital in Jerusalem. He commissioned work from Donatello, the sculptor of genius who was eventually to be buried alongside him, and also from Friar Giovanni of Fiesole, better known as Fra Angelico, to whom he entrusted the painting of the frescoes of San Marco. He was also the patron of a number of other great painters and artists of his day.

Florence was the scene of many of the greatest products of the new Renaissance art: for example the doors of the Baptistery, sculpted by some of the greatest artists of the early fifteenth century; the revolutionary frescoes in Santa Maria del Carmine by Masaccio, who made brilliant use of the new techniques of perspective. and – most spectacular of all – Brunelleschi's cupola for the cathedral. As this is not the place to embark on a history of Florentine Quattrocento art, I have limited myself to naming just a few of the most outstanding artists and their creations. I must also mention the neo-Platonic movement which was encouraged by the Medicis, as we have seen, and was fueled by the arrival in Europe of Greek scholars fleeing the Turks after the fall of Constantinople. Neo-Platonism evolved in Florence, around Marsilio Ficino in particular, and was one of the great innovations at this moment that bridged the Middle Ages and the Renaissance. In truth, it prolonged an intellectual practice that was characteristic of the Middle Ages: the presentation of new ideas in an ancient guise was a great European tradition handed on through a series of minor renaissances from the Carolingian period right down to the end of the eighteenth century, which inspired André Chénier to say: "Sur des pensers nouveaux / Faisons des vers antiques" (Let us write ancient verse about new thinking).

The frenetic, tormented, but passionate fifteenth century was a seething cauldron of ideas and creative works. Let me spotlight two figures from it to whom historiography has not paid the attention that they deserve.

Two Open Minds: Nicholas of Cusa...

The first was a philosopher, Nicholas of Cusa (1401–1464). He was born in Cusa, a little village on the bank of the River Moselle. He studied the liberal arts in Heidelberg, canon law in Padua, and theology in Cologne. He took part in the Council of Basel, which began in 1432, and played a role of the first importance alongside several popes, first Eugenius IV, but above all Pius II, his friend Enea Silvio Piccolomini, who was pope from 1458 to 1464. But the political and administrative activities of this cardinal took second place to his ideas and the works that he wrote. In the first place, Nicholas of Cusa was a great scholar of theological and mystical literature, both ancient and medieval, upon which he drew in his own thinking. As Jean Michel Counet has observed, he reckoned that "true theology only begins once one has moved beyond Aristotelianism and its logic of noncontradiction, which may be suitable for the finite world but is totally inadequate for the study of God." Nicholas of Cusa recommended a "learned ignorance" (the title of his treatise was *Docta ignorantia*). He stressed man's inability to understand God fully, but at the same time underlined the need for learning. As he saw it, learned ignorance not only made an intellectual approach to God possible but also led to a new conception of the world. He rejected Aristotle's and Ptolemy's idea of an immobile earth at the center of the world. Without being a precursor to Copernicus, he did propose "an infinite universe the center of which is everywhere, the circumference no-where [a definition that Pascal was to take over], a universe that is the cosmological basis of subjectivity." He was also deeply interested in mathematics, particularly insofar as studies on the quadrature of the circle might resolve that problem. Nicholas believed that with the mathematics he sought to develop he might complement rational mathematics by a transcendental, intellectual variety. The work that he undertook to some extent prefigured the infinitesimal calculus of Leibniz and Newton. Like his friend Pius II, Nicholas was very worried by the Turkish conquest and wanted to work toward the realization of "peace within faith." According to him, what we need to do is move beyond the intrinsic limits of each separate belief and see that all beliefs are based on the same presuppositions. Nicholas thought that in truth the doctrinal divergences between Islam, Judaism, Zoroastrianism, and even paganism and philosophy only constituted divergences at the level of rites. Deep down, the common faith to which all those religions were linked was Christianity. Even if Nicholas of Cusa preserved or even reinforced the primacy of Christianity, his endeavor to come to terms with the multiplicity of religions was more vigorous and innovative than those of anyone else. Not only was he a harbinger of the ecumenical movement, he also laid the foundations for a tolerance unknown to the Middle Ages.

... Pawel Wlodkowic

The other figure I wish to focus on was not one of the fifteenth century's great intellectuals but the author of a book that historiography often passes over but that seems to me remarkable in the evolution of European political thought. This was a tract presented to the Council of Constance by the rector of the university of Kraców, Pawel Wlodkowic. It should be set within the context of the conflict between Poland and the Teutonic monk/knights who had just been crushed in the battle of Grünwald (Tannenberg, 1410). Having examined the Teutonic Knights' behavior toward the pagans of Prussia and Lithuania, Wlodkowic proposed that a general attitude be adopted toward pagans. Basing his remarks on the fruit of his studies in Padova, he underlined the existence of natural laws among the pagans and the immorality of the wars waged against them, and he went on to justify their claim to civil and political rights. No doubt this gave him a chance to praise the attitude of the Polish kings, in opposition to the Teutonic Knights, but more importantly, Wlodkowic laid the foundations for a "modern" view of international law. As he saw it, Europe should endeavor to integrate pagans and schismatics. The Europe that he recommended no longer coincided exactly with Christendom.

The Waning of the Empire?

It should not be imagined that the Holy Roman Empire was about to disappear from the realities of the territorial and political scene or from how these were perceived by the Europeans of the fourteenth and fifteenth centuries. But historians have certainly noted its decadence and even waning, or at least the fragmentation of this empire which, despite the consolidation of, in particular, the English and French national monarchies, and the German and Italian towns, still represented European unity in a more than symbolic fashion. Through the Golden Bull of December 25, 1356, Emperor Charles IV (who reigned from 1347 to 1378) had reformed the structure and functioning of the assembly of the emperor's Electors. There were now seven of these: the archbishops of Mainz, Cologne, and Trier, the king of Bohemia, the margrave of Brandenburg, the duke of Saxe-Wittenberg, and the count-palatine of the Rhine. The emperor was assisted by an imperial Diet. Since the early fourteenth century, this had been composed solely of what were called "states," that is to say the secular and ecclesiastical princes and the towns of the Empire. Charles IV tried to impose an imperial peace (*Reichslandfriede*) upon the entire territory of the Empire but, as it turned out, the only peace treaties that were observed were regional ones (*Landfrieden*). Also, the princes each controlled the ecclesiastical affairs of their own territories and from the mid-fifteenth century on there was no one "Empire Church." What probably affected the European nature of Germany most was the fragmentation of the Empire. In the fifteenth century Germany was divided into 350 territories (*Landschaften*), the leaders of which in effect wielded sovereign power with respect to their clergy, ordinances, justice, army, and taxation; and these sovereign powers were clearly of very unequal influence in the life of Germany as a whole.

In the course of the fifteenth century, three new powers, flanking the Electors, arose in eastern Germany. These were Brandenburg, Saxony, and Austria. The marquesses of Brandenburg, the Hohenzollern, brought the towns, in particular Berlin, to heel (1442), gained control of the Teutonic Knights, reorganized justice and finance, extended their power to Lusatia, overcame the coalition formed by their neighbors, and, in 1473, established their dynastic succession in accordance with the law of primogeniture. The small electoral duchy of Saxe-Wittenberg was still modest at the end of the fifteenth century despite the fact that at the beginning of the century

Emperor Sigismond had placed it under the control of the powerful house of Wettin.

The most successful of these three new powers was Austria. For close on 27 years Maximilian, the son of Emperor Frederick III (ruled 1438–93), had not been seen in Germany, as he had been absorbed by Austrian problems. But, following many ups and downs, Maximilian of Austria set about creating Austrian power. Through his marriage to the heiress of Charles the Rash , the duke of Burgundy, he was in possession of the Netherlands. By 1486 he had got himself elected king of the Romans. After the death in 1490 of the king of Hungary, Matthias Corvinus, he retook Vienna and inherited control of the Tyrol. The treaty of Pressburg in 1491 recognized his rights over Bohemia and Hungary and in 1493, at the death of his father, he became the master of a vast domain stretching all the way from Trieste to Amsterdam. By the eve of modern times the imperial House of Austria had established itself in the first rank of the great powers of Europe. The immediate future was to be marked both territorially and politically by attempts to find a balance between these great powers.

A Simplification of the Map of Europe

Apart from the fragmentation of the Empire described above, the political map of Europe was redrawn in the fifteenth century, and, instead of following the German trend toward fragmentation, was, on the contrary, somewhat simplified.

The first thing to note is that, although the people of the fifteenth century did not realize it, the long conflict between the two principal monarchies, England and France, in which a large portion of the French territory had been under dispute ever since the twelfth century, came to an end with a conclusion to the Hundred Years' War that was favorable to France.

Since 1435 Charles VII had been winning back his kingdom. In 1436 he took Paris, in 1449 he reconquered Normandy, and in 1451 he recovered Bayonne. The French triumph was confirmed by victories in the battles of Formigny (April 15, 1450) and Castillon (1492), in which cannon fire played an all-important role. Following the failure of an attack on Boulogne by King Henry VII of England, the treaty of Étaples, which confirmed England's abandonment of all its territories on the continental mainland (except Calais), brought the Hundred Years' War to a definitive end.

Meanwhile, the French monarchy was no longer threatened by the creation, on its eastern flank, of a kingdom of Burgundy that would have included some of its eastern territories. After the death of Charles the

Rash (1477), France suffered a semisetback when Charles's daughter Marie, the heiress to the kingdom of Burgundy, finally married Maximilian of Habsburg. However, in return for leaving the Netherlands to Maximilian, France obtained Picardy, the Boulogne region, the duchy of Burgundy, Artois, and Franche-Comté, through the treaty of Arras (1482). The French monarchy furthermore benefited from the extinction of the House of Anjou. Having no direct heir, King René of Anjou left Anjou to the king of France, and Maine and Provence to another of his nephews. When the last of the Angevins died in 1481, those two regions were reunited with France. Once France's southern frontier with Navarre and Aragon had been recognized, only the duchy of Brittany remained outside the French monarchy. The marriage of its only heir, Anne, to King Charles VIII of France in 1491 and her remarriage to his successor Louis XII (1499) ensured Brittany's integration into the kingdom of France.

Events in the Iberian peninsula led to further simplification. After many ups and downs, the treaty of Alcaçovas preserved the independence of Portugal, which, however, renounced all its claims to Castile. In 1464, Catalonia was reintegrated into Aragon, and Ferdinand, the king of Aragon, married Isabella, the queen of Castile, in Valladolid. These were to be the "Catholic monarchs" and their union held out the promise of unification for Spain.

Finally, and above all, amid a new crusading atmosphere, the Catholic monarchs launched an attack against the last remaining Muslim kingdom in Spain, the kingdom of Granada. In 1487 they captured Malaga, in 1489 Baza and Almeria, and finally, on January 2, 1492, after a very long siege, they captured Granada itself. At this point, I feel bound to mention two other events of that same year, 1492: the Jews were expelled from Castile; and Christopher Columbus, with the backing of the monarchs of Spain, discovered the land that was to become America.

The long implantation of Muslims in Europe, dating from the eighth century, should now have come to an end. However, as Muslim domination in the southwest collapsed, another Muslim threat loomed in the southeast: the threat of the Turks.

The Turkish Threat

Since the mid-fourteenth century the threat of an attack on the European Balkans by the Ottoman Turks had been growing ever more acute. They had captured Gallipoli and southern Thrace between 1353 and 1356, Salonica in 1387, and in 1389 had inflicted a bloody defeat on the Serbs at the battle of Kosovo, the cruel awareness of which has remained in the latter's collect-ive memory right down to the present day. At the instigation of Emperor Sigismund, a crusade against the Turks was launched. What has been called the very "flower of European chivalry" took part in this, but in 1396, all were massacred at Nicopolis, in present day Bulgaria. This was the last crusade. The congress of the Christian princes of Europe convened by Pius II in Mantova in 1459 was a total failure. The Turks' capture of Constantin-ople in 1453 created huge shock waves in the West, but produced no strong resistance on the part of the Christian Europeans. The Turks seized Bosnia between 1463 and 1466, raided Friuli and Styria in 1478 and 1479, and captured Otranto in 1480. With the fall of Caffa in the Crimea, in 1475, Genoa lost its colonial empire. As I have already mentioned, Pius II was the pope who wrote the only medieval treatise with a title that contained and was even dominated by the word "Europa." Immediately after the fall of Constantinople, on July 21, 1453 Pius II wrote to Nicholas of Cusa. He stressed the threat that the Turks posed to the Italian, that is European, coast of the Adriatic and expressed his fear that Venice would be weakened, which would be disastrous for Christendom as a whole. He concluded as follows: "The Turkish sword is now suspended over our heads, yet mean-while we are engaging in internal wars, harassing our own brothers, and leaving enemies of the Cross to unleash their forces against us." In even more pointed terms, in a letter to Leonardo Benvoglienti, the Sienese am-bassador to Venice, dated September 25 of that same year, Pius II painted a catastrophic picture of the divisions within a Christendom under threat from the Turks, and in this exceptional and exemplary context he pointedly used the word "Europe": "Such is the face of Europe and such is the situation of the Christian religion."

The European Plan of George Podiebrad

Also at about this time, the king of Bohemia, George Podiebrad, who was a Hussite moderate, proposed a plan to contain if not repulse the Turks. He suggested creating an assembly which, although it was not specifically called European and instead focused primarily on the common Catholic faith, in effect constituted the very first plan for an assembly that would represent a united Europe. This text, which in its 1464 Latin version is entitled *Universitas,* has been called a *Tractatus* for Europe in a translation by Konstantin Gelinek, edited by Jean-Pierre Faye in his work *L'Europe une* (One Europe), which was published in 1992. In his treatise, the king of Bohemia explicitly declared that the cessation of warfare between the

European states should be both the goal and the means of such a union. This treatise written five centuries ago called for a Europe of peace and identified peace as the principal advantage that would stem from a united Europe. In the event of conflicts between members of the assembly, it envisaged intervention by a joint European arbitration force. It called for an official seat for the assembly. It suggested that the original assembly should be able to admit new Christian members. It proposed the creation of special taxes and financial provision to fund the assembly. It suggested that five-yearly assemblies should meet successively in different European towns, the first time in Basel, next in a French town, next in an Italian one. It also called for the institution of a common emblem, a seal, a treasury, archives, a general council, a procurator fiscal, and other officials. It proposed one vote for every "nation" (in the first instance France, Germany, Italy, eventually Spain, and so on). Decisions would be taken by majority votes, and when no clear majority emerged "the votes of the delegates representing the lords with the greatest titles and greatest merit would prevail"; the rest of the signatories to the pact would choose between the two parties. It was an astonishing text. Sadly, however, no moves were ever made even to begin to put the project into effect. The notion of a united Europe was well ahead of its time in the mid-fifteenth century, but it is remarkable that this prince, who was (to put it mildly) atypical, should have produced an idea so strikingly modern.

Italy, at once the Beacon and the Prey of Europe

Of all the regions of fifteenth-century Europe, it was Italy above all that attracted the attention of many contemporaries at the time, and ever since it has captured the interest of countless historians. Despite its inability to form a nation, it continued to inspire many intellectual humanists, including Machiavelli, with feelings of patriotism. But in reality Italy was divided into many separate units. Its position in the fifteenth century was a paradox, for it was a fragmented land. Yet it was the brilliant home of not only humanism but also the great Renaissance, as the flowering of Florence shows. Italy attracted many Europeans, most of them with religious goals that were supplemented by what we could call a touristic interest. Religion provided them with an opportunity to satisfy both. Most of the many European pilgrims who passed through on their way to the Holy Land would arrive one month before embarking in Venice for their destination, in order to visit Italy's many superb churches and revere the countless relics that they contained.

In the fifteenth century, the fragmentation of Italy was somewhat simplified. Florence united more or less the whole of Tuscany, particularly once it had taken possession of Pisa and Livorno, thereby acceding to the rank of a maritime power. In the northeast of the peninsula Venice also extended its domination on *terra firma*, taking control of Bergamo and Brescia in 1428. Filippo Maria Visconti reunited the region around Milan and in 1421 seized Genoa. King René of Anjou, who had captured Naples in 1438, was forced in 1443 to hand it over definitively to Alfonso of Aragon, who restored the unity of the "Two Sicilies" (Naples, Sardina, and Sicily), which then remained for many years under Aragonese domination. The states and the lords who were their leaders, such as Francesco Sforza, the successor to the Viscontis of Milan, and Cosimo de' Medici in Florence, engaged in interminable conflicts in which they would frequently appeal to the king of France for help. Eventually, on April 9, 1454, Venice joined a "very Holy League," set up by the Peace of Lodi for 25 years, under the patronage of the pope. This established a measure of equilibrium between the various Italian powers that was more or less to endure right down to 1860, apart from the temporary upheavals of the Napoleonic period.

This brilliant but divided Italy certainly exerted a powerful attraction on much of the rest of Europe, but it was an attraction compounded of envy as much as admiration. Italy, the beacon to others, was to become more than ever Italy, the prey of others, as Girolamo Arnaldi has shown in his excellent essay *L'Italia e suoi invasori* (Italy and its invaders). The aggressors were first Aragon, later the Empire, but also and above all France. In 1489, Pope Innocent VIII appealed for help to Charles VIII, begging him to intervene in the kingdom of Naples, as did Ludovico "il Moro," the new master of Milan, who was seeking aid in his Milanese territories. On August 29, 1494, King Charles VIII of France left Lyon, ostensibly bound for a crusade. However, he never embarked on this, but instead made his way to Naples, bent on regaining the rights over it that he claimed to have inherited from the House of Anjou. This marked the beginning of the Italian Wars.

Philippe de Commynes, the European

Meanwhile, this Europe, a structure that combined a Christian ideology of unity with concretely separate nationalities, was increasingly conceived as an entity by its intellectuals, historians, and statesmen. Philippe de Commynes, the great European historian of this period, after surveying the state of the Christian world of his day, concluded by declaring, "I have spoken only of Europe, since I am not well informed on the other two parts [of the world]." He simply remarked that, so far as he knew, the latter two continents were also afflicted by the main unfortunate characteristics of Europe, "wars and divisions." He added that Africa moreover suffered from another misfortune, for its people sold one another to the Christians, while the Portuguese traded in Blacks on a daily basis. A new phase was looming for the Europe that had discovered Africa: it was about to discover America and was beginning to acquire infamous renown as it supplied the New World with slaves abducted from the African continent.

Europe Encountering the Outside World

With historical hindsight we can see that the most striking development in late fifteenth-century Europe was its rapidly increasing expansion beyond European territory. Michel Mollat has produced a fine book devoted to the explorers of the Middle Ages. But in truth neither the term "explorer" nor the explorer's role existed at that time. The forays outside Europe made by Roman Christians had been mostly missionary expeditions, such as those undertaken by the Franciscan Jean de Plan Carpin, in the thirteenth century. He conducted missions in recently converted countries such as Scandinavia, Bohemia, Poland, and Hungary. But he also carried letters from Pope Innocent IV to Russian princes and to the Mongol khans Batu and Güyük, inviting them – albeit without success – to enter into an entente between their religions and the Roman Church. (When Jean de Plan Carpin returned to Lyon in 1247, he told Saint Louis of his voyage and what he had learned from it. The king, who was about to set out on a crusade, was thinking of possibly concluding an *entente* with the Mongols and so to attack the Muslims from the rear.) Apart from those missionary expeditions, a number of merchants had ventured forth. Among these were the Venetian Polo brothers, accompanied by their nephew Marco, who had gone to do business in Ceylon and then placed themselves at the service of the Mongols, possibly traveling as far as China.

Apart from the ephemeral Latin states of Palestine, the only truly expansionist medieval European ventures were undertaken by merchants from the great Italian ports, above all Genoa and Venice. These set up a veritable commercial, and at times territorial empire within Byzantium and its possessions and elsewhere in the Near East. The eastern Mediterranean's chief attraction for Europeans was the possibility of purchasing, among many other products, spices. According to a tract, *La Practica della mercatura* (The practice of trading) written by the Florentine Pegolotti in about 1340, known spices numbered 286. However, given that some were mentioned more than once, the real total came to 193. These spices were used above all in medieval pharmacopoeia, but also in dying processes and perfumery – and in cooking. The men and women of the Middle Ages seem to have been very partial to spicy dishes. Medieval spices included citrus fruits and cane sugar. More than a quarter of these products came from India, China, and other parts of the Far East. They were extremely costly, bought from the Indians by the Arabs and from the Arabs by Christian Europeans who traveled to the Near East for this purpose. The chief ports in which spices were sold and from which they were exported were Acre, Beirut, and above all, Alexandria, for these were the cities to which the ancient silk road led.

In the late Middle Ages, the European spice merchants were primarily Venetians, who annually invested 400,000 ducats in this trade and each year dispatched three to five galleys to fetch the cargoes. Considering that, although extremely costly, the spices took up very little space, that was a very large consignment. After the Venetians, the next most deeply involved were the Genoese, the Catalans, and the people of Ancona, each dispatching one or two galleys every year.

At the end of the fifteenth century, businessmen and wealthy consumers were eager to find new sources of spices and sugar, and also, it must be added, new sources of gold and precious metals to meet their growing monetary needs.

The Attraction of the Atlantic and Africa

So Europeans rather turned away from the Mediterranean horizon, the more so because it was disturbed by the Turkish conquest. By the end of the fifteenth century Europe was increasingly looking toward the Atlantic. Initially this interest in the Atlantic was directed toward western Africa. The image of Africa among Christian Europeans had been unfavorable ever since antiquity and its negative aspect increased in the Middle Ages. Because of the color of their skin, Africans, who were often called "Ethiopians," were considered examples of ugliness. Furthermore, Africa was believed to be full of snakes and monstrous beasts, whereas in the East, where monsters likewise abounded, there were at least marvels as well. In 1245, Gossuin of Metz, in his *Image du monde* (Image of the world), described "Ethyope," that is to say Africa, as a country inhabited by people "blacker than pitch," where the heat was such that "it seems that the earth is on fire" and, beyond a northern fringe, there was nothing but deserts full of "vermin and wild animals." The only fruitful relations with Africa, which were limited to a minority of specialist merchants, involved bartering for Sudanese gold, chiefly in Sijilmassa.

In the fourteenth century, the Europeans' image of Africa underwent considerable modification. Africa became an object of covetous greed. Earlier efforts to exploit it had failed. In 1291 the Genoese merchant brothers Ugolino and Vanino Vivaldi had crossed the straits of Gibraltar and struck out southward, but were never seen again. In 1346 Jaime Ferrer likewise mounted an expedition that was a failure.

At the beginning of the fifteenth century, the Canary Islands were explored by the Norman Jean de Béthencourt (in 1402–6) and were subsequently gradually colonized by the Castilians. This kind of activity speeded up once the Portuguese became interested. On August 20, 1415, Ceuta, which commanded the straits of Gibraltar and was an essential staging post in the importation of gold from the Sahara, was captured by the Portuguese. This marked the beginning of the Portuguese expansion. It led to a number of conflicts however, prefigurations of those that were to follow at the time of the major European expeditions of colonization, between on the one hand the Portuguese who wished above all to establish themselves in Morocco and exploit it, and on the other, those determined to push as far as possible southward and explore the western coast of Africa and its outlying islands. All this Portuguese activity was orchestrated by a leader who planned and directed the movement of expansion and exploration from his Portuguese residences, in particular Sagres in the Algarve. This director of operations was the Portuguese *infante* Henry the Navigator (1394–1460), the son of John I. Between 1418 and 1433, the Portuguese established themselves in Madeira and the Azores. Gil Eanes rounded Cape Bojador in 1435. Dinis Dias reached Cape Verde in 1444 and sailed up the Senegal estuary that had been discovered by Nuño Tristao. In 1461 Diago Afonso explored the Cape Verde archipelago. In 1471 Joao de Santarém and Pero Escobar reached the equator. In 1487 Bartolomeo Dias rounded the Cape of Storms, which Vasco da Gama, who repeated this exploit in 1497–8, on his way to India, renamed the Cape of Good Hope. In the meantime, between 1470 and 1483, Castile had completed its conquest of the Canaries. King Alfonso V of Portugal stuck to the earlier political program and limited his interest to Morocco, where he seized Tangier in 1471, and to the unsuccessful Castilian adventure.

All this Spanish and, above all, Portuguese expansion along the African coasts should be set in the context of a vaster fifteenth-century movement that drew European eyes away from the Mediterranean and directed them toward the Atlantic. Economic activities and projects involving a mixture of economic greed, missionary zeal, and a spirit of adventure had brought

Portugal and western Andalusia to the centre of the European stage. Lisbon and Seville became powerful business centers oriented toward not only the Atlantic but Europe as well.

The Progress and Archaism of Ships and Navigation

The interest in the Atlantic seaboard of Europe and whatever lay beyond it was encouraged by improvements in shipping and navigation. Decisive progress was made in the thirteenth century. The lateral rudder was replaced by the stern-post rudder, which afforded ships greater maneuverability and stability, and square yardarm sails were introduced. The surface area of these sails could be increased or diminished by means of ropes known as ring-tails and reef-points. However, systematic use of these improvements , which began in the fourteenth century, only became general in the fifteenth. Europe had now embarked on research aimed at improving maritime transport. As Jean-Claude Hocquet has shown, every 30 or 40 years improved performance resulted from modifications in the types of ships in use and in the composition of fleets. One crucial improvement was the juxtaposition of square sails and lateen sails on a ship's mast, making it possible to tack against the wind instead of having to overwinter. The Caravelle, of quasi-mythical European fame, was the champion vessel that exemplified this progress. A Caravelle had three masts instead of one. Its sides were clad by planks that met edge to edge instead of overlapping. Its capacity was between 40 and 60 nautical tons and its principal quality was speed. Of the three vessels that Christopher Columbus took to what turned out to be America, two, the *Niña* and the *Pinta* were Caravelles. The emergence of Spain and Portugal as the states most capable of moving on from the Mediterranean to tackle the Atlantic was blessed by the papacy. In 1493 the papal bull *Inter aetera* announced Pope Alexander Borgia VI's decision that lands so far not claimed by European Christian princes and situated to the west or the east of a line drawn west of the Azores would be assigned respectively to Portugal and to Spain. In the following year, the treaty of Tordesillas between the Spanish and the Portuguese shifted the demarcation line drawn by Alexander VI further west in the Atlantic Ocean. This was the start of the carving-up of the world by the Europeans, which may be considered to mark the end of the Middle Ages and the beginning of Modern Times. But we should not forget that the mentalities and attitudes that presided over this European appropriation of the world were deeply steeped in medieval prejudice and ignorance. What people imagined beyond the Atlantic and beyond Africa were not new lands but extremely ancient ones that were a product of the medieval imagination. Beyond the Cape of Good Hope was the land of Prester John, a fabulous figure who ruled over a world of marvels. What men went forth to seek beyond the Atlantic was the ancient East and China. Above all, at a time when, despite some progress, European cartography remained extremely inaccurate and still much confused by myth and fables, the targets of these journeys of exploration and discovery were believed to lie quite close at hand. In his annotations to Pierre d'Ailly's extremely inaccurate *Imago mundi*, Christopher Columbus wrote: "The extremity of Spain and the beginning of India are not so very far apart, but close to each other and it is clear that, with a favorable wind, the sea between them may be traversed in just a few days."

Christopher Columbus presents the finest example of a mentality steeped in the kind of medieval imaginary representations and errors that may well have constituted a powerful incentive encouraging him to embark on his voyages of discovery. He believed that the distance between the Canaries and China was no more than 5,000 sea miles, whereas in reality it is 11,766 miles. The Europe of Atlantic adventure and discovery was profoundly medieval.

Conclusion

From the vantage point of the twenty-first century – but not forgetting that the concept of a "century" was not invented until the end of the sixteenth century – the Europe of the late fifteenth century seems to have been, as it were, torn apart by new tensions: on the one hand the friction behind the internal splits in store for Europe (the Italian Wars, the Peasants' Wars in Germany, and the Reforms of Luther and Calvin), and on the other, the mirage of distant horizons affording promising perspectives in Africa, the Indian Ocean, and what we know to have been a New World that in a few years' time would be called America. Was this juncture in time sufficiently affected by new discoveries and breaks with the past for it to be reasonable to believe that Europe was about to move on from one long period of human life to another: should we conclude that the Middle Ages were over?

With historical hindsight, the fifteenth century may indeed be considered as the beginning of another long period now known as Modern Times. But before winding up our reflections on the question of whether Europe was born in the Middle Ages, as our title implies, we should ask ourselves whether this really was the end of the Middle Ages, for only if that is indeed so are we in a position to evaluate the relations between this Middle Ages and the elaboration of Europe. I have in the past already suggested that the notion of a *long* medieval period comes the closest to the historical reality. There can be no doubt that, as the great Polish historian Witold Kula felicitously puts it, every period is marked by "the coexistence of asynchronisms." I myself accordingly use the term "crisis" as little as possible, for it frequently masks the absence of any attempt to analyze the changes taking place within a society. However, I do believe that mutations and turning points can be identified. Are these in evidence at the end of the fifteenth century? This brings us to the (in my opinion unfortunate) term "Renaissance," which was coined by the Swiss historian Burckhardt at the end of the nineteenth century and has since enjoyed such success. In the first place, it should be remembered that other periods of the Middle Ages too may and indeed have been described as "renaissances," notably the Carolingian period and the twelfth century.

Next, let us see what characterizes this Renaissance with a capital R. It has, justifiably, been detected above all in the domain of art and thought. But in Italy, at the very least, had not art been undergoing a rebirth ever since the thirteenth century, and did not the humanism that characterizes the Renaissance begin in the fourteenth century?

Furthermore, in all the fundamental areas of the history of European society and civilization, do not the basic phenomena spill over the dividing line of the end of the fifteenth century? The Black Death appeared in Europe between 1347 and 1348 and continued to ravage it right down to 1720. Marc Bloch made a study of a ritual that was inherent to royal power in the Middle Ages, the rite of the royal touch of "miracle-working kings." This made its appearance in the eleventh century, was adopted in France and England in the thirteenth century, and continued to be practiced in England right down to 1825, although by then most people admittedly did regard it as anachronistic.

But let us consider some more weighty examples. We have noted the great surge of medieval urban development and its important impact on Europe. Bernard Chevalier has studied the chief towns in France that were linked to the crown. They were known as "good towns" (bonnes villes). He shows that the term itself and the urban network that it defined appeared in the thirteenth century and had virtually lost all meaning by the early seventeenth. The most famous attempt to divide Europe into separate historical periods was that proposed by Marx. In his view, the Middle Ages, identified with Feudalism, lasted from the end of the Roman Empire, which was characterized by its slave-based mode of production, right down to the Industrial Revolution. This medieval period was also that in which the trifunctional Indo-European schema described by Georges Dumézil appeared. It was detectable in England in the ninth century and triumphed in the eleventh, with the formula "oratores, bellatores, laboratores" (those who pray, those who fight, those who work), that is to say priests, warriors, and peasants. This survived down to the time of the Three Estates of the French Revolution. But after the Industrial Revolution an altogether different trifunctionality was set in place, that of primary, secondary, and tertiary activities as defined by economists and sociologists. In the domain of teaching, universities appeared in the twelfth century and remained by and large unchanged down to the French Revolution, while at the primary and secondary stages of education literacy was slowly continuing to spread right down to the nineteenth century, when schooling was generalized.

This long medieval period was also when Europe saw the appearance of popular folk culture, and this lingered on until the folkloric revival of the nineteenth century. Stories using the theme of the Angel and the Hermit were transmitted from a twelfth-century fable to Voltaire's *Zadig*, and later also to storytellers of nineteenth-century Brittany. As we have seen, the Middle Ages constituted a period dominated by Christianity and the Church. To be sure, the first great turning point was to come in the sixteenth century when Christianity was split between Catholicism and Protestantism; moreover, the place and role of religion has certainly not remained unchanged in the various European countries. It does, nevertheless, seem fair to say that, in relation to religion, Europe by and large was to continue in the line of development the roots of which were already discernible in the Middle Ages, that is to say pursuing the establishment of a more or less clear separation between Church and State, with Christians rendering to Caesar whatever belonged to him. This, in contrast to Islam or Byzantine Christianity, involved the rejection of theocracy, and the promotion of children, women and lay people, and of a balance between faith and reason. However, up until the French Revolution all this was to remain more or less masked by the power and influence of the Roman Church; and, in fact, the power and influence of the reformed, Protestant Church had exactly the same effect. Clearly, in this respect there was no break introduced by the Renaissance. I would therefore suggest that we regard the end of the fifteenth century simply as an important pause in medieval history – not that that disqualifies us from raising the question of whether Europe was indeed born in the Middle Ages, as the title of this book implies.

What we have noted so far is the construction and flowering of the European Middle Ages. I think it reasonable to halt at this point of the fifteenth century, to take stock of the situation and see if we can find an answer to the above-mentioned question.

It seems to me that there are two fundamental aspects to the relations between Europe and History. The first is that of territory. History always takes place within a particular space, and a civilization is always elaborated and diffused within a territory. Essentially, the fifteenth century put the finishing touches to the medieval creation of a European space, a creation that began with the "great invasions" of the early Middle Ages. By the fifteenth century there were no longer any pagans, nor would there have been any Muslims had not the Turkish conquest got underway. That conquest had a twofold and contradictory effect. On the one hand it posed a threat to Europe; but on the other, even if European resistance was not as strong as Pope Pius II would have hoped, given that a collective identity is generally constructed as much on the basis of opposition to "the other" as upon internal convergences, the Turkish threat was to turn out to contribute to the unification of Europe. Universities were now diffusing the same kind of knowledge across the board from the Mediterranean to the Baltic, just as humanism, once it had abandoned Latin for vernacular languages, was penetrating European culture everywhere, from Sweden to Sicily. Antwerp was the centre of a world-economy which, as Fernand Braudel has shown, for a long time still remained essentially European, before eventually meshing with the entire world.

One uncertainty remained outstanding, although at the end of the fifteenth century the issue may have seemed clearer. Where did the eastern frontier of Europe lie? First we should recognize that, even if the fall of Constantinople in 1453 was keenly felt by Europeans and particularly by its elite groups, it did not, as traditional history would have it, simply constitute the catastrophic end of a whole world, that of Byzantium. In the long term it also turned out to release European unity from a handicap. For although the Greek Orthodox religion is still observed in eastern Europe today, it is no longer linked to the double center of political and religious power that the Byzantine Empire used to constitute. In 1453 a potential obstacle to a future united Europe was, paradoxically enough, removed.

Elsewhere, the Slavic states were elaborating territorial policies that were to alter the problem of Europe's eastern frontier. Poland, a fully European state by virtue of its conversion, and united with Lithuania by the Polish-Lithuanian Jagiellon dynasty, in the late fourteenth century adopted a policy of territorial expansion to the north (Prussia) and to the east and the southeast (Volhynia and Podolia). By the fifteenth century Poland extended all the way from the Baltic Sea to the Black Sea.

Meanwhile Russia, which had thrown off the Mongol yoke, was evolving into a centralized state in the Moscovite region. Ivan III (ruled 1462–1505) continued the unification of Russian territories by gaining control of Novgorod (1478) and Tver (1485). He set up a powerful and centralized state based on a solid administrative and judicial system, which was largely instituted by the Code of 1497.

The question that thus arises is whether, from a historical point of view, at the end of the fifteenth century the threats that hung over the past achievements of the Middle Ages outweighed the promises held out for Europe by the long medieval period that I am proposing, or whether the reverse was the case. Of course, we must take into account the vagaries of History and the impact of unpredictable eventualities, but I believe that it is possible to assess what Europe's chances were at the end of the fifteenth century. I do not think that the threats stemmed either from the emergence of nations or from the religious dissent that was in danger of degenerating into schism. I hope that this book has by now shown that, notwithstanding those two factors, Europe had begun to take shape in the Middle Ages, fueled by ideas of unity and "nationhood" and encouraged by real instances of them, even if the development of the concept of sovereignty and its applications did, from the thirteenth century on, introduce a problem for Europe's future. Furthermore, the end of the monopoly of the Catholic Church did not spell the end of a common Christian culture, or of its civilization and values: in that respect, the laity played a double role for on the one hand it was the heir and disseminator of Christian values, but on the other, it was forced to become their adversary in the course of the bitter struggles that were ahead, at the end of the fifteenth century. Rather, the source of any threat to a future Europe was constituted by armed clashes between its various nations and the warlike nature of the Europeans themselves, which Hippocrates had detected and described even in antiquity. Europe's future was also unquestionably threatened by the way in which the expansion and colonization initiated in the fifteenth century evolved and by Europe's relations with its possessions elsewhere in the world.

As for progress, here the Middle Ages manifested a tension at the deepest level – to the point of presenting a paradoxical image. The dominant ideology, or perhaps one should say medieval mentalities in general, tended to condemn as an error and a sin all that was progressive and unheard of. But at the same time, with respect to both the material and the spiritual worlds, the Middle Ages constituted a period of creativity, innovations, and extraordinary progress. I believe that we should recognize that the most advantageous asset for the development of the concept of Europe and its realization was the European ability to progress that became evident in the Middle Ages and was further strengthened in the fifteenth century. The term "progress" may be found surprising. It is generally recognized that a sense of progress and the latter's promotion as an ideal was a phenomenon of the late seventeenth and above all the eighteenth centuries, a flower that, in order to bloom, needed the climate of the Enlightenment. And yet, I believe that progress had begun to burgeon in the Middle Ages. What medieval Europe elaborated and began to demonstrate stands in stark contrast to what was to happen in the Muslim world, and above all in China. In the fifteenth century China was the most powerful, rich, and advanced country in the world. But it then remained closed within itself and became etiolated, leaving domination of the world, including the East, to the Europeans. Despite the establishment of the powerful Ottoman Empire and the diffusion of Islam in Africa and Asia, the Muslim world, apart from the Turks, lost the dynamism of its medieval period. Christian Europe, in contrast, acquired ideas and practices that were to ensure its incomparable expansion from the fifteenth century onward. Despite its internal rivalries and the injustices and even crimes that it perpetrated abroad, that expansion was a major positive factor in the creation of Europe's self-awareness and consolidation. Peter Biller's *The Measure of Multitude: Population in Medieval Thought* (Oxford University Press, 2000) has shown how fourteenth-century Europe took the measure of its population and realized the role that the latter could play in the conduct of human affairs. Despite the fact that, by reason of the agricultural crisis and the plague, the fourteenth century was a period of stark demographic regression, the Europe of the end of the Middle Ages took to regarding the number of its inhabitants and their way of living together and reproducing themselves as a factor of power. A recent collective work, *Progrès, réaction, décadence dans l'Occident médiéval* (essays collected by Emmanuelle Baumgartner and Laurence Harf-Lancher, Paris/Geneva: Droz/Champion, 2003) studies the notions and aspects of "progress, reaction, and decadence" in the medieval West. While agreeing with the traditional idea that "the mental frameworks [of the Middle Ages] were hardly compatible with the idea of progress," this work notes notwithstanding that Christianity ascribed a direction to History (and I have, myself, stressed the "progressive" side to Joachim's of Fiore's Utopias). Christianity also demolished the ancient myth of eternal return and the cyclical concept of history. In a classic work, *La Théologie au XIIe siècle*, Father M. D. Chenu showed how medieval thought restarted history in the twelfth century. The quest for salvation was envisaged as a progress, of a moral nature of course, but also beneficial in every way. Scorn for the world, despite all its theoreticians and emulators, need not imply a rejection of material progress. Medieval dynamism resulted from the interaction of oppositions and tensions that produced progress (even if that was not what it was called). The collective work distinguishes a number of dualisms such as progress–reaction, progress–decadence, past–present, and ancient–modern that fueled medieval dynamism. As we have seen, the thirteenth-century Mendicant Orders dared, in provocative fashion, to proclaim their own novelty, while their opponents formed by more monastic attitudes considered such novelty to be sinful and evil. Medieval civilization and attitudes did not scorn technology and, as soon as an economic domain emerged, applied themselves to encouraging productivity and growth. Already in the Middle Ages, peasants were required to satisfy "contracts *ad meliorandum*," that is to say contracts that demanded that whoever benefited from the land should work to improve its yield.

As we have seen, in the fourteenth century interest in agricultural progress encouraged the reappearance of treatises on agriculture. The Middle Ages, despite their bad name, were in truth a period of inventions generally, ranging from the applications of mills to the camshaft system, which could convert continuous movements into alternate ones. Some remarkable pages written by Marc Bloch testify to this medieval inventiveness. In the Middle Ages everything was steeped in religion; in fact, religion was so omnipresent that there was no word to distinguish it. The whole of civilization, starting with the material variety, was, as the great economist Karl Polanyi puts it, "embedded" in religion. However, as I have suggested above, once values came down from heaven to earth, the handicap that this religious throttle inflicted on progress was increasingly replaced by a springboard aimed at progress. The interplay between providence and chance was less and less propelled by means of a wheel connected to circular time, and more and more geared to the creative individual and collective efforts of the Europeans themselves. In no domain did the creativity of the Europeans make more progress than in that of time. For one thing, although the past, given the lack of any rational study (which would be applied to it only in the eighteenth century), was not the object of any true historical science, it was used for the elaboration of a store of memories that took on the dimensions of a culture. Medieval Europe used the past as a springboard from which to propel itself better and further forward. Mastery of the measurement of time also provided it with the means to progress. Although it continued to use Caesar's Julian calendar, an innovation prompted by the Old Testament and Judaism introduced a rhythm that still regulates our lives, even today: this was the weekly rhythm, which establishes between the time for work and the time for rest a relationship that not only makes allowances with regard to the religious time of Sundays, but probably ensures the best possible use of human energy. The medieval Christian calendar furthermore introduced the two great festivals of Christmas and Easter into Europe: Christmas which, in contrast to the pagan Halloween festival of death, is a festival of birth and life, and Easter, the festival of resurrection, revival – not to mention Whitsun, the festival of the Spirit (which took the place of feudal festive customs such as "dubbing day").

In the fifteenth century, the great Italian architect and humanist Leon Battista Alberti put the following words into the mouth of one of his heroes:

Gianozzo: There are three things that a man can claim to belong to him: wealth, his body ...

Leonardo: And what is the third?

Gianozzo: Ah! Something very precious. Even these hands and eyes are not so much mine.

Leonardo: Wonder of wonders! Whatever is it?

Gianozzo: Time, my dear Leonardo, time, my children.

The value of time praised in this text is no doubt of an economic nature (for time is money), but it is also a cultural and existential value. The Europe of the late fifteenth century was a Europe of precious time, time that was appropriated by the individuals and groups that were to constitute Europe in the future.

Chronology

European events

276 First great wave of Germanic invasions into the Roman Empire.

313 The Edict of Milan grants Christians freedom of worship.

325 At the Council of Nicea, Constantine champions Orthodox Christianity against Aryanism.

330 Constantine establishes the empire's new capital in Constantinople.

379–95 Theodosius I recognizes Christianity as the state religion and, at his death, splits the Roman Empire into a Western Empire and an Eastern Empire.

407–29 A new wave of Germanic invasions.

410 Alaric's Visigoths take and sack Rome.

415 The Visigoths settle in Spain.

432–61 Saint Patrick converts Ireland.

ca. 440 Germanic peoples, Angles, Jutes, and Saxons settle in Great Britain; Britons withdraw to the continental mainland.

451 The Roman general Aetius halts Attila's Huns at the Catalaunic Fields.

476 The Herulian Odoacer deposes Emperor Romulus Augustulus and returns the insignia of the Western Empire to Constantinople.

488–526 The reign of the Ostrogoth Theodoric in Ravenna.

betw. 496 and 511 Baptism of the Frankish leader Clovis.

527–65 The Byzantine Emperor Justinian engages upon a partial and temporary reconquest of the West (southern Italy and Andalusia).

The so-called "Justinian plague," originating in the East, devastates Europe to the south of the Alps and the Loire.

ca. 529 Benedict of Nursia founds the abbey of Monte Cassino and produces a *Rule* for his monks, who were to become the Benedictine Order.

ca. 555 The Visigoths, having recaptured Andalusia, establish their capital in Toledo.

ca. 570–636 Isidore of Seville, the father of medieval Christian encyclopedism.

590–604 The pontificate of Gregory the Great.

ca. 590–615 The Irish monk Columban goes forth to found monasteries in Gaul (Luxeuil), southern Germany (Constance), and northern Italy (Bobbio).

568–72 The Lombards conquer northern and part of central Italy and found a kingdom with Pavia as its capital.

711–19 Muslim Berbers conquer Spain as far as the River Ebro.

726 The start of the iconoclastic quarrel in the Byzantine Empire.

732 Charles Martel, the mayor of the Frankish palace, halts the Muslims close to Poitiers.

757 Pepin the Short, the palace mayor, is consecrated king of the Franks by Pope Stephen II, whom he supports in Italy, where a pontifical state, known as "the patrimony of Saint Peter," is created.

759 The Muslims lose Narbonne, their last stronghold in Gaul.

771 Charlemagne becomes the sole king of the Franks.

774 Charlemagne becomes king of the Lombards.

778 The Frankish rear guard, led by Roland, Charlemagne's nephew, suffers a surprise attack by the Basques at Roncesvalles.

787 Second council of Nicea. Charlemagne authorizes the use of images in Christian art.

788 Charlemagne annexes Bavaria.

793–810 The first Norman attacks on Great Britain and Gaul.

796 Charlemagne conquers the Avars.

796–803 Construction of the palace and chapel of Aix-la-Chapelle, on Charlemagne's orders.

800 Charlemagne is crowned emperor in Rome.

827 The start of the Saracen conquest of Sicily.

ca. 830 The body of Saint James is claimed to be discovered in Galicia.

842 The Strasburg oath, sworn in the Frankish and Germanic vernacular languages.

843 The Treaty of Verdun seals the birth of Germany and France.

2nd half 9th C. The term *miles* (soldier, knight) is applied to vassals.

881 First appearance of the word "fief" (*feudum*).

885–6 Paris beseiged by Normans.

895 Hungarians settle in the Danubian plain.

910 Foundation of the abbey of Cluny.

911 The Treaty of Saint-Clair-sur-Epte: Charles the Simple cedes the Seine estuary to the Normans led by Rollo.

929 Creation of the Caliphate of Córdoba.

948 Foundation of the archbishopric of Hamburg, the religious metropolis for the conversion of the Scandinavians.

ca. 950 The start of major land clearance operations. Introduction of the plough north of the River Loire.

955 Otto I's victory over the Hungarians at Lechfeld.

960 Construction of the Córdoba mosque.

962 The imperial coronation of Otto the Great founds the Germanic Holy Roman Empire.

967 Baptism of the Polish duke Mieszko.

972 Foundation of the bishopric of Prague.

987 Accession of the Capetian dynasty in Gaul (Hugh Capet).

989 Prince Vladimir of Kiev is baptized by Byzantine Orthodox priests.

1000 The pair formed by Sylvester II (Gerbert of Aurillac, pope from 999 to 1003) and Otto III (emperor from 983 to 1002) dominates Latin Christendom.

The start of the construction of a "white mantle of churches" (as the Cluniac monk Raoul Glaber put it).

Creation of the archbishopric of Gniezno, the religious metropolis of Poland.

1001 Saint Stephen is crowned king of Hungary.

1005–6 Widespread famine in western Europe.

1015–28 Olav II Haraldsson, the saint, tries to impose Christianity on Norway by force.

1019–35 Cnut the Great, king of Denmark and England.

1020 Avicebron (Salomon Ibn Gabirol), Jewish philosopher, in Malaga ca. 1020, Valencia ca. 1058.

The lintel of Saint-Genès-des Fontaines (Catalonia), the oldest dated Romanesque sculpture in France.

ca. 1020 Gui of Arezzo invents a new system of musical notation.

1023 Under Church pressure, Robert the Pious has Manichean heretics burnt at the stake in Orléans.

1028 King Cnut of Denmark conquers Norway and completes his conquest of England.

betw. 1028 and 1072 Miniatures of the Apocalypse are produced in Saint-Sever.

1029 The first Norman principality in southern Italy (Averso).

ca. 1030 Start of the communal movement in Italy (Cremona).

1031 End of the Umayyad caliphate of Córdoba.

1032–3 Famine in western Europe.

ca. 1035 Construction of a stone bridge in Albi.

1037 Emperor Conrad II institutes hereditary fiefs in northern Italy.

1054 Definitive schism between the Roman Latin and the Greek Orthodox Churches.

1060–91 The Normans conquer Sicily.

1066 Led by William the Conqueror, the Normans conquer England.

1069 A "communal" demonstration in Le Mans.

1071 The relics of Saint Nicholas are brought to Bari from the East.

1072 The *colleganza* contract is introduced in Venice.

1073–85 Pontificate of Gregory VII. The Gregorian reform.

1077 Emperor Henry IV is humiliated before Pope Gregory VII in Canossa.

ca. 1080 The Guild of Saint Omer.

1081 Bourgeois "consuls" in Pisa.

1085 Alfonso VI of Castile seizes Toledo.

1086 First mention of a fulling mill, in Normandy (Saint-Wandrille).

late 11th C. Draught horses replace oxen in northern France

after 1088 Irnerius teaches Roman law in Bologna.

1093 The construction of Durham cathedral begins: the first Gothic arch.

1095 In Clermont, Urban II preaches in favor of a crusade.

1098 A wave of anti-Semitism: pogroms perpetrated by popular crusaders on their way to Palestine.

Foundation of the Cistercian order by Robert of Molesmes.

1099 The merchants of Genoa form a *compagna*.

ca. 1100 The marshes of Flanders begin to be drained: polders.

1108 The foundation, near Paris, of the abbey of Saint-Victor, the home of pre-scholasticism.

1112 Communal revolution in Laon. The bishop-count is killed.

1120–50 The first professional statutes in the West.

1126–98 Averroës, the Arabic philosopher from Córdoba, author of an Aristotelian commentary, who died in Marrakech.

1127 Flemish towns obtain franchise charters.

1132–44 Suger rebuilds Saint-Denis, introducing the Gothic style.

1135–1204 Maimonides, the Jewish theologian and philosopher from Córdoba, who wrote in Arabic and died in Cairo.

1140 Formation of the kingdom of Portugal.

ca. 1140 *Decretum Gratiani* (Gratian's decree), the basis for the corpus of canon law.

1141 Peter the Venerable, abbot of Cluny, has the Koran translated into Latin.

1143 Foundation of Lübeck.

1154 Frederick Barbarossa grants privileges to the masters and students of Bologna.

1154–1224 The Anglo-French "empire" of the Plantagenets.

1165 Canonization of Charlemagne.

1170 Construction of the Giralda minaret in Seville.

after 1175 Introduction of contract orders in Genoa.

1180 Death of John of Salisbury, the bishop of Chartres and patron of its school.

1183 The Peace of Constance. Frederick Barbarossa recognizes the liberty of the Lombard towns.

1200 Foundation of Riga.

1202 Death of Joachim of Fiore, theorist of millenarianism.

1204 Constantinople is seized and sacked by the crusaders of the Fourth Crusade. Foundation of the Latin Empire of Constantinople (1204–60).

1207 Saint Dominic's mission to the Albigensian Cathars.

1209 First Franciscan community.

1209–29 Albigensian crusade.

1212 The Christians of Spain defeat the Moors at Las Navas de Tolosa.

1214 The University of Oxford is granted its first privileges.

1215 The University of Paris receives statutes from Robert de Courson.
Fourth Lateran Council rules on marriage and confession and takes measures against the Jews and heretics.
The Magna Carta in England.

1215–18 William of Morbeke translates Aristotle into Latin.

1216 Foundation of the Friars Preachers (Dominicans).

1223 The papacy accepts the revised Franciscan Rule.

1229–31 The University of Paris is on strike.

1231 Gregory IX organizes the Inquisition.

after 1232 The Muslims of Granada build the Alhambra.

1238 Valencia is seized by the Aragonese.

1241 Mongols raid Silesia, Poland, and Hungary.

1242 The first graphical representation of a stern-post rudder (on the Elbing seal).

1248 Seville seized by the Castilians.

1252 Gold coins minted in Genoa and Florence (florins).

1252–9 Thomas Aquinas teaching in the University of Paris.

1253 Foundation of a college for poor theology students by Canon Robert de Sorbonne in the University of Paris (the future Sorbonne).

1254 Pope Urban IV institutes the festival of Corpus Christi.

1261 The Latin Empire of Constantinople collapses.

1266 Battle of Benevento. Charles of Anjou becomes king of Sicily.

1268 The first paper mills, in Fabriano.

1270 The first mention of a marine map of the Mediterranean.

1276 Raymond Lulle founds a college for the teaching of Arabic to Christian missionaries.

1280 A wave of urban strikes and riots (Bruges, Douai, Tournai, Provins, Rouen, Caen, Orléans, Béziers).

1281 Hanseatic fusion of the merchants of Cologne, Hamburg, and Lübeck.

1282 The Sicilian Vespers: the French are forced to cede Sicily to the Aragonese.

1283 The Teutonic knights complete the conquest of Prussia.

1284 Gold ducats are minted in Venice.
The arched roof of Beauvais cathedral collapses (48 meters).

1290 The Jews are expelled from England.

1298 Regular sea links begin to be established between Genoa, England, and Flanders.

1300 The first certain mention of eye-spectacles.

early 14th C. Letters of monetary exchange circulating in Italy.

1306 Jews are expelled from France.

ca. 1306 Piero of Crescenza produces a summary of medieval agricultural knowledge.

1309 The papacy is installed in Avignon.

1310 The first representation of the Passion in front of Rouen cathedral.

1313 Henry VII dies in Pisa. The end of the imperial dream.

ca. 1313 Dante completes the *Divina Commedia*.

1315 The battle of Morgarten: Swiss infantrymen defeat the Habsburgs.
1315–17 Widespread famine in Europe: the beginning of the fourteenth-century "crisis."
1321 Jews and lepers accused of poisoning wells are massacred.
1337 The start of the Hundred Years' War between England and France.
1341 Cola di Rienzo eventually fails to restore an ancient-style government in Rome.
1347–8 The start of the great Black Death epidemics (that continue down to 1720).
1348 The Black Death gives rise to pogroms.
1353 The Turks gain a foothold in Europe at Gallipoli.
1355 Nicholas Oresme's *Treatise on Money*.
1358 Parisian revolt against the royal regent.
Étienne Marcel is murdered. Peasant *jacquerie* in northeastern France.
1368 Jagiello, prince of Lithuania, marries Jadwiga of Poland, the daughter and heir of Casimir the Great.
1378 The beginning of the Great Schism.
Ciompi revolt in Florence.
Pope Urban VI returns to Rome.
1379 Philippe Van Artevelde's revolt in Ghent.
1381 Wat Tyler's peasant revolt in England.
1382 Wycliffe condemned for heresy.
1389 The Turks defeat the Serbs in Kosovo.
1394 The Jews are definitively expelled from France.
1397 The three Scandinavian countries agree to union, in Kalmar.
1409 The Germans leave the University of Prague, following the Kutna Hora decree, influenced by Jan Hus, which favors the Czechs.
1410 The Teutonic Knights are defeated by the Poles at Tannenberg (Grünwald).
1414–18 Council of Constance.
Jan Hus is condemned for heresy and executed.
1420–36 Brunelleschi builds the cupola of the Duomo in Florence.
1431 Death of Joan of Arc, burnt at the stake in Rouen.
1431–7 Council of Basel.
1434 Cosimo de' Medici, master of Florence.
1439–43 The councils of Florence and Rome bring the Great Schism to an end.
1450 Gutenberg puts the finishing touches to the Mainz printing press.
1453 Constantinople captured by the Turks.
1456 Marsilio Ficino's *Institutiones Platonicae*.
1458–64 Pontificate of Pius II (Enea Silvio Piccolomini), a promoter of Europe.
1458–71 George Podiebrad, king of Bohemia.
His plan for European union.
1458–90 Matthias Corvinus, king of Hungary.
1462–1505 The reign of Ivan III, grand duke of Moscow.
1464 Death of Nicholas of Cusa, a "modern" theologian who favored religious tolerance.

1468 Death of the Albanian Skanderbeg, a great leader of the resistance to the Turks.
1469 The Catholic monarchs (Ferdinand and Isabella) marry in Spain.
1475 Treaty of Picquigny. End of the Hundred Years' War.
1476 Marriage of Maximilian of Austria and Marie of Burgundy.
1477 Botticelli paints his *Primavera*.
1483 The Dominican Torquemada is appointed Grand Inquisitor of Spain.
1492 Granada is captured by the Catholic monarchs.
   End of the Muslim presence in the Iberian peninsula.
1494 The treaty of Tordesillas: Spain and Portugal divide the world between them under the auspices of Pope Alexander VI Borgia.
1495 The French King Charles VIII's short-lived conquest of the kingdom of Naples. The start of the Italian Wars.

Events outside Europe

America

700–800 The Mayan civilization in central America is at its peak.
800–925 Collapse of the Mayan civilization.
1000–200 The Toltec civilization in Mexico is at its peak.
12th C. Semilegendary origins of the Inca dynasty in Peru.
1370 The Aztecs found Teotihuacan in Mexico.
15th C. A succession of Aztec confederations in Mexico.
1492 Christopher Columbus "discovers America."

Africa

6th–8th C. The Zulu kingdom of Zimbabwe is at its peak.
   The Arabs conquer Europe and found Fustat (Cairo), which becomes the capital of the Fatimid Shiites (969–1171).
709 The Arabs complete their conquest of northern Africa.
ca. 800 Foundation of the kingdom of Kanem in the region of Lake Chad.
1057 Hilalian Arabs destroy Kairouan, the capital of the Aghlabids.
1062 Foundation of Marrakech by the Berber dynasty of the Almoravids, who conquer Muslim Spain. They were later succeeded by the Berber dynasties of Almohads (late twelfth century) and Marinids (1269).
   Collapse of a Muslim state incorporating Algeria.
1171 The Kurd, Saladin, reestablishes Sunnism in Egypt and founds the Ayyubid dynasty (1171–1250).

early 13th C. Lalibila, king of the Christian kingdom of Ethiopia, under pressure from Islam, transfers his capital from Aksum to Roha.

1250 Mamluks seize power in Egypt.

14th C. Foundation to the west of Lake Chad of the kingdom of Bornu, which absorbs Kanem.

1312–37 The peak of the Muslim kingdom of Mali under Kouta Mousa, who absorbs the kingdom of Ghana.

1402 The Norman Jean de Béthencourt conquers the Canaries.

1415 The Portuguese conquer Ceuta.

1418 The Portuguese occupy Madeira.

1456 The Portuguese reach the Gulf of Guinea.

1477 The Canaries pass under Spanish domination.

1488 Bartholomew Diaz discovers the Cape of Good Hope.

Asia: The Far East

320–480 Reign of the Gupta dynasty in northern India.

3rd to 9th C. Domination of the Pallava dynasty, centred in Madras.

581–618 Yang Jian restores the unity of China, with a new capital, Chang'an (Xian). Construction of canals and great city walls.

618–907 Tang dynasty. Central administration is strengthened. Victories in Korea. Tibet's independence is recognized. Diffusion of Buddhism.

710 Nara becomes the imperial capital of Japan.

mid-8th C. to 824 The Shailendra sovereigns have the Buddhist stupa of Borobudur built in central Java.

777 Buddhism becomes the religion of the Japanese court.

794 Heian (Kyoto) the new capital of the Japanese emperor.

858 Start of Fujiwara domination in Japan.

907 The Chola dynasty supplants the Pallava dynasty in India. Its power extends to Ceylon (Sri Lanka) and Malaysia until the thirteenth century.

907–60 Anarchy of the "five dynasties" in China.

960–1279 Song dynasty. Mandarinate. Construction of the Grand Canal.

1024 Paper money first printed in China.

1086 First mention of movable characters for Chinese printing presses.

1181–1218 Peak of the Khmer empire under Jayavarman VII, who built Angkor Thom, following on Suryavarman II's Angkor Wat.

1185–92 The Kamakura shogunate becomes established.

1192 Muhammad Ghori defeats the rajput of Prithvi Raj. The Muslims become the masters of northern India.

1206–1526 Muslim sultanates in Delhi, India.

1206–79 Formation of the Mongol Empire.

1254–5 The Venetian merchants Niccolò and Matteo Polo and their son and nephew Marco Polo travel in China and southeast Asia.

1279–1368 The Mongol Yuan dynasty in China. Beijing (Khanbalik) had become the capital in 1264.

1314–30 The Franciscan Odoric of Pordenone travels in India and China.

1371 Overseas travel is forbidden for the Chinese.

1392 Shogunate of Muromachi in Japan. Diffusion of Zen culture. Creation of Noh theater.

1400–1700 Ming dynasty in China.

1470–80 The Great Wall is built in northern China.

The Muslim Near East

622 Muhammad leaves Mecca for Medina: the Hegira.

630 The Byzantine Emperor Heraclius defeats the Persians and takes the "True Cross" back to Jerusalem.

632 Death of Muhammad.

634 The Muslims leave Arabia.
Start of the Muslim conquest from North Africa (completed in 712) to Tashkent (709).

636–724 Umayyad caliphate in Damascus.

638 Jerusalem seized by Arabs.

661 Murder of Ali, Muhammad's son-in-law.

680 Hussein, Ali's son, is massacred at Kartala. Beginning of the Shiite religion.

762 Abbasid caliphate in Baghdad.

786–809 Caliphate of Harun al-Rashid.

1009 The caliph Hakem destroys the Holy Sepulcher of Jerusalem.

1055 The Seljuq Turks seize Baghdad and reestablish Suniism.

1071 The Seldjuq Turks defeat the Byzantines at Mantzikert.

1099 Crusaders capture Jerusalem.

1187 The Kurd Saladin defeats the Christians at Hattsin and seizes Jerusalem.

1191 Collapse of the Third Crusade (apart from the installation of Christians in Cyprus).

1250–4 Saint Louis is in the Holy Land.
The failure of Saint Louis's crusades (Egypt 1250), Tunis (1270).

1291 Mamluks seize Saint John of Acre, the last Christian stronghold in Palestine.

1354–1403 The Ottoman sultan Bayezid I conquers and unites the Turkish emirates of Anatolia.

A Selective Thematic Bibliography

This is not a full bibliography of medieval history. Rather, it is a list, organized into themes, of the works (and a few articles) that I have found stimulating and useful during the composition of this book. Some constitute general panoramas, others express suggestive points of view.

André Segal's reaction to the problem of periodization that arises here is to reject any idea of it. See his nihilistic article, "Périodisation et didactique: le 'moyen âge' comme obstacle à l'intelligence de l'Occident," *Actes du Colloque d'Histoire au présent* (Paris, 1989), Paris: Éditions de l'ÉHÉSS, 1991, pp. 105–14.

My own considered opinion is that there can be no historiography without periodization, although we do need to recognize the latter's artifical nature and the fact that it depends on the way that history evolves. In criticizing the traditional notion of the Middle Ages, I prefer my own hypothesis of a *long* medieval period (see the concluding pages of chapter 6).

Abbreviations

Gauvard-deLibera-Zink: *Dictionnaire du Moyen Age.* Paris: PUF, 2002.
Le Goff-Schmitt: *Dictionnaire raisonné de l'Occident médiéval.* Paris: Fayard, 1999.
Linehan-Nelson: *The Medieval World.* London–New York: Routledge, 2001.
Vauchez: *Dictionnaire encyclopédique du Moyen Age.* 2 vols, Paris: Cerf, 1997. In English as *Encyclopedia of the Middle Ages,* ed. André Vauchez with Barrie Dobson and Michael Lapidge, trans. Adrian Walford, 2 vols, Chicago–London: Fitzroy Dearborn, 2000.

CNRS: Centre National de la Recherche Scientifique

ÉHÉSS: École des Hautes Études en Sciences Sociales
SHMES(P): Société des Historiens Médiévistes de l'Enseignement Supérieur (Public)

Studies on Europe (and the idea of Europe), particularly the medieval period

Bloch, Marc, "Projet d'un enseignement d'histoire comparée des sociétés européennes," 16pp., in *Dernières nouvelles de Strasbourg* (1934), repr. in Étienne Bloch and Marc Bloch (eds), *Histoire et historiens*, Paris: Armand Colin, 1995.

Bloch, Marc, "Problèmes d'Europe," *Annales HES*, 7 (1935), pp. 471–9.

Braudel, Fernand, *L'Europe. L'espace, le temps, les hommes*. Paris: Arts et métiers graphiques, 1987.

Carpentier, Jean and Lebrun, François (eds), *Histoire de l'Europe*. Paris: Seuil, 1990.

Chabod, Federico, *Storia dell'idea d'Europa*. Bari: Laterza, 1961.

Elias, Norbert, *State Formation and Civilization*, vol. 2 of *The Civilizing Process*, 2 vols. Oxford: Blackwell, 1978–82.

Febvre, Lucien, *L'Europe. Genèse d'une civilization* (a course of lectures at the Collège de France in 1944–5), preface by Marc Ferro. Paris: Perrin, 1999.

Le Goff, Jacques, *La Vieille Europe et la nôtre*. Paris: Seuil, 1994.

Pagden, Anthony (ed.), *The Idea of Europe: From Antiquity to the European Union*. Baltimore: Johns Hopkins University, Woodrow Wilson Center Press, 2002.

Villain-Gandossi, Christiane (ed.), *L'Europe à la recherche de son identité* (in particular, Robert Fossier, "L'Europe au Moyen Age," pp. 35–40). Paris: Éditions du Comité des travaux historiques et scientifiques, 2002.

Europe and the Middle Ages

Barraclough, Geoffrey (ed.), *Eastern and Western Europe in the Middle Ages*. London: Thames and Hudson, 1970.

Bartlett, Robert, *The Making of Europe: Conquest, Colonisation and Cultural Change, 950–1350*. London: Allen Lane, 1993.

Bosl, Karl, *Europa im Mittelalter*. Vienna–Heidelberg: Carl Uebersenter, 1970.

Compagnon, Antoine and Seebacher, Jacques, *L'Esprit de l'Europe*. 3 vols, Paris: Flammarion, 1993.

Duroselle, Jean-Baptiste, *L'Idée d'Europe dans l'histoire*. Paris: Denoël, 1965.

Edson, Evelyn, *Mapping Time and Space: How Medieval Mapmakers Viewed their World*, British Library Studies in Map History, vol. 1. London: British Library, 1998.

Geremek, Bronislaw, *The Common Roots of Europe*. Cambridge: Polity, 1991.

Hay, Denys, *The Emergence of an Idea: Europa*. Edinburgh: Edinburgh University Press, 1957 (1st edn), 1968 (2nd edn).

Hersant, Yves and Durand-Bogaert, Fabienne, *Europes. De l'Antiquité au XXe siècle. Anthologie critique et commentée*. Paris: Robert Laffont, 2000.

Le Goff, Jacques, *L'Europe racontée aux jeunes*. Paris: Seuil, 1996.

Mackay, Angus and Ditchburn, David, *Atlas of Medieval Europe*. London: Routledge, 1996.

Menestò, Enrico (ed.), *Le radici medievali della civiltà europea* (Congress Ascoli Piceno, 2000). Spoleto: Centro italiano di studi sull'alto medioevo, 2002.

Mitterauer, Michael, *Warum Europa? Mittelalterliche Grundlagen eines Sonderwegs*. Munich: Beck, 2000.

Past and Present, special issue (Nov. 1992) (in particular Karl Leyser, "Concept of Europe in the Early and High Middle Ages," pp. 25–47).

Pastoureau, Michel and Schmitt, Jean-Claude, *L'Europe. Mémoire et Emblèmes*. Paris: Éditions de l'Epargne, 1990.

Storia d'Europa. 3. Il Medioevo, secoli V–XV. Turin: Einaudi, 1994.

Middle Ages, in general

Bartlett, Robert (ed.), *Le Monde médiéval*. Paris: Éditions du Rocher, 2002. See in English, Robert Bartlett (ed.), *Medieval Panorama*, London: Thames & Hudson, 2001.

Borst, Arno, *Lebensformen im Mittelalter*. Frankfurt–Berlin: Ullstein, 1973.

Dalarun, Robert (ed.), *Le Moyen Age en lumière*. Paris: Fayard, 2002.

Delort, Robert, *Le Moyen Age. Histoire illustrée de la vie quotidienne*. Lausanne: Edita, 1972. New edn as *La Vie au Moyen Age*, Paris: Seuil, 1981.

Gatto, Ludovico, *Viaggio intorno al concetto di Medioevo*. Rome: Bulzoni, 1992.

Gourevitch, Aaron J., *Les Catégories de la culture médiéval* (1972). Paris: Gallimard, 1983 (translated from Russian).

Heer, Friedrich, *L'Univers du Moyen Age*, [1961], Paris: Fayard, 1970 (translated from German).

Kahl, Hubert D., "Was bedeutet 'Mittelalter'?" *Seculum*, 40 (1989), pp. 15–38.

Le Goff, Jacques, *La Civilisation de l'Occident médiéval*. Paris: Arthaud, 1964.

Le Goff, Jacques, "Pour un long Moyen Age," in *L'Imaginaire médiéval*, Paris: Gallimard, 1985, pp. 7–13.

Le Goff, Jacques (ed.), *L'Homme médiéval*. Italian edn, Bari: Laterza, 1987; French edn, Paris: Seuil, 1989, 1994.

Linehan, Peter and Nelson Janet L. (eds), *The Medieval World*. London–New York: Routledge, 2001.

Lopez, Robert, *Naissance de l'Europe*. Paris: Armand Colin, 1962.

Méhu, Didier, *Gratia Dei, les chemins du Moyen Age*. Quebec: Fides, 2003.

Pirenne, Henri, *L'Histoire de l'Europe des invasions au XVe siècle*. Paris–Brussels, 1936.

Sergi, Giuseppe, *L'Idée de Moyen Age. Entre sens commun et pratique historique* (1998). Paris: Flammarion, 2000 (translated from Italian).

Southern, Richard W., *The Making of the Middle Ages*. London: Hutchinson, 1953.
Tabacco, Giovanni and Merlo, Grado Giovanni, *La civiltà europea nella storia mondiale. Medioevo, v/xv secolo*. Bologna: Il Mulino, 1981.

The Middle Ages after the Middle Ages

Amalvi, Christian, *Le Goût du Moyen Age*. Paris: Plon, 1996.
Amalvi, Christian, "Moyen Age," in Le Goff-Schmitt.
Apprendre le Moyen Age aujourd'hui, special issue of *Médiévales*, no. 13 (autumn 1987).
Boureau, Alain, "Moyen Age," in Gauvard-de Libera-Zink.
Branca, Vittore (ed.), *Concetto. Storia. Miti e immagini del medioevo*. Florence, Sansoni, 1973.
Capitani, Ovidio, *Medioevo passato prossimo. Appunti storiografici, tra due guerre e molte crisi*. Bologna: Il Mulino, 1979.
Eco, Umberto, "Dieci modi di sognare il medioevo," in *Sugli sprechi e altri saggi*, Milan: Bompiani, 1985, pp. 78–89.
Eco, Umberto, "Le Nouveau Moyen Age," in *La Guerre du faux*, Paris: Grasset, 1985, pp. 87–116.
Europe, special issue, *Le Moyen Age maintenant* (Oct. 1983).
Fuhrmann, Horst, *Überall ist mittelalter. Von der Gegenwart einer vergangenen Zeit*. Munich: Beck, 1996.
Goetz, Hans-Werner (ed.), *Die Aktualität des Mittelalters*. Bochum: D. Winckler, 2000.
Guerreau, Alain, *L'Avenir d'un passé incertain. Quelle histoire du Moyen Age au XXIe siècle?* Paris: Seuil, 2001.
Heinzle, Joachim, *Modernes Mittelalter. Neue Bilder einer populären Epoche*. Frankfurt–Leipzig: Insel, 1994.
Le Goff, Jacques and Lobrichon, Guy (eds), *Le Moyen Age aujourd'hui. Trois regards contemporains sur le Moyen Age: histoire, théologie, cinéma* (Proceedings of the Cérisy-la-Salle colloquium, July 1991). Paris: Cahiers du Léopard d'Or, 1998.
Lire le Moyen Age, ed. Alain Corbellari and Christopher Lucken, special issue of *Equinoxe*, no. 16 (autumn 1996).
Moyen Age, mode d'emploi, special issue of *Médiévales*, no. 7 (autumn 1984).

The Middle Ages and the cinema

Airlie, Stuart, "Strange Eventful Histories: The Middle Ages in the Cinema," in Peter Linehan and Janet L. Nelson (eds), *The Medieval World*, London–New York: Routledge, 2001, pp. 163–81.

La Bretèque, François de, "Le regard du cinéma sur le Moyen Age," in Jacques Le Goff and Guy Lobrichon (eds), *Le Moyen Age aujourd'hui*. *Trois regards contemporains sur le Moyen Age: histoire, théologie, cinéma* (Proceedings of the Cerisy-la-Salle colloquium, July 1991), Paris: Cahiers du Léopard d'Or, 1998, pp. 283–326.

Le Moyen Age au cinéma, special issue of *Cahiers de la Cinémathèque*, nos 42–3 (1985).

Early Middle Ages

Banniard, Michel, *Genèse culturelle de l'Europe, Ve–VIIIe siècle*. Paris: Seuil, 1989.

Brown, Peter, *The Rise of Western Christendom: Triumph and Diversity*, AD 200–1000. Oxford: Blackwell, 1997.

Herrin, Judith, *The Formation of Christendom*. Princeton: Princeton University Press, 1987.

Hillgarth, J. N. (ed.), *The Conversion of Western Europe, 350–750*. Englewood Cliffs: Prentice Hall, 1969.

Leguay, Jean-Pierre, *L'Europe des États barbares (Ve–VIIIe siècle)*. Paris: Belin, 2003.

Pohl, Walter, *Die Völkerwanderung. Eroberung und Integration*, Stuttgart–Berlin–Cologne: Kohlhammer, 2002.

Pohl, Walter and Diesenberger, Maximilien (eds), *Integration und Herrschaft. Ethnische Identitäten und soziale Organisation im Frümittelalter*. Vienna: Verlag der Osterreichischen Akademie der Wissenschaften, 2002.

Charlemagne and Carolingian civilization

Barbero, Alessandro, *Carlo Magno. Un padre dell'Europa*. Rome–Bari: Laterza, 2000.

Braunfels, Wolfgang (ed.), *Karl der Grosse. Lebenswerk und Nachleben*. 5 vols, Dusseldorf: 1965–68.

Ehlers, Joachim, *Charlemagne l'Européen entre la France et l'Allemagne*. Stuttgart: Thorbecke, 2001.

Favier, Jean, *Charlemagne*. Paris: Fayard, 1999.

Fichtenau, Heinrich, *L'Empire carolingien*. Paris: 1958.

Intellectuels et Artistes dans l'Europe carolingienne, IXe–XIe siècle. Auxerre: Abbaye Saint-Germain, 1990.

McKitterick, Rosamund, *The Carolingians and the Written Word*. Cambridge: Cambridge University Press, 1989.

McKitterick, Rosamund (ed.), *Carolingian Culture: Emulation and Innovation*. Cambridge: Cambridge University Press, 1994.

Morissey, Robert, *L'Empereur à la barbe fleurie. Charlemagne dans la mythologie et l'histoire*, Paris: Gallimard, 1997.

Nelson, Janet L., "Charlemagne: 'Father of Europe?'" *Quaestiones Medii aevi novae*, 7 (2002), pp. 3–20.

Pirenne, Henri, *Mahomet et Charlemagne*. Paris–Brussels, 1937.

Riché, Pierre, *Les Carolingiens. Une famille qui fit l'Europe*. Paris: Hachette, 1983.

Werner, Karl-Ferdinand, *Karl der Grosse oder Charlemagne? Von der Aktualität einer überholten Fragestellung*. Munich: Verlag der bayerischen Akademie der Wissenschaften, 1995.

The year 1000

Bourin, Monique and Parisse, Michel, *L'Europe de l'an Mil*. Paris: Livre de Poche, 1999.

Duby, Georges, *L'An Mil*. Paris: Gallimard, 1967.

Duby, Georges and Frugoni, Chiara, *Mille e non più Mille. Viaggio tra le paure di fine millennio*. Milan: Rizzoli, 1999.

Gerbert l'Européen (Proceedings of the Aurillac colloquium). Aurillac: Éditions Gerbert, 1997.

Gieysztor, Aleksander, *L'Europe nouvelle autour de l'an Mil. La papauté, L'Empire et les "nouveaux venus."* Rome: Unione internazionale degli Istituti di archeologia storia, e storia dell'arte, 1997.

Guyotjeannin, Olivier and Poulle, Emmanuel (eds), *Autour de Gerbert d'Aurillac, le pape de l'An Mil*. Paris: École des Chartes, 1996.

Riché, Pierre (ed.), *L'Europe de l'An Mil*. Saint-Léger-Vauban: Zodiaque, 2001.

The twelfth-century renaissance

Benson, R. L. and Constable, Giles (eds), *Renaissance and Renewal in the Twelfth Century*. Oxford: Clarendon Press, 1982.

Haskins, C. H., *The Renaissance of the Twelfth Century*. Cambridge: Harvard University Press, 1927.

Le Goff, Jacques, "What Does the Twelfth Century Renaissance Mean?" in Linehan-Nelson, pp. 635–47.

Moore, Robert I., *The First European Revolution (c. 970–1215)*. Oxford: Blackwell, 2000.

Moos, Peter von, "Das 12. Jahrhundert: eine 'Renaissance' oder ein 'Auflärungszeitalter'?" in *Mittelalterliches Jahrbuch* 23 (1988), pp. 1–10.

Ribémont, Bernard, *La Renaissance du XIIe siècle et l'Encyclopédisme*. Paris: Honoré Champion, 2002.

Thirteenth century

Génicot, Léopold, *Le XIIIe siècle européen*. Paris: PUF, 1968.

Le Goff, Jacques, *L'Apogée de la chrétienté v. 1180–v. 1330*. Paris: Bordas, 1982.

Le Goff, Jacques, "Du ciel sur la terre: la mutation des valeurs du XIIe au XIIIe dans l'Occident médiéval," in *Odysseus* (1990) (in Russian), repr. in "Quarto", *Le Roi, le Saint*, Paris: Gallimard, 2003.

Mundy, J.-H., *Europa in the High Middle Ages* (1973). London: Longman, 1991.

Fourteenth to fifteenth century: mutations, conflicts, violence

Abel, Wilhelm, *Die Wüstungen des ausgehenden Mittelalters*, 2nd edn. Stuttgart, 1955.

Gauvard, Claude, *"De grace especial." Crime, État et société en France à la fin du Moyen Age*. 2 vols, Paris: Publications de la Sorbonne, 1991.

Graus, Frantisek, *Pest, Geiszler, Juenmorde. Das 14. Jahrhundert als Krisenzeit*, 2nd edn. Göttingen: Vandenhoeck & Ruprecht, 1988.

Hilton, Rodney H., *Bond Men Made Free: Medieval Peasant Movements and the English Rising of 1381*. London: Methuen, 1973.

Hilton, Rodney H. and Aston, T. H., *The English Rising of 1381*. Cambridge: Past and Present Publications, 1984.

Jordan, William Chester, *The Great Famine: Northern Europe in the Early Fourteenth Century*. Princeton: Princeton University Press, 1996.

Leff, Gordon, *The Dissolution of the Medieval Outloo:. An Essay on Intellectual and Spiritual Change in the Fourteenth Century*; New York: Harper & Row, 1976.

Malowist, Marian, *Croissance et répression en Europe, XIVe–XVIIe siècle*. Paris: Armand Colin, 1972.

Martines, Lauro (ed.), *Violence and Civil Disorder in Italian Cities, 1200–1500*. Berkeley–Los Angeles: University of California Press, 1972.

Mollat, Michel and Wolff, Philippe, *Ongles bleus, Jacques et Ciompi. Les révolutions populaires en Europe aux XIVe et XVe siècles*. Paris: Calmann-Lévy, 1970.

Stella, Alessandro, *La Révolte des Ciompi. Les hommes, les lieux, le travail*. Paris: ÉHÉSS, 1993.

Valdeón Baruque, Julio, *Los conflictos sociales en el reino de Castilla en los siglos XIV y XV*. Madrid: Siglo veintiuno, 1975.

Villages désertes et Histoire économique, XIe–XVIIIe siècle, preface by Fernand Braudel. Paris: SEVPEN, 1965.

Wolff, Philippe, *Automne du Moyen Age ou Printemps des temps nouveaux? L'économie européenne aux XIVe et XVe siècles*. Paris: Aubier, 1986.

The genesis of the modern state

Coulet, Noël and Genet, Jean-Pierre (eds), *L'État moderne. Territoire, droit, système politique*. Paris: Éditions du CNRS, 1990.

Culture et Idéologie dans la genèse de l'État moderne (Rome Round Table, 1984). Rome: École française de Rome, 1985.

Genet, Jean-Pierre (ed.), *L'État moderne. Genèse. Bilans et perspectives*. Paris: Éditions du CNRS, 1990.

Guenée, Bernard, *L'Occident aux XIVe et XVe siècles. Les États*. Paris: PUF, 1971 (1st edn) and 1991 (4th edn).

Strayer, Joseph R., *On the Medieval Origins of the Modern State*. Princeton: Princeton University Press, 1970.

Wilks, M. J., *The Problem of Sovereignty in the Later Middle Ages*. Cambridge: Cambridge University Press, 1963.

Was the end of the fifteenth century the end of the Middle Ages?

Brown, Elizabeth A. R., "On 1500," in Linehan-Nelson, pp. 691–710.

Cardini, Franco, *Europa 1492. Ritratto di un continente cinquecento anni fa*. Milan: Rizzoli, 1989.

Vincent, Bernard, *1492, l'année admirable*. Paris: Aubier, 1991.

* * *

Animals

Berlioz, Jacques and Polo de Beaulieu, Marie-Anne, *L'Animal exemplaire au Moyen Age. Bestiares du Moyen Age*, trans. G. Bianciotto. Paris: Stock, 1980.

Delort, Robert, *Les animaux ont une histoire*. Paris: Seuil, 1984.

Delort, Robert, "Animaux," in Le Goff-Schmitt, pp. 55–66.

Guerreau, Alain, "Chasse," in Le Goff-Schmitt, pp. 166–78.

Il Mondo animal. Micrologus VIII, 2 vols (2000).

Ortalli, Gherardo, *Lupi gente culture. Uomo e ambiente nel medioevo*. Turin: Einaudi, 1997.

Voisenet, Jacques, *Bestiaire chrétien. L'imagerie animale des auteurs du haut Moyen Age (Ve–XIe siècle)*. Toulouse: Presses universitaires du Mirail, 1994.

Art, aesthetics

Baral i Altet, Xavier, *L'Art médiéval*. Paris: PUF, 1991.

Caillet, Jean-Pierre (ed.), *L'Art du Moyen Age*. Paris: Réunion des Musées nationaux, Gallimard, 1995.

Castelnuovo, Enrico, "L'Artiste," in Jacques Le Goff (ed.), *L'Homme médiéval*. Italian edn, Bari: Laterza, 1987; French edn, Paris: Seuil, 1989, pp. 233–66.

Castelnuovo, Enrico and Sergi, Giuseppe (eds), *Arti e storia nel Medioevo*. Vol. 1: *Tempi, spazi, istituzioni*. Turin: Einaudi, 2002.

De Bruyne, Edgar, *Études d'esthétique médiévale*. 3 vols, Bruges, 1946.

De Bruyne, Edgar, *L'Esthétique du Moyen Age*. Louvain, 1947.

Duby, Georges, *L'Art et la société. Moyen Age–XXe siècle*. Paris: Gallimard, 2002.

Eco, Umberto, *Le Problème esthétique chez Thomas d'Aquin* (1970), new trans. Paris: PUF, 1993.

Eco, Umberto, *Art et Beauté dans l'esthéthique médiévale* (1987). Paris: Grasset, 1997 (translated from Italian).

Ladner, G. B., *Ad imaginem Dei: The Image of Man in Medieval Art*. Latrobe: Archabbey Press, 1965.

Panofsky, Erwin, *Architecture gothique et pensée scolastique* (with a contribution by Pierre Bourdieu). Paris: Minuit, 1967.

Recht, Roland, *Le Croire et le Voir. L'art des cathédrales, XIIe–XVe siècle*. Paris: Gallimard, 1999.

Scobeltzine, André, *L'Art féodal et son enjeu social*. Paris: Gallimard, 1973.

Von den Steinen, Wolfram, *Homo caelestis. Das Wort der Kunst im Mittelalter*. 2 vols, Berne–Munich, 1965.

Arthur

Barber, Richard, *King Arthur: Hero and Legend*. Woodbridge: Boydell Press, 1986.

Berthelot, Anne, *Arthur et la Table Ronde. La force d'une légende*. Paris: Gallimard, 1996.

Boutet, Dominique, *Charlemagne et Arthur ou le roi imaginaire*. Paris: Champion, 1992.

Loomis, R. S. (ed.), *Arthurian Literature in the Middle Ages*. Oxford: Clarendon Press, 1959.

The Bible

Dahan, Gilbert, *L'Exégèse chrétienne de la Bible en Occident médiéval, XIIe–XIVe siècle*, Paris: Cerf, 1999.

Lobrichon, Guy, *La Bible au Moyen Age*. Paris: Picard, 2003.

Riché, Pierre and Lobrichon, Guy (eds), *Le Moyen Age et la Bible*. Paris: Beauchesne, 1984.

Smalley, Beryl, *The Study of the Bible in the Middle Ages*, 3rd edn. Oxford: Blackwell, 1983.

Body: medicine, sexuality

Agrimi, Jole and Crisciani, Chiara, *Medicina del corpo e medicina dell'anima*. Milan: Episteme Editrice, 1978.

Agrimi, Jole and Crisciani, Chiara, *Malato, medico e medicina nel Medioevo*. Turin: Loescher, 1980.

Brown, Peter, *Body and Society: Men, Women and Sexual Renunciation in Early Christianity*. London: Faber, 1989.

Brundage, J. A., *Law, Sex and Christian Society in Medieval Europe*. Chicago–London: University of Chicago Press, 1987.

Bullough, Vern L. and Brundage, James (eds), *Handbook of Medieval Sexuality*. New York–London: Garland, 2000.

Bynum, Caroline W., *The Resurrection of the Body in Western Christianity, 200–1336*. New York: Columbia University Press, 1995.

Casagrande, Carla and Vecchio, Silvana, *Anima e corpo nella cultura medievale*. Florence: Sismel, 1999.

I discorsi dei corpi, in *Micrologus I* (1993).

Flandrin, Jean-Louis, *Un temps pour embrasser. Aux origines de la morale sexuelle occidentale. VIe–XIe siècle*. Paris: Seuil, 1983.

Jacquart, Danielle and Thomasset, Claude, *Sexualité et savoir médical au Moyen Age*. Paris: PUF, 1985.

Le Goff, Jacques and Truong, Nicolas, *Une histoire du corps au Moyen Age*. Paris: Liana Levi, 2003.

Poly, Jean-Pierre, *Le Chemin des amours barbares. Genèse médiévale de la sexualité européenne*. Paris: Perrin, 2003.

Rossiaud, Jacques, *La Prostitution médiévale*. Paris: Flammarion, 1988.

Castles

Albrecht, U., *Der Adelstz im Mittelalter*. Munich–Berlin: Deutscher Kunstverlag, 1995.

Brown, A. R., *English Castles*, 3rd edn. London: Batsford, 1976.

Chateaux et peuplements en Europe occidentale du Xe au XVIIIe siècle. Auch: Centre culturel de l'abbaye de Floran, 1980.

Comba, Rinaldo and Settia, Aldo, *Castelli, storia e archeologia*. Turin: Turingraf, 1984.

Debord, André, *Aristocratie et pouvoir. Le rôle du chateau dans la France médiévale*. Paris: Picard, 2000.

Fournier, Gabriel, *Le Château dans la France médiévale*, Paris: Aubier-Montaigne, 1978.

Gardelles, Jacques, *Le Château féodal dans l'histoire médiévale*. Strasbourg: Publitotal, 1988.

Mesqui, Jean, *Châteaux et enceintes de la France médiévale. De la défense à la résidence*. 2 vols, Paris: Picard, 1991–3.

Pesez, Jean-Michel, "Château," in Le Goff-Schmitt, pp. 179–98.

Poisson, Jean-Michel (ed.), *Le Château médiéval, forteresse habitée (XIe–XVIe siècle)*. Paris: Éditions de la Maison des sciences de l'homme, 1992.

Cathedrals

Erlande-Brandenburg, Alain, *La Cathédrale*. Paris: Fayard, 1989.

Vingt siècles en cathédrales (catalogue of the Rheims exhibition). Paris: Monum, 2001.

Children

Alexandre-Bidon, Danièle and Lett, Didier, *Les Enfants au Moyen Age, Ve–XV siècle*. Paris: Hachette, 1997.

Ariès, Philippe, *L'Enfant et la vie familiale sous l'Ancien Régime*. Paris: Seuil, 1960.

Boswell, John, *The Kindness of Strangers: The Abandonment of Chidren in Western Europe from Late Antiquity to the Renaissance*. London: Allen Lane, 1989.

Enfant et société, special issue of *Annales de la démographie historique* (1973).

Lett, Didier, *L'Enfant des miracles. Enfance et société au Moyen Age (XIIe–XIIIe siècle)*. Paris: Aubier, 1997.

Riché, Pierre and Alexandre-Bidon, Danièle, *L'Enfance au Moyen Age*. Paris: Seuil–BNF, 1994.

Shahar, Shulamith, *Childhood in the Middle Ages*. London: Routledge, 1990.

Chivalry, civilization

Bumke, Joachim, *Höfische Kultur, Literatur und Gesellschaft im hohen Mittelalter*. Munich: Deutscher Taschenbuchverlag, 1986.

Elias, Norbert, *The History of Manners*, vol. 1 of *The Civilizing Process*, 2 vols. Oxford: Blackwell, 1978–82.

Paravicini, Werner, *Die ritterlich-höfische Kultur des Mittelalters*. Munich: Oldenbourg, 1994.

Romagnoli, Daniela (ed.), *La Ville et la cour. Des bonnes et des mauvaises manières* (1991). Paris: Fayard, 1995 (translated from Italian).

Schmitt, Jean-Claude, *La Raison des gestes dans l'Occident médiéval*. Paris: Gallimard, 1990.

Church

Arnaldi, Girolamo, "Church, papacy," in Le Goff-Schmitt, p, 322–45.

Congar, Yves, *L'Ecclésiologie du Haut Moyen Age*. Paris, 1968.

Guerreau, Alain, *Le Féodalisme, un horizon théorique*. Paris: Le Sycomore, 1980, pp. 201–10.

Le Bras, Gabriel, *Institutions ecclésiastiques de la chrétienté médiévale* (section 12 of *Histoire générale de l'Eglise*). 2 vols, Paris: Fliche et Martin.

Lubac, Henri de, *Corpus mysticum. L'Eucharistie et l'Église au Moyen Age, étude historique*. Paris, 1944.

Schmidt, Hans-Joachim, *Kirche, Staat, Nation. Raumgliederung der Kirche im mittelalterlichen Europe*. Weimar: H. Böhlaus Nachf, 1999.

Southern, Richard W., *Western Society and the Church in the Middle Ages*. Harmondsworth: Penguin, 1970.

Courtly love

Bezzola, Reto R., *Les Origines et la formation de la littérature courtoise en Occident*. 5 vols, Paris: 1944–63.

Cazenave, Michel, Poirion, Daniel, Strubel, Armand and Zink, Michel, *L'Art d'aimer au Moyen Age*. Paris: Philippe Lebaud, 1997.

Duby, Georges, *Mâle Moyen Age. De l'amour et autres essais*, Paris: Flammarion, 1988.

Huchet, Jean-Charles, *L'amour discourtois. La "fin'amor" chez les premiers troubadours*. Toulouse: Privat, 1987.

Köhler, Erich, *L'Aventure chevaleresque. Idéal et réalité dans le roman courtois* (1956). Paris: Gallimard, 1974 (translated from German).

Régnier-Bohler, Danielle, "Amour courtois," in Le Goff-Schmitt, pp. 32–41.

Rey-Flaud, Henri, *La Névrose courtoise*. Paris: Navarin, 1983.

Rougemont, Denis de, *L'Amour et l'Occident*, new edn. Paris: Plon, 1994.

Crusades

Alphandéry, Pierre and Dupront, Alphonse, *La Chrétienté et l'idée de croisade*. 2 vols, Paris: Albin Michel, 1954; repr. 1995 as 1 vol.

Balard, Michel, *Les Croisades*. Paris, 1968.

Chroniques arabes des Croisades, texts collected and introduced by Francisco Gabrieli (1963). Paris: Sindbad, 1977 (translated from Italian).

Dupront, Alphonse, *Du sacré, croisades et pélérinages, images et langages*. Paris: Gallimard, 1987.

Flori, Jean, *Les Croisades. Origines, réalisation, institutions, déviations*. Paris: Jean-Paul Gisserot, 2001.

Flori, Jean, *Guerre sainte, Jihad, Croisade. Violence et religion dans le christianisme et l'islam*. Paris: Seuil, 2002.

Hillenbrand, Carole, *The Crusades: Islamic Perspectives*, Edinburgh: Edinburgh University Press, 1999.

Kedar, Benjamin Z., *Crusade and Mission: European Approaches toward the Muslims*. Princeton: Princeton University Press, 1984.

Lobrichon, Guy, *1099, Jérusalem conquise*. Paris: Cerf, 1998.

Riley-Smith, Jonathan, *The Crusades*. London: Athlone Press, 2001.

Siberry, Elizabeth, *Criticism of Crusading, 1095–1274*. Oxford: Clarendon Press, 1985.

Sivan, Emmanuel, *L'Islam et la croisade*. Paris, 1968.

Tyerman, Christopher, "What the Crusades Meant to Europe," in Linehan-Nelson, pp. 131–45.

Dance

Horowitz, Jeannine, "Les danses cléricales dans les églises au Moyen Age," *Le Moyen Age* 95 (1989), pp. 279–92.

Sahlin, Margit, *Étude sur la carole médiévale*. Uppsala, 1940.

Death and the beyond

Alexandre-Bidon, Danièle and Treffort, C. (eds), *La Mort au quotidien dans l'Occident médiéval*. Lyon: Presses universitaires de Lyon, 1993.

Ariès, Philippe, *L'Homme devant la mort*. Paris: Seuil, 1977.

Baschet, Jérôme, *Les Justices de l'au-delà. Les représentations de l'enfer en France et en Italie (XIIe–XVe siècle)*. Rome: École française de Rome, 1993.

Bernstein, Alan, *The Formation of Hell*. Ithaca–London: Cornell University Press, 1993.

Borst, Arno (ed.), *Tod im Mittelalter*. Konstanz: Konstanz Universität-Verlag, 1993.

Carozzi, Claude, *Le Voyage de l'âme dans l'au-delà d'après la littérature latine (Ve–XIIIe siècle)*. Rome: École française de Rome, 1994.

Chiffoleau, Jacques, *La Comptabilité de l'au-delà, les hommes, la mort et la religion dans la région d'Avignon à la fin du Moyen Age*. Rome: École française de Rome, 1980.

Death in the Middle Ages. Leuven: Leuven University Press, 1993.

Delumeau, Jean, *Une Histoire du Paradis*. 2 vols, Paris: Fayard, 1992.

Dies illa. Death in the Middle Ages (Manchester colloquium, 1983). Liverpool: Cairns, 1984.

Erlande-Brandenburg, Alain, *Le roi est mort. Étude sur les funerailles, les sépultures et les tombaux des rois de France jusqu'à la fin du XIIIe siècle*. Geneva: Droz, 1975.

Goody, Jack, *Death, Property and the Ancestors*. Stanford: Stanford University Press, 1962.

Lauwers, Michel, *La Mémoire, les ancêtres, le souci des morts. Morts, rites et société au Moyen Age (diocèse de Liège, XIe–XIIIe siècle)*. Paris: Beauchesne, 1997.

Lauwers, Michel, "Mort," in Le Goff-Schmitt, pp. 771–89.

Le Goff, Jacques, *La Naissance du Purgatoire*. Paris: Gallimard, 1981.

Le Goff, Jacques, "Au-delà," in Le Goff-Schmitt, pp. 89–102.

Mitre Fernández, Emilio, *La Muerte vencida. Imagines y historia en el Occidente medieval (1200–1348)*. Madrid: Encuentro, 1988.

Morgan, Alison, *Dante and the Medieval Other World*. Cambridge: Cambridge University Press, 1990.

Ohler, Norbert, *Sterben und Tod im Mittelalter*. Munich: Artemis Verlag, 1990.

Schmitt, Jean-Claude, *Les Revenants, les vivants et les morts dans la société médiévale*. Paris: Gallimard, 1994.

Treffort, Cécile, *L'Église carolingienne et la mort. Christianisme, rites funéraires et pratiques commémoratives*. Lyon: Presses universitaires de Lyon, 1996.

The devil

Le Diable au Moyen Age. Sénéfiance (Aix-en-Provence), no. 6 (1979).

Graf, Arturo, *Il diavolo*, new edn. Rome: Salerno, 1980.

Muchembled, Robert, *Une histoire du diable, XIIe–XXe siècle*. Paris: Seuil, 2000 (1st edn), 2002 (2nd edn).

Muchembled, Robert, *Diable!* Paris: Seuil–Arte, 2002.

Discovery of the world

Chaunu, Pierre, *L'Expansion européenne du XIIIe au XVe siècle*. Paris: PUF, 1969.

Duteil, Jean-Pierre, *L'Europe à la découverte du monde du XIIIe au XVIIe siècle*. Paris: Armand Colin, 2003.

Heers, Jacques, *Marco Polo*. Paris: Fayard, 1983.

Magalhaes-Godihno, Vitórino, *Les Découvertes: XVe–XVIe siècle. Une révolution des mentalités*. Paris: Autrement, 1990.

Mollat du Jourdain, Michel, *Les Explorateurs du XIIIe au XVIe siècle. Premiers regards sur des mondes nouveaux*. Paris: J.-C. Lattès, 1984.

Philips, J. R. S., *The Medieval Expansion of Europe*. Oxford: Oxford University Press, 1988.

Roux, Jean-Paul, *Les Explorateurs au Moyen Age*. Paris: Seuil, 1961.

Dreams

Dinzelbacher, Peter, *Mittelalteriche Visionsliteratur*. Darmstadt: Wiss, 1985.
Gregory, Tullio (ed.), *I sogni nel Medioevo*. Rome: dell'Ateneo, 1985.
Le Goff, Jacques, "Rêves," in Le Goff-Schmitt, pp. 950–8.
Paravicini Bagliani, Agostino and Stabile, Giorgio, *Träume im Mittelalter. Chronologische Studien*. Stuttgart–Zurich: Belser Verlag, 1989.

The economy

Abel, Wilhelm, *Crises agraires en Europe (XIIIe–XXe)* (1966). Paris: Flammarion, 1973 (translated from German).
Bloch, Marc, *Esquisse d'une histoire monétaire de l'Europe*. Paris, 1954.
The Cambridge Economic History of Europe, vol. 1: *The Agrarian Life of the Middle Ages*, 2nd edn (1966); vol. 2: *Trade and Industry in the Middle Ages* (1952); vol. 3: *Economic Organization and Policies in the Middle Ages* (1963). Cambridge: Cambridge University Press.
Cipolla, Carlo M. *Storia economica dell'Europa pre-industriale*. Bologna: Il Mulino, 1974.
Cipolla, Carlo M., *Before the Industrial Revolution: European Society and Economy, 1000–1700*. New York: W. W. Norton, 1976.
Contamine, Philippe et al., *L'Economie médiévale*. Paris: Armand Colin, 1993.
Day, John, *The Medieval Market Economy*. Oxford: Blackwell, 1987.
Duby Georges, *L'Économie rurale et la vie des campagnes dans l'Occident médiéval (France, Angleterre, Empire, IXe–XVe siècle)*. 2 vols, Paris, 1962.
Fournial, Étienne, *Histoire monétaire de l'Occident médiéval*. Paris: Nathan, 1970.
Latouche, Robert, *Les Origines de l'économie occidentale*. Paris: Albin Michel, 1970.
Lopez, Roberto S., *La Révolution commerciale dans L'Europe Médiévale*. Paris: Aubier-Montaigne, 1974.
Pounds, N. J. G., *An Economic History of Medieval Europe*. New York: Longman, 1974.

The economy and religion

Ibanès, Jean, *La Doctrine de l'Eglise et les réalités économiques au XIIIe siècle*. Paris, 1967.
Langholm, Odd, *Economics in the Medieval Schools: Wealth, Exchange, Money and Usury according to the Paris Theological Tradition, 1200–1350*. Leiden: Brill, 1992.

Le Goff, Jacques, *La Bourse et la vie. Economie et religion au Moyen Age.* Paris: Hachette, 1986 (1st edn), "Pluriel," 1997.

Little, Lester K., *Religious Poverty and the Profit Economy in Medieval Europe.* London: Cornell University Press, 1978.

Todeschini, Giacomo, *Il prezzo della savezza. Lessici medievali del pensiero economico,* Rome: La Nuova Italia Scientifica, 1994.

Todeschini, Giacomo, *I mercanti e il Tempio. La società cristiana e il circolo virtuoso della richezza fra Medioevo,* ed. *Età moderna.* Bologna: Il Mulino, 2002.

Empire

Ehlers, Joachim, *Die Entstehung des deutschen Reiches.* Munich: Oldenbourg, 1994.

Folz, Robert, *L'Idée d'Empire en Occident du Ve au XIVe siècle.* Paris: Aubier, 1972.

Parisse, Michel, *Allemagne et Empire au Moyen Age.* Paris: Hachette, 2002.

Rapp, Francis, *Le Saint Empire romain germanique, d'Otton le Grand à Charles Quint.* Paris: Tallendier, 2000.

Encyclopedism

Bartholomew the Englishman, *On the Properties of Things* (19 vols, translated into English ca. 1495); in French as Barthélemy l'Anglais, *Le Livre des propriétés des choses, une encyclopédie du XIVe siècle,* translated into modern French and annotated by Bernard Ribémont. Paris: Stock, 1999.

Beonio-Brocchieri Fumagalli, Maria Teresa, *Le Enciclopedie dell'Occidente medioevale.* Turin: Loescher, 1981.

Boüard, Michel de, "Encyclopédies médiévales," *Revue des questions historiques,* 3rd s., no. 16 (1930), pp. 258–304.

Boüard, Michel de, "Réflexions sur l'enciclopédisme médiéval," in Annie Becq (ed.), *L'Encyclopédisme* (Proceedings of the Caen colloquium, 1987). Paris: Klincksiek, 1991.

Meier, Christel, "Grundzüge der mittelalterlichen Enzyklopädie. Zu Inhalten, Formen und Funktionen einer problematischen Gattung," in *Literatur und Laienbildung im Spätmittelalter* (Wolfenbüttel Symposium, 1981), Stuttgart: Metzler, 1984, pp. 467–500.

Picone, Michelangelo (ed.), *L'Enciclopedismo medievale* (Proceedings of the San Gimigniano Colloquium, 1992). Ravenna: Longo, 1994.

Ribémont, Bernard, "L'Encyclopédisme médiéval et la question de l'organisation du savoir," in *L'Écriture du savoir* (Proceedings of the Bagnoles-de-l'Orme Colloquium, 1990), Le Menil-Brout: Association Diderot, 1991, pp. 95–107.

Family, kinship, marriage

Aurell, Martin, *Les Noces du comte. Mariage et pouvoir en Catalogne (785–1213)*. Paris: Publications de la Sorbonne, 1995.

Burguière, André (ed.), *Histoire de la famille*. Paris: Armand Colin, 1986.

Duby, Georges, *Le Chevalier, la femme et le prêtre. Le mariage dans la France féodale*. Paris: Hachette, 1961.

Duby, Georges and Le Goff, Jacques (eds), *Famille et parenté dans l'Occident médiéval*. Paris: Hachette, 1961.

Flandrin, Jean-Louis, *Familles. Parenté, maison et sexualité dans l'ancienne société*. Paris: Hachette, 1976; Seuil, 1984.

Gaudemet, Jean, *Le Mariage en occident*. Paris: Cerf, 1987.

Goody, Jack, *The European Family: An Historico-Anthropological Essay*. Oxford: Blackwell, 2001.

Guerreau-Jalabert, Anita, "Sur les structures de parenté dans l'Europe médiévale," in *Annales ESC*, 1981, pp. 1028–49.

Guerreau-Jalabert, Anita, "Parenté," in Le Goff-Schmitt, pp. 861–76.

Herlihy, David, *Medieval Households*. Cambridge: Harvard University Press, 1985.

Il matrimonio nella società altomediovale, Settimane di studi sull'alto medioevo, Spoleto, XXIV, 1977.

Le Jan, Régine, *Famille et pouvoir dans le mode franc (VIIe–Xe siècle)*. Paris: Publications de la Sorbonne, 1995.

Lett, Didier, *Famille et parenté dans l'Occident médiéval, Ve–XVe siècle*. Paris: Hachette, 2000.

Feudalism

Barthélémy, Dominique, *L'Ordre seigneurial, XI–XIIe siècle*. Paris: Seuil, 1990.

Barthélémy, Dominique, "Seigneurie," in Le Goff-Schmitt, pp. 1056–66.

Bloch, Marc, *La Société féodale*. Paris: Albin Michel, 1939–40 (1st edn), 1968 (2nd edn).

Duby, Georges, *Les Trois ordres ou l'imaginaire du féodalisme*. Paris: Gallimard, 1978.

Guerreau, Alain, *Le Féodalisme, un horizon théorique*. Paris: Le Sycomore, 1980.

Guerreau, Alain, "Féodalité," in Le Goff-Schmitt, pp. 387–406.

Le Goff, Jacques, "Les trois fonctions indo-européennes, l'historien et l'Europe féodale," *Annales ESC* (Nov.–Dec.1979), pp. 1187–215.

Poly, Jean-Pierre and Bournazel, Eric, *La Mutation féodale, Xe–XII siècle*. Paris: PUF, 1980.

Reynolds, Susan, *Fiefs and Vassals*. New York–Oxford: Oxford University Press, 1994.

Toubert, Pierre, *Les Structures du Latium médiéval. Le Latium méridonial et la Sabine du IXe à la fin du XIIIe siècle*. Rome: École française de Rome, 1973.
Toubert, Pierre (ed.), *Structures féodales et féodalisme dans l'Occident méditerranéaen (Xe–XIIIe)* (1978 colloquium). Rome: École française de Rome, 1980.

Frontiers

Abulafia, David and Berend, Nora (eds), *Medieval Frontiers: Concepts and Practices*. Aldershot: Ashgate, 2002.
Barnavi, Elie and Goosens, Paul (eds), *Les Frontières de l'Europe*. Brussels: De Noeck, 2001.
Berend, Nora, *At the Gate of Christendom: Jews, Muslims, and "Pagans" in Medieval Hungary, c.1000–c.1300*. Cambridge: Cambridge University Press, 2001.
Buresi, Pascal, "Nommer, penser les frontières en Espagne aux XIe–XIII siècles," in Carlos de Ayala Martinez, Pascal Buresi and Philippe Josserand (eds), *Identidad y presentación de la frontera en la España medieval (siglos XI–XIV)*, Madrid: Casa de Velázquez, 2001.
Les Frontières et l'espace national en Europe du Centre-Est. Lublin: Institut de l'Europe du Centre-Est, 2000.
Guénée, Bernard, "Des limites féodales aux frontières politiques," in Pierre Nora (ed.), *Les Lieux de mémoire*, vol 2: *La Nation*. Paris: Gallimard, 1986, pp. 10–33.
Linehan, Peter, "At the Spanish Frontier," in Linehan-Nelson, pp. 37–59.
Marchal, Guy P. (ed.), *Grenzen und Raumvorstellungen / Frontières et conceptions de l'espace (XIe–XXe siècle)*. Lucerne: Chronos, Historisches Seminar, Hochschule, n.d.
Mitre Fernandez, Emilio, "La cristianidad medieval y las formulaciones fronterizas," in E. Mitre Fernandez et al., *Fronteras y Fronterizos en la Historia*, Valladolid: Universidad de Valladolid, 1997.
Power, Daniel and Standon, Naomi, *Frontiers in Question: Eurasian Borderlands, 700–1700*. London: Macmillan, 1999.
Ruiz, Teófilo F. "Fronteras de la comunidad a la nación en la Castilla bajomedieval," *Annuario de estudios medievales*, 27, no. 1 (1997), pp. 23–41.
Sénac, Philippe, *La Frontière et les hommes (VIIIe–XIIe siècle). Le peuplement musulman au nord de l'Èbre et les débuts de la reconquête aragonaise*. Paris: Maisonneuve et Larose, 2000.
Las Sociedades de frontera en la España medieval. Zaragoza: Universidad de Zaragoza, 1993.
Sullivan, R. E., "The Medieval Monk as Frontiersman," in R. E. Sullivan (ed.), *Christians' Missionary Activity in the Early Middle Ages*. London: Variorum, 1994.
Tazbir, Janusz, *Poland as the Rampart of Christian Europe: Myths and Historical Reality*. Warsaw: Interpress, 1983.

Toubert, Pierre, "Frontière et frontières. Un objet historique," in *Castrum*, 4, *Frontière et peuplement dans le monde méditerranéen au Moyen Age* (Evian colloquium, Sept. 1988), Rome–Madrid: École française de Rome–Casa Velásquez, 1992, pp. 7–9.

God

Boespflug, François, *Dieu dans l'art*. Paris: Cerf, 1984.
Boyer, Régis, *Le Christ des barbares. Le monde nordique (IXe–XIIIe siècle)*. Paris: Cerf, 1987.
Le Goff, Jacques and Pouthier, Jean-Luc, *Dieu au Moyen Age*. Paris: Fayard, 2003.
Pellegrin, Marie-Frédérique, *Dieu* (selected texts). Paris: Flammarion, 2003.
Rubin, Miri, *Corpus Christi: The Eucharist in Late Medieval Culture*. Cambridge: Cambridge University Press, 1991.
Schmitt, Jean-Claude, "Dieu," in Le Goff-Schmitt, pp. 273–89.

Heraldry

Pastoureau, Michel, *Traité d'héraldique*. Paris: Picard, 1993.

Heretics

Biget, Jean-Louis, "Réflexions sur 'l'hérésie' dans le Midi de la France au Moyen Age," *Hérésies*, nos 36–7 (2002), pp. 29–74.
Borst, Arno, *Les Cathares* (1953). Paris: Payot, 1974 (translation from German).
Borst, Arno, *Effacement du catharisme*. Cahiers de Fanjeaux, 20 (1985).
Le Goff, Jacques (ed.), *Hérésies et Sociétés dans L'Europe pré-industrielle, XIe–XVIIIe siècle*. Paris–The Hague: Mouton, 1968.
Moore, Robert, *The Origins of European Dissent*. London: Allen Lane, 1977 (1st edn); Oxford: Blackwell, 1985 (2nd edn).
Moore, Robert I., "A la naissance de la société persécutrice: les clercs, les cathares et la formation de l'Europe," in *La Persécution du catharisme* (Proceedings of the 6th session of medieval history organized by the Centre d'études cathares). Carcassonne: Centre d'études cathares, 1996, pp. 11–37.
Oberste, Jörg, *Der Kreuzzug gegen die Albigenser. Ketzerei und Machtpolitik im Mittelalter*. Darmstadt: Primus Verlag, 2003.
Schmitt, Jean-Claude, *Mort d'une hérésie. L'Église et les clercs face aux Béguines et aux Beghards du Rhin supérieure du XIVe au XVe siècle*. Paris–The Hague: Mouton, 1978.

Vauchez, André, "Orthodoxie et hérésie dans l'Occident médiéval (Xe–XIIIe siècle)," in Susanna Elm, Eric Rebillard and Antonella Romano (eds), *Orthodoxie, Christianisme, Histoire*, Rome: École française de Rome, 2000, pp. 321–32.

Zerner, Monique (ed.), *Inventer l'hérésie?* (Nice, CEM colloquium, vol. 2). Centre d'études médiévales, 1998.

Zerner, Monique, "Hérésie," in Le Goff-Schmitt, pp. 464–82.

History

Borst, Arno, *Geschicte in mittelalterlichen Universitäten*. Konstanz, 1969.

Guenée, Bernard, *Le Métier d'historien au Moyen Age*. Paris: Publication de la Sorbonne, 1977.

Guenée, Bernard, *Histoire et culture historique dans l'Occident médiéval*. Paris: Aubier, 1991.

Guenée, Bernard, "Histoire," in Le Goff-Schmitt, pp. 483–96.

Images

Bascher, Jérôme and Schmitt, Jean-Claude (eds), "L'Image. Fonctions et usages des images dans l'Occident médiéval," *Cahiers du Léopard d'Or* (Paris), no. 5 (1996).

Belting, Hans, *Image et culte. Une histoire de l'image avant l'époque de l'art* (1990). Paris: Cerf, 1998 (translated from German).

Belting, Hans, *L'Image et son public au Moyen Age*. Paris: G. Montfort, 1998 (translated from German).

Boespflug, François (ed.), *Nicée II, 787–1987. Douze siècles d'images religieuses*. Paris: Cerf, 1987.

Camille, Michael, *Image on the Edge: The Margins of Medieval Art*. London: Reaktion Books, 1992.

Garnier, François, *Le Langage de l'image au Moyen Age*. Vol. 1: *Signification et symbolique* (1982); vol. 2: *Grammaire du geste*, Paris: Le Léopard d'Or, 1989.

Ladner, Gerhart B., *Images and Ideas in the Middle Ages*. Rome: Edizioni di storia e letteratura, 1983.

Le Goff, Jacques, *Pour l'image*, special issue of *Médiévales*, nos 22–3 (1992).

Le Goff, Jacques, *Un Moyen Age en images*. Paris: Hazan, 2000.

Schmitt, Jean-Claude, "Image," in Le Goff-Schmitt, pp. 497–511.

Schmitt, Jean-Claude, Bonne, Jean-Claude, Barbu, Daniel and Baschet, Jérôme, "Images médiévales," *Annales HSS* (1996).

Wirth, Jean, *L'Image médiévale. Naissance et développement (VIe–XVe siècle)*. Paris: Klincksieck, 1989.

Wirth, Jean, *L'Image à l'époque romane*. Paris: Cerf, 1999.

Immobilism (Progress, see Techniques and innovation)

Baumgartner, Emmanuelle and Harf-Lancner, Laurence (eds), *Progrès, réaction, décadence dans l'Occident médiéval*. Paris–Geneva: Droz–Champion, 2003.

Bultot, Robert, *Christianisme et valeurs humaines. La doctrine du mépris du monde.* 4 vols, Leuven–Paris, 1964.

Le Goff, Jacques, "Antico-Moderno," in *Enciclopedia*, vol. 1, Turin: Einaudi, 1977, reprinted in French in *Histoire et Mémoire*, Paris: Gallimard, 1988.

Le Goff, Jacques,"Progresso-Reazione," in *Enciclopedia*, vol. 11, Turin: Einaudi, 1980.

Smalley, Beryl, "Ecclesiastical Attitudes to Novelty, c.1100–c.1150," in Derek Baker (ed.), *Church, Society and Politics*, Studies in Church History 12, Oxford: Blackwell for the Ecclesiastical History Society, 1975, pp. 113–31.

The individual

Benton, J. E., *Self and Society in Medieval France: The Memoir of Abbot Guibert de Nogent*. New York: Harper & Row, 1970.

Boureau, Alain, "Un royal individu," *Critique*, 52 (1996), pp. 845–57.

Bynum, Caroline W., "Did the Twelfth Century Discover the Individual?" in *Jesus as Mother: Studies in the Spirituality of the High Middle Ages*. Berkeley: University of California Press, 1982, pp. 82–109.

Coleman, Janet (ed.), *L'Individu dans la théorie politique et dans la pratique*. Paris: PUF, 1996, pp. 1–90.

Duby, Georges and Ariès, Philippe (eds), *Histoire de la vie privée*, vol. 2, Paris: Seuil, 1985: "L'émergence de l'individu," pp. 503–619. See in English *A History of Private Life*, vol. 2, Cambridge: Belknap, 1988.

Gourevitch, Aron J., *La Naissance de l'individu dans l'Europe médiévale*. Paris: Seuil, 1997 (translated from Russian).

Le Goff, Jacques, *Saint Louis*. Paris: Gallimard, 1996.

Melville, Gert and Schürer, Markus (eds), *Das Eigene und das Ganze. Zum Individuellen im mittelalterlichen Religiösentum*. Münster: LIT, 2002.

Morris, Colin, *The Discovery of the Individual, 1050–1200*. London: SPCK for the Church Historical Society, 1972.

Schmitt, Jean-Claude, "La découverte de l'individu, une fiction historiographique?" in Pierre Mengal and Françoise Parot (eds), *La Fabrique, la figure et la feinte. Fictions et statut de la fiction en psychologie*, Paris: Vrin, 1989, pp. 213–36.

Ullmann, Walter, *The Individual and Society in the Middle Ages*. Baltimore: Johns Hopkins University Press, 1966.

Zink, Michel, *La Subjectivité littéraire. Autour du siècle de Saint Louis*. Paris: PUF, 1985.

Islam, Arabs and medieval Christianity

Agius, D. A. and Hitchcock, Richard (eds), *The Arab Influence in Medieval Europe*. Reading: Ithaca Press, 1994.

Bresc, Henri and Bresc-Bautier, Geneviève (eds), *Palerme, 1070–1492*. Paris: Autrement, 1993.

Cardini, Franco, *Europe et Islam* (French version). Paris: Seuil, 1994.

Clément, François and Tolan, John (eds), *Réflexions sur l'apport de la culture arabe à la construction de la culture européenne*. Paris, 2003.

Sénac, Philippe, *L'Occident médiéval face à l'Islam. L'Image de l'Autre*, 2nd edn. Paris: Flammarin, 2000.

Southern, Richard, *Western Views of Islam in the Middle Ages*. Cambridge: Harvard University Press, 1962.

Tolan, John, *Saracens: Islam in the Medieval European Imagination*. New York: Columbia University Press, 2002.

Tolan, John and Josserand, Philippe, *Les relations entre le monde arabo-musulman et le monde latin (milieu du Xe–milieu du XIIe siècle)*. Paris: Bréal, 2000.

Jews

Barros, Carlos (ed.), *Xudeus y conversos na historia* (Ribadavia congress, 1991). 2 vols, Santiago de Compostela: Editorial de la Historia, 1994.

Blumenkranz, Bernhard, *Juifs et chrétiens dans le monde occidental, 430–1096*. Paris–The Hague: Mouton, 1960.

Blumenkranz, Bernhard, *Juden und Judentum in der mittelalterlichen Kunst*. Stuttgart: Kohlhammer, 1965.

Dahan, Gilbert, *Les Intellectuels chrétiens et les Juifs au Moyen Age*. Paris: Cerf, 1990.

La Famille juive au Moyen Age, Provence-Languedoc, special issue of *Provence historique*, 37, 150 (1987).

Gli Ebrei e le scienze, special issue of *Micrologus*, 9 (2001).

Grayzel, Solomon, *The Church and the Jews in the XIIIth Century*. 2 vols, New York–Detroit: Hermon Press, 1989.

Jordan, William Chester, *The French Monarchy and the Jews from Philip Augustus to the Last Capetian*. Philadelphia: University of Pennsylvania Press, 1989.

Katz, Jacob, *Exclusiveness and Tolerance: Studies in Jewish–Gentile Relations in Medieval and Modern Times*. Oxford: Oxford University Press, 1961.

Kriegel, Maurice, *Les Juifs à la fin du Moyen Age dans l'Europe méditerranéenne*. Paris: Hachette, 1979.

Schmitt, Jean-Claude, *La Conversion d'Hermann le Juif. Autobiographie, Histoire et Fiction*. Paris: Seuil, 2003.

Toaff, Ariel, *Le Marchand de Pérouse. Une communauté juive du Moyen Age* (1988). Paris: Balland, 1993 (translated from Italian).

Todeschini, Giacomo, *La richezza degli Ebrei. Merci e denaro nella riflessione ebraica e nella definizione cristiana dell'usura alla fine del Medioevo.* Spoleto: Centro italiano di studi sull'alto medioevo, 1989.

Trachtenberg, Joshua, *The Devil and the Jews: The Medieval Conception of the Jew and its Relations to Modern Antisemitism.* New Haven: Yale University Press, 1943.

Justice

Bartlett, Robert, *Trial by Fire and Water: The Medieval Judicial Ordeal.* Oxford: Oxford University Press, 1986.

Chiffoleau, Jacques, *Les Justices du pape. Délinquence et criminalité dans la région d'Avignon aux XIVe et XVe siècles.* Paris: Publications de la Sorbonne, 1984.

Gauvard, Claude, *"De grace especial." Crime, État et société en France à la fin du Moyen Age.* 2 vols, Paris: Publications de la Sorbonne, 1991.

Gauvard, Claude, "Justice et paix," in Le Goff-Schmitt, pp. 587–94.

Gauvard, Claude and Jacob, Robert (eds), *Les Rites de la justice. Gestes et rituels judiciaires au Moyen Age.* Paris: *Cahiers du Léopard d'Or,* 2000.

Gonthier, Nicole, *Le Châtiment du crime au Moyen Age, XIIe–XVI siècle.* Rennes: Presses universitaires de Rennes, 1998.

Guenée, Bernard, *Tribuneaux et gens de justice dans le bailliage de Senlis à la fin du Moyen Age (vers 1380–vers 1550).* Paris, 1963.

Jacob, Robert, *Images de la justice. Essai sur l'iconographie judiciaire du Moyen Age à l'âge classique.* Paris: Le Léopard d'Or, 1994.

Jacob, Robert, "Le jugement de Dieu et la formation de la fonction de juger dans l'histoire européenne," *Archives de philosophie et de droit* (1994).

La Justice au Moyen Age (sanction ou impunité?). Sénéfiance, no. 16 (1986).

La Preuve. Recueils de la Société Jean-Bodin, vol. 17. Brussels, 1965.

Knights

Bumke, Joachim, *Studien zum Ritterbegriff im 12. und 13. Jahrhundert.* Heidelberg, 1964.

Cardini, Franco, "Le guerrier et le chevalier," in Jacques Le Goff (ed.), *L'Homme médiéval,* Paris: Seuil, 1989, pp. 87–128.

Duby, Georges, *Guillaume le Maréchal ou le meilleur chevalier du monde.* Paris: Fayard, 1984.

Fleckenstein, Joseph, *Das ritterliche Turnier im Mittelalter.* Göttingen: Vandenhoeck & Ruprecht, 1985.

Flori, Jean, *Chevalier et chevalerie au Moyen Age.* Paris: Hachette, 1998.

Flori, Jean, *L'Idéologie du glaive. Préhistoire de la chevalerie.* Geneva: Droz, 1981.
Gies, Frances, *The Knight in History.* New York: Harper & Row, 1984.
Keen, Maurice, *Chivalry.* New Haven: Yale University Press, 1984.
Köhler, Eric, *L'Aventure chevaleresque. Idéal et réalité dans le roman courtois.* Paris: Gallimard, 1974 (translated from German).
Reuter, Hans Georg, *Die Lehre vom Ritterstandzum Ritterbegriff in Historiographie und Dichtung vom 11. bis zum 13. Jahrhundert.* Cologne–Vienna: Böhlau, 1971.

Laity

Lobrichon, Guy, *La Religion des laïcs en Occident, XIe–XIVe siècle.* Paris: Hachette, 1994.
Meersseman, G. G., *Ordo fraternitatis. Comfraternite e pietà dei laici nel Medioevo.* Rome: Herder, 1977.
Vauchez, André, *Les Laïcs au Moyen Age. Pratiques et expériences religieuses.* Paris: Cerf, 1987.

Language(s), literature

Banniard, Michel, *Viva voce.* Paris: Institut des études augustiniennes, 1992.
Banniard, Michel, *Du Latin aux langues romanes.* Paris: Nathan, 1997.
Borst, Arno, *Der Turmbau von Babel. Geschicte der Meinungen über Ursprung und Vielfalt der Sprachen und Völker.* 2 vols, Stuttgart, 1957–63.
Cavallo, Guglielmo, Leonardo, Claudio and Menestò, Enrico, *Lo Spazio letterario del Medioevo. I. Il Medioevo latino.* 5 vols, Rome: Salerno, 1992–8.
Chaurand, Jacques (and, for the thirteenth to fifteenth centuries, Serge Lusignan), *Nouvelle Histoire de la langue française.* Paris: Seuil, 1999.
Curtius, E. R., *La Littérature européenne et le Moyen Age latin.* Paris, 1956 (translated from German).
Gally, Michèle and Marchello-Nizia, Christiane, *Littératures de l'Europe médiévale.* Paris: Magnard, 1985.
Jonin, Pierre, *L'Europe en vers au Moyen Age.* Paris: Honoré Champion, 1996.
Redon, Odile et al., *Les langues de l'Italie médiévale,* L'Atelier du médiéviste 8. Turnhout: Brepols, 2002.
Walter, Henriette, *L'Aventure des langues en Occident. Leur origine, leur histoire, leur géographie.* Paris: Laffont, 1994 (1st edn), 1996 (2nd edn).
Wolff, Philippe, *Les Origines linguistiques de l'Europe occidentale,* 2nd edn. Toulouse: Publications de l'université de Toulouse-Le Mirail, 1982.
Zumthor, Paul, *La Lettre et la voix. De la "littérature" médiévale.* Paris: Seuil, 1987.

Law

Bellomo, Manlio, *L'Europea del diritta commune*. Rome: Il Cigno Galileo Galilei, 1988 (1st edn), 1996 (7th edn).

Calasso, Francesco, *Medioevo del diritto*. I. *Le Fonti*. Milan, 1954.

Chiffoleau, Jacques, "Droit," in Le Goff-Schmitt,, pp. 290–308.

Gaudemet, Jean, *La Formation du droit canonique médiéval*. London: Variorum Reprints, 1980.

Grossi, Paolo, *L'Ordine giuridico medievale*. Rome–Bari: Laterza, 1995.

Legendre, Pierre, *La Pénétration du droit romain dans le droit canonique classique de Gratien à Innocent IV (1140–1254)*. Paris, 1964.

Legendre, Pierre, *Écrits juridiques du Moyen Age occidental*. London: Variorum Reprints, 1988.

Post, Gaines, *Studies in Medieval Legal Thought: Public Law and the State, 1100–1322*. Princeton: Princeton University Press, 1964.

Radding, Charles M., *The Origin of Medieval Jurisprudence. Pavia and Bologna: 850–1150*. New Haven, Yale University Press, 1988.

Reynold, Susan, "Medieval Law," in Linehan-Nelson, pp.485–502.

Memory

Carozzi, Claude and Taviani-Carozzi, Huguette (eds), *Faire mémoire. Souvenir et commémoration au Moyen Age*. Aix-en-Provence: Publications de l'université de Provence, 1994.

Carruthers, Mary, *The Book of Memory*. Cambridge: Cambridge University Press, 1940.

Carruthers, Mary, *The Craft of Thought: Meditatio: Thinking and the Making of Images, 400–1200*. Cambridge: Cambridge University Press, 1998.

Clanchy, Michel, *From Memory to Written Record: England, 1066–1907*, 2nd edn. London: Edward Arnold, 1996.

Geary, Patrick J., *Phantoms of Rememberance: Memory and Oblivion at the End of the First Millenium*. Princeton: Princeton University Press, 1994.

Lauwers, Michel, *La Mémoire des ancêtres, le souci des morts. Morts, rites et société au Moyen Age*. Paris: Beauchesne, 1997.

Le Goff, Jacques, *Histoire et Mémoire*. Italian version 1981; French version, Paris: Gallimard, 1988.

Oexle, Otto Gerhard (ed.), *Memoria als Kultur*. Göttingen: Vandenhoeck & Ruprecht, 1995.

Restaino, Rosangela, "Ricordare e dimenticare nella cultura del Medioevo" (a record of the Trent colloquium of April 4–6, 2002: Memoria. Ricordare e dimenticare nella cultura del Medioevo), *Quaderni medioevali*, 54 (Dec. 2002), pp. 221–38.

Yates, Frances A., *The Art of Memory*. Harmonsworth: Penguin, 1978.
Zinn Jr, Grover A., "Hugh of Saint-Victor and the Art of Memory," *Viator*, 5 (1974), pp. 211–34.

Merchants

L'Argent au Moyen Age (SHMES congress, Clermont-Ferrand, 1997). Paris: Publications de la Sorbonne, 1998.
Dollinger, Philippe, *La Hanse, XIIe–XVIIe siècle*. Paris, 1964.
Jorda, Henri, *Le Moyen Age des marchands. L'utile et le nécessaire*. Paris: L'Harmattan, 2002.
Lebecq, Stéphane, *Marchands et Navigateurs frisons du haut Moyen Age*. 2 vols, Lille: Presses universitaires de Lille, 1983.
Le Goff, Jacques, *Marchands et banquiers du Moyen Age*, new edn. Paris: PUF, 2000.
Le Marchand du Moyen Age (SHMES congress, Rheims, 1988). Paris: SHMES, 1992.
Monnet, Pierre, "Marchands," in Le Goff-Schmitt, pp. 624–38.
Renouard, Yves, *Les Hommes d'affaires italiens au Moyen Age*. Paris, 1968.
Sapori, Armando, *Le Marchand italien au Moyen Age*. Paris, 1952.
Tangheroni, Marco, *Commercio e navigazione nel Medioevo*. Rome–Bari: Laterza, 1996.

Millenarianism, apocalypse

Boureau, Alain and Piron, Sylvain (eds), *Pierre de Jean Olivi (1248–1298). Pensée scolastique, dissidence spirituelle et société*. Paris: Vrin, 1999.
Bynum, Caroline W. and Freedman, Paul, *Last Things: Death and the Apocalypse in the Middle Ages*. Philadelphia: University of Pennsylvania Press, 2000.
Capitani, Ovicio and Miethke, Jürgen (eds), *L'Attesa della fine dei tempi nel Medioevo*. Bologna: Il Mulino, 1990.
Carozzi, Claude, *Apocalypse et salut dans le christianisme ancien et médiéval*. Paris: Aubier, 1996.
Cohn, Norman, *Cosmos, Chaos and the World to Come: The Ancient Roots of Apocalyptic Faith*. New Haven–London: Yale University Press, 2001.
Head, Thomas and Landes, Richard, *The Peace of God: Social Violence and Religious Response in France around the Year 1000*. London: Cornell University Press, 1992.
Manselli, Raoul, *La "Lectura super Apocalipsim" di Pietro di Giovanni Olivi*. Rome, 1955.
Mendel, Arthur P., *Vision and Violence (on the Millennium)*. Ann Arbor: University of Michigan Press, 1992 (1st edn), 1999 (2nd edn).

Reeves, Marjorie, *Joachim of Fiore and the Prophetic Future*. London: Sutton, 1976.

Les Textes prophétiques et la prophécie en Occident, XIIe–XVIe siècle (Chantilly Round Table, 1988). Rome: École française de Rome, 1990.

Töpfer, Bernhard, *Das kommende Reich des Friedens*. Berlin, 1964.

Verbeke, Werner, Verhelst, Daniel and Welkenhuysen, Andries, *The Use and Abuse of Eschatology in the Middle Ages*. Leuven: Leuven University Press, 1988.

Miracles, monsters and marvels

Démons et Merveilles au Moyen Age (Nice colloquium, 1987). Nice: Faculté des lettres et sciences humaines, 1990.

Dubost, Francis, "Merveilleux," in Gauvard-de Libera-Zink, pp. 905–10.

Friedman, J. B., *The Monstrous Races in Medieval Art and Thought*. Cambridge: Harvard University Press, 1981.

Kappler, Claude, *Monstres, démons et merveilles à la fin du Moyen Age*. Paris: Payot, 1980.

Lecouteux, Claude, *Les Monstres dans la pensée médiévale européenne*. Paris: Presses de l'université Paris-Sorbonne, 1993.

Miracles, prodiges et merveilles au Moyen Age (25th congress of the SHMESP, Orleans, 1994). Paris: Publications de la Sorbonne, 1995.

Poirion, Daniel, *Le Merveilleux dans la littérature française de Moyen Age*. Paris: PUF, 1982.

Sigal, Pierre-André, *L'Homme et le miracle dans la France médiévale (XIe–XIIe siècle)*. Paris: Cerf, 1985.

Vauchez, André, "Miracle," in Le Goff-Schmitt, pp. 725–40.

Music

Cullin, Olivier, *Brève Histoire de la musique au Moyen Age*. Paris: Fayard, 2002.

Gagnepain, Bernard, *Histoire de la musique au Moyen Age. II. XIIIe–XIVe siècle*. Paris: Seuil, 1996.

Hoppin, Richard, *Medieval Music in the Middle Ages*. New York: Norton, 1978.

Nations

Beaune, Colette, *La Naissance de la nation France*. Paris: Gallimard, 1985.

Geary, Patrick J., *The Myths of Nations: The Medieval Origins of Europe*. Princeton: Princeton University Press, 2002.

Gieysztor, Alexander, "Gens Poloniae: aux origines d'une conscience nationale," in *Mélanges E. R. Labande*, Poitiers: Centre d'études supérieurs de civilisation médiévale, 1974, pp. 351–62.

Moeglin, Jean-Marie, "De la 'nation allemande' au Moyen Age," *Revue française d'histoire des idées politiques*, special issue, *Identités et spécificités allemandes*, no. 14 (2001), pp. 227–60.

Zientara, Benedykt, *Swit naradow europajskich* (The dawn of European nations). Warsaw: PIW, 1985 (translated into German).

Nature

Alexandre, Pierre, *Le Climat en Europe au Moyen Age. Contribution à l'histoire des variations climatiques de 1000 à 1425 d'après les sources narratives de l'Europe occidentale*. Paris: ÉHÉSS, 1987.

Alexandre, Pierre, *Comprendre et maîtriser la nature au Moyen Age. Mélanges d'histoire des sciences offerts à Guy Beaujouan*. Geneva: Droz, 1994.

Fumagalli, Vito, *L'uomo e l'ambiente nel Medioevo*. Bari: Laterza, 1992.

Fumagalli, Vito, *Paesaggi della paura. Vita e natura nel Medioevo*. Bologna: Il Mulino, 1994.

Gregory Tullio, *Milieux naturels, espaces sociaux. Études offertes à Robert Delort*, Paris: Publications de la Sorbonne, 1997.

Gregory, Tullio, "Nature," in Le Goff-Schmitt, pp. 806–20.

Solère, Jean-Luc, *Il teatro della Natura*, special issue of *Micrologus*, 4 (1996).

Solère, Jean-Luc, "Nature," in Gauvard-de Libera-Zink, pp. 967–76.

Nobility

Adel und Kirche, Festschrift für Gert Tallenbach. Fribourg–Basel–Vienna: Herder, 1968.

Aurell, Martin, *La Noblesse en Occident (Ve–XVe siècle)*. Paris: Armand Colin, 1996.

Contamine, Philippe (ed.), *La Noblesse au Moyen Age*. Paris: PUF, 1976.

Génicot, Léopold, *La Noblesse dans l'Occident médiéval*. London: Variorum Reprints, 1982.

Génicot, Léopold, "Noblesse," in Le Goff-Schmitt, pp. 821–33.

Werner, Ernest F., *Naissance de la noblesse. L'essor des élites politiques en Europe*, Paris: Fayard, 1998 (translated from German).

Papacy

Arnaldi, Girolamo, "Église et Papauté," in Le Goff-Schmitt, pp. 322–45.

Barraclough, Geoffrey, *The Medieval Papacy*. London: Thames & Hudson,1968.

De Rosa, Gabriele and Cracco, Giorgio, *Il Papato e l'Europa*. Suveria Mannelli, Rubbetino Editore, 2001.

Guillemain, Bernard, *Les Papes d'Avignon, 1309–1376*. Paris: Cerf, 1998.

Miccoli, Giovanni, *Chiesa gregoriana*. Rome: Herder, 1999.

Pacaut, Marcel, *Histoire de la Papauté*. Paris: Fayard, 1976.

Paravicini Bagliani, Agostino, *La Cour des papes au XIIIe siècle*. Paris: Hachette, 1995.

Paravicini Bagliani, Agostino, *Il trono di Pietro. L'universalità del papato da Alessandro III a Bonifazio VIII*. Rome: La Nuova Italia Scientifica, 1996.

Persecution, marginalization, exclusion

Albaret, Laurent, *L'Inquisition, rempart de la foi?* Paris: Gallimard, 1998.

Bennassar, Bartolomé (ed.), *L'Inquisition espagnole*. Paris: Hachette, 1979.

L'Étranger au Moyen Age (SHMES colloquium, Göttingen, 1999). Paris: Publication de la Sorbonne, 2000.

Gauvard, Claude, "Torture," in Gauvard-de Libera-Zink, p. 1397.

Geremek, Bronislaw, *Les Marginaux parisiens aux XIVe et XVe siècles*. Paris: Flammarion, 1976.

Iogna-Prat, Dominique, *Ordonner et exclure. Cluny et la société chrétienne face à la hérésie, au judaïsme et à l'Islam*. Paris: Aubier, 1998.

Mitre Fernández, Emilio, *Frontierizos de Clio (Marginados, Oisidentes y Desplazados en la Edad Media)*. Granada, Universidad de Granada, 2003.

Moore, Robert I., *Formation of a Persecuting Society: Power and Deviance in Western Europe, 950–1250*. Oxford: Blackwell, 1987.

Schmieder, Felicitas, *Europa und die Fremden. Die Mongolen im Urteil des Abendlandes vom 13. bis in das 15. Jahrhundert*. Sigmaringen, 1994.

Vincent, Bernard (ed.), "Les marginaux et les exclus dans l'histoire," *Cahiers Jussieu* (Paris), no. 5 (1979).

Vodola, Elisabeth, *Excommunication in the Middle Ages*. Berkeley: University of California Press, 1986.

Wiedenfeld, Katia, "Police," in Gauvard-de Libera-Zink, pp. 639–54.

Zaremska, Hanna, *Les Bannis du Moyen Age*. Paris: Aubier, 1996.

Zaremska, Hanna, "Marginaux," in Le Goff-Schmitt, pp. 639–54.

Pilgrimages

Barriero Rivas, José Luis, *La Función politica de los caminos de peregrinación en la Europa medieval. Estudio del camino de Santiago*. Madrid: Editorial Tecnos, 1997.

Barriero Rivas, José Luis, *The Construction of Political Space: Symbolic and Cosmological Elements (Jerusalem and Santiago in Western History)*. Jerusalem–Santiago: Al-Quds University, Araguaney Foundation, 1999.

Benassar, Bartolomé, *Saint-Jacques-de-Compostelle. Puissance du pélerinage*. Turnhout: Brepols, 1985.

Gicquel, Bernard, *La Légende de Compostelle. Le livre de saint Jacques*. Paris: Tallandier, 2003.

Oursel, Raymond, *les Pélerins du Moyen Age. Les hommes, les chemins, les sanctuaires*. Paris, 1957.

Vásquez de Parga, Luis, Lacarra, José Maria and Uría Ríu, Juan, *Las Peregrinaciones a Santiago de Compostela*. 3 vols, Madrid, 1948–50.

Vielliard, Jeanne, *Le Guide du pélerin de Saint-Jacques-de-Compostelle*. Mâcon–Paris: Protat, 1981 (5th edn).

Popular culture

Boglioni, Pierre (ed.), *La Culture populaire au Moyen Age* (Montreal colloquium). Montreal: L'Aurore, 1979.

Cardini, Franco, *Magia, stregoneria, superstizioni nell'Occidente medievale*. Florence: La Nuova Italia, 1979.

Cohn, Norman, *Europe's Inner Demons*. St Albans: Paladin, 1976.

Gurjewitsch, Aaron J., *Mittelalterliche Volkskultur. Problem der Forschung*. Dresden: UEB Verlag der Kunst, 1986.

Kaplan, Steven L. (ed.), *Understanding Popular Culture*. New York: de Gruyter Press, 1984.

Kieckhefer, Richard, *Magic in the Middle Ages*. Cambridge: Cambridge University Press, 1989.

Lecouteux, Claude, *Fées, sorciéres et loups-garous au Moyen Age. Histoire du double*. Paris: Imago, 1992.

Manselli, Raoul, *La Religion populaire au Moyen Age*. Paris–Montreal: Vrin, 1975.

Population

Bairoch, Paul, Batou, Jean and Chèvre, Pierre, *La population des villes européennes. Banque de données et analyse des résultats, 800–1850*. Geneva: Droz, 1988.

Bardet, Jean-Pierre and Dupâquier, Jacques (eds), *Histoire des populations de l'Europe. I: Des origines aux prémices de la révolution démographique*. Paris: Fayard, 1997.

Biller, Peter, *The Measure of Multitude: Population in Medieval Thought*. Oxford: Oxford University Press, 2000.

Poverty

Brown, Peter, Capitani, Ovidio, Cardini, Franco and Rosa, Mario, *Povertà e carità della Roma tardo-antica al'700 italiano*. Abano Terme: Francisci Ed., 1983.

Capitani, Ovidio (ed.), *La Concezione della povertà nel medioevo*. Bologna: Padron, 1983.

Geremek, Bronislaw, *La Potence ou la pitié. L'Europe et les pauvres du Moyen Age à nos jours*. Paris: Gallimard, 1987.

Little, Lester K., *Religious Poverty and the Profit Economy in Medieval Europe*. London: Paul Elek, 1975.

Mollat, Michel (ed.), *Études sur l'histoire de la pauvreté (Moyen Age XIIe siècle)*. 2 vols, Paris: Publications de la Sorbonne, 1974.

Mollat, Michel, *Les Pauvres au Moyen Age, étude sociale*. Paris: Hachette, 1978.

La povertà del secolo XIIe, Francesco d'Assisi (collective papers). Assisi: Società internazionale di studi francescani, 1975.

Royalty, kings

Bak, János (ed.), *Coronations: Medieval and Early Modern Monarchic Rituals*. Berkeley: University of California Press, 1990.

Bloch, Marc, *Les Rois thaumaturges. Étude sur le caractère surnaturel attribué à la puissance royale, particulièrement en France et en Angleterre* (1924), new edn. Paris: Gallimard, 1983.

Bourreau, Alain, *Le Simple Corps du roi. L'impossible sacralité des souverains français, XVe–XVIIIe siècles*. Paris: Éd. de Paris, 1998.

Boureau, Alain and Ingerflom, Claudio-Sergio (eds), *La Royauté sacrée dans le monde chrétien*. Paris: ÉHÉSS, 1992.

Folz, Robert, *Les Saints rois du Moyen Age en Occident (VIe–XIIIe)*. Brussels: Société des Bollandistes, 1989.

Kantorowicz, Ernest, *The King's Two Bodies: A Study in Medieval Political Theory*. Princeton: Princeton University Press, 1957.

Klaniczay, Gabor, *The Uses of Supernatural Power*. Cambridge: Polity, 1990.

Le Goff, Jacques, "Le roi dans l'Occident médiéval; caracteres originaux," in Anne J. Duggan, *King and Kingship in Medieval Europe* (colloquium 1992), London: King's College, 1993.

Le Goff, Jacques, "Roi," in Le Goff-Schmitt, pp. 985–1004.

Saints

Boesch-Gajano, Sofia, *La santità*. Rome–Bari: Laterza, 1999.

Brown, Peter, *The Cult of Saints: Its Rise and Function in Latin Christianity.* London: SCM Press, 1981.

Brown, Peter, *Les Fonctions des saints dans le monde occidental (IIIe–XIIIe siècle).* Rome: École française de Rome, 1991.

Geary, Patrick J., *Living with the Dead in the Middle Ages.* Ithaca–New York: Cornell University Press, 1994.

Kleinberg, A. M., *Prophets in their Own Country: Living Saints and the Making of Sainthood in the Later Middle Ages.* Chicago–London: University of Chicago Press, 1992.

Mitterauer, Michael, *Ahnen und Heilige. Namengebung in der europäischen Geschichte.* Munich: Beck, 1993.

Schmitt, Jean-Claude, *Le Saint Lévrier. Guinefort guérisseur d'enfants depuis le XIIIe siècle.* Paris: Flammarion, 1979.

Vauchez, André (ed.), *Histoire des saints et de la sainteté chrétienne,* vols 1–11. Paris: Hachette, 1986–8.

Vauchez, André, "Le Saint," in Jacques Le Goff (ed.), *L'Homme médiéval,* Paris: Seuil, 1989 (Italian edn Bari: Laterza, 1987).

Vauchez, André, *Saints, prophètes et visionnaires. Le pouvoir surnaturel au Moyen Age.* Paris: Albin Michel, 1999.

Scholasticism

Alessio, Franco, "Scolastique," in Le Goff-Schmitt, pp.1039–55.

Baldwin, John W., *The Scholastic Culture of the Middle Ages, 1000–1300.* Lexington: D. C. Heath, 1971.

Le Goff, Jacques, *Les Intellectuels au Moyen Age.* Paris: Seuil, 1957, new edn 1985.

Libera, Alain de, *Penser au Moyen Age.* Paris: Seuil, 1991.

Solère, Jean-Luc, "Scolastique," in Gauvard-de Libera-Zink, pp. 1299–310.

Southern, R. W., *Scholastic Humanism and the Unification of Europe. I. Foundations.* Oxford: Blackwell, 1995.

Vignaux, Paul, *Philosophie au Moyen Age.* Paris: Vrin, 2002.

Science, the scientific spirit

Beaujouan, Guy, "La science dans l'Occident médiéval chrétien," in René Taton, (ed.), *La Science antique et médiévale des origines à 1450,* Paris: PUF, 1966 (1st edn); 1994 (2nd edn).

Beaujouan, Guy, *Par raison de nombres. L'art du calcul et les savoirs scientifiques médiévaux.* Aldershot–Brookfield: Variorum Reprints, 1991.

Crombie, Alistair C., *Augustine to Galileo: Medieval and Early Modern Science*. London: Heinemann, 1952 (1st edn), 1959 (2 vols, revised and expanded), 1979 (repr.).

Crombie, Alistair C., *Robert Grosseteste and the Origins of Experimental Science, 1100–1700*. Oxford: Clarendon Press, 1953 (1st edn), 1971 (3rd edn).

Crombie, Alistair C., *Scientific Change: Historical Studies in the Intellectual, Social and Technical Conditions for Scientific Discovery and Technical Invention from Antiquity to the Present* (symposium on the history of science, Oxford, 1961). London: Heinemann Educational Books; New York: Basic Books, 1963.

Crombie, Alistair C., "The Relevance of the Middle Ages to the Scientific Movement," in *Science, Optics, and Music in Medieval and Early Modern Thought*, London: Hambledon Press, 1990, pp. 41–71.

Grant, Edward, *Physical Science in the Middle Ages*. New York–London: Wiley, 1971.

Lindberg D. C. (ed.), *Science in the Middle Ages*. Chicago–London: University of Chicago Press, 1978.

Minois, Georges, *L'Église et la science. De saint Augustin à Galilée*. Paris: Fayard, 1990.

Murray, Alexander, *Reason and Society in the Middle Ages*. Oxford: Clarendon Press, 1978.

Murray, Alexander, "Raison," in Le Goff-Schmitt, pp.934–49.

Stock, Brian, *Myth and Science in the Twelfth Century: A Study of Bernard Silvester*. Princeton: Princeton University Press, 1972.

Sin(s)

Bloomfield, M. W., *The Seven Deadly Sins: An Introduction to the History of a Religious Concept, with Special References to Medieval English Literature*. East Lansing: Michigan State College Press, 1952.

Casagrande, Carla and Vecchio Silvana, *Les Péchés de la langue* (1987). Paris: Cerf, 1991 (translated from Italian).

Casagrande, Carla and Vecchio, Silvana, *Histoire des péchés capitaux au Moyen Age* (2000). Paris: Aubier, 2003 (translated from Italian).

Delumeau, Jean, *Le Péché et la peur. La culpabilisation en Occident (XIIIe–XVIIe s.)*. Paris: Fayard, 1983.

Levelleux, Corinne, *La Parole interdite. Le blasphème dans la France médiévale (XIIe–XVII s.), du péché au crime*. Paris: De Boccard, 2001.

Schimmel, Solomon, *The Seven Deadly Sins: Jewish, Christian and Classical Reflections on Human Nature*. New York: Maxwell Macmillan International, 1992.

Tentler, T. N., *Sin and Confession on the Eve of the Reformation*. Princeton: Princeton University Press, 1977.

Vogel, Cyrille, *Le Pécheur et la pénitence au Moyen Age*. Paris: Cerf, 1969.

Techniques and innovation

Amouretti, Marie-Claire and Comet, Georges, *Hommes et techniques de l'Antiquité à la Renaissance*. Paris: Armand Colin, 1993.

Antiqui und Moderni. Traditionsbewusstsein und Fortschrittsbewusststein im späten Mittelalter. Miscellanea Medievalia, 9. Berlin, 1974.

Beck, Patrice (ed.), *L'Innovation technique au Moyen Age*. Paris: Errance, 1998.

Bloch, Marc, "Avènement et conquêtes du moulin à eau," *Annales HES* (1935), pp. 538–63.

Bloch, Marc, "Les 'inventions' médiévales," *Annales HES* (1935), pp. 634–43.

Europäische Technik im Mittelalter, 800 bis 1400. Tradition und Innovation. Ein Handbuch, ed. U. Lindgren. Berlin: Gebr. Mann Verlag, 1997.

Gille, Bertrand, *Histoire des techniques*. Paris: Gallimard, Encyclopédie de la Pléiade, 1978.

Lardin, Philippe and Bührer-Thierry, Geneviève (eds), *Techniques. Les paris de l'innovation. Médiévale*s, 39 (autumn 2000).

Long, Pamela D. (ed.), *Science and Technology in Medieval Society. Annals of the New York Academy of Sciences*, 441 (1985).

White, Lynn Jr, *Medieval Technology and Social Change*. Oxford: Clarendon Press, 1962.

Theology and philosophy

Aertsen, J. A. and Speer, Andreas (eds), *Was ist Philosophie im Mittelalter?* Berlin–New York: de Gruyter, 1998.

Boulbach, Libère, "Philosophie," in Gauvard-de Libera-Zink, pp. 1081–94.

Chenu, Marie-Dominique, *La Théologie au XIIe siècle*. Paris, 1957.

Chenu, Marie-Dominique, *La Théologie comme science au XIIIe siècle*, 3rd edn. Paris, 1957.

De Rijk, L. M., *La Philosophie au Moyen Age*. Leiden: Brill, 1985.

Ghisalberti, Alessandro, *Medioevo teologico*. Rome–Bari: Laterza, 1990.

Gilson, Étienne, *L'Esprit de la philosophie médiévale*, 2nd edn. Paris: Vrin, 1978.

Jeauneau, Edouard, *La Philosophie au Moyen Age*, 3rd edn. Paris: PUF, 1976.

Libera, Alain de, *La Philosophie médiévale*, Paris: PUF, 1993.

Solère, Jean-Luc and Kaluza, Zénon (eds), *La Servante et la Consolatrice. La philosophie au Moyen Age et ses rapports avec la théologie*. Paris: Vrin, 2002.

Vignaux, Paul, *Philosophie au Moyen Age*. Paris: Vrin, 2002.

Time

Cipolla, Carlo M., *Clock and Culture, 1300–1700*. London: Collins, 1967.

Landes, David, *Revolution in Time: Clocks and the Making of the Modern World*. Cambridge: Harvard University Press, 1983.

Le Goff, Jacques, "Au Moyen Age: temps de l'Église et temps du marchand," *Annales ESC* (1960), repr. in *Pour un autre Moyen Age. Temps, travail et culture en Occident*, Paris: Gallimard, 1977, pp. 46–65.

Le Goff, Jacques, "Temps," in Le Goff-Schmitt, pp. 1113–22.

Mane, Perrine, *Calendriers et techniques agricoles. France–Italie, XIIe-XIIIe s.* Paris: Le Sycomore, 1983.

Pietri, Charles, Dagron, Gilbert and Le Goff, Jacques (eds), *Le Temps chrétien de la fin de l'Antiquité au Moyen Age, IIIe–XIIIe s.* Paris: CNRS, 1984.

Pomian, Krzysztof, *L'Ordre du temps*. Paris: Gallimard, 1984.

Ribemont, Bernard (ed.), *Le Temps. Sa mesure et sa perception au Moyen Age* (Orléans colloquium, 1991). Caen: Paradigme, 1992.

Tiempo y memoria en la edad media, special issue of *Temas medievales* (Buenos Aires), 2 (1992).

Towns

Barel, Yves, *La Ville médiévale, système social, système urbain*. Grenoble: Presses universitaires de Grenoble, 1975.

Benevolo, Leonardo, *La Ville dans l'histoire européenne*. Paris: Seuil, 1993.

Bulst, Neithard and Genet, Jean-Philippe (eds), *Ville, État, bourgeoisie dans la genèse de l'État moderne*. Paris: CNRS, 1988.

Chevalier, Bernard, *Les Bonnes Villes de France du XIVe au XVIe siècle*. Paris: Aubier, 1982.

Dutour, Thierry, *La Ville médiévale*. Paris: Odile Jacob, 2003.

Les Elites urbaines au Moyen Age (27th SHMES congress, Rome, May 1996). Paris–Rome: Publications de la Sorbonne, École française de Rome, 1997.

Ennen, Edith, *Die europäische Stadt des Mittelalters*. Göttingen, Vandenhoeck & Ruprecht, 1972.

Francastel, Pierre (ed.), *Les Origines des villes polonaises*. Paris–The Hague: Mouton, 1960.

Gonthier, Nicole, *Cris de haine et rites d'unité. La violence dans les villes, XIIe–XIVe siècles*. Turnhout: Brepols, 1992.

Guidoni, Enrico, *La Ville européenne. Formation et signification du IVe au XIe siècle*. Brussels: Mardaga, 1981.

Heers, Jacques, *La Ville au Moyen Age en Occident. Paysages, pouvoirs et conflits*. Paris: Fayard, 1990.

Hilton, Rodney H., *English and French Towns in Feudal Society: A Comparative Study*. Cambridge: Cambridge University Press, 1992.

Lavedan, Pierre and Hugueney, Jeanne, *L'Urbanisme au Moyen Age*. Paris: Arts et Métiers graphiques, 1974.

Le Goff, Jacques, "Ville," in Le Goff-Schmitt, pp. 1183–200.

Le Goff, Jacques and De Seta, Cesare (eds), *La Città e le mure*. Rome–Bari: Laterza, 1959.

Le Goff, Jacques, Chédeville, André and Rossiaud, Jacques, in Duby, Georges (ed.), *Histoire de la France urbaine*. II: *La ville médiévale*, Paris: Seuil, 1980 (1st edn), 2000 (2nd edn).

Lopez, Roberto S., *Intervista sulla città medievale (a cura di Mario Berengo)*. Bari: Laterza, 1984.

Maire-Vigueur, Jean-Claude (ed.), *D'une ville à l'autre. Structures matérielles et organisation de l'espace dans les villes européennes, XIIIe–XVI siècle*. Rome: École française de Rome, 1989.

Monnet, Pierre and Oexle, Otto Gerhard (eds), *Stadt und Recht im Mittelalter*, Veröffentlichungen des Max-Plank-Instituts für Geschichte, 174. Göttingen: Vandenhoeck & Ruprecht, 2003.

Pirenne, Henri, *Les Villes et les institutions urbaines*. 2 vols, Paris, 1969.

Poirion, Daniel (ed.), *Milieux universitaires et mentalité urbaine au Moyen Age*. Paris: Presses de l'université Paris-Sorbonne, 1987.

Romagnoli, Daniela (ed.), *La Ville et la cour. Des bonnes et des mauvaises manières* (1991). Paris: Fayard, 1995 (translated from Italian).

Romero, José Luis, *La revolició burguesa en el mundo feudal*. Buenos Aires, 1969.

Rörig, Fritz, *Die europäische Stadt und die Kultur des Burgertums im Mittelalter*. Göttingen, 1955.

Rossi, Pietro, *Modelli di città. Strutture e funzioni politiche*. Turin: Einaudi, 1987.

Roux, Simone, *Le Monde des villes au Moyen Age, XIe–XVe siècle*. Paris: Hachette, 1994.

Towns–countryside

Dutour, Thierry, *La Ville médiévale*. Paris: Odile Jacob, 2003.

Duvosquel, Jean-Marie and Thoen, Erik (eds), *Peasants and Townsmen in Medieval Europe. Studia in honorem Adrian Verhulst*. Ghent: Snoeck-Ducaju, 1995.

Villes et campagnes au Moyen Age. Mélanges Georges Despy. Liège: Perron, 1991.

Troubadours

Bec, Philippe, *Anthologie des troubadours*. Paris: Hachette, 1979.

Bec, Pierre, *Burlesque et obscénité chez les troubadours. Le contre-texte au Moyen Age*. Paris: Stock, 1984.

Brunel-Lobrichon, Geneviève and Duhamel-Amado, Claudie, *Au temps des troubadours, XIIe–XIIIe siècle*. Paris: Hachette, 1947.

Gouiran, Gérard, *L'Amour et la guerre. L'oeuvre de Bertran de Born*. Aix-en-Provence: Publications de l'université de Provence, 1985.

Huchet, Jean-Charles, *L'Amour discourtois. La "fin'amor" chez les premiers troubadours*. Toulouse: Privat, 1987.
Nelli, René, *L'Erotique des troubadours*. Toulouse: Privat, 1963 (1st edn), 1984 (2nd edn).
Payen, Jean-Charles, *Le Prince d'Aquitaine. Essai sur Guillaume IX, son oeuvre et son érotique*. Paris: Honoré Champion, 1980.
Roubaud, Jacques, *La Fleur inverse. L'art des troubadours*. Paris: Les Belles Lettres, 1994.
Zuchetto, Gérard, *Terre des troubadours, XIIe–XIIIe siècles*. Paris: Éditions de Paris, 1996.

Universities, schools

Arnaldi, Girolamo (ed.), *Le origine dell'Università*. Bologna: Il Mulino, 1974.
Brizzi, Gian Paolo and Verger, Jacques (eds), *Le Università d'Europa*. 5 vols, Milan: Amilcare Pizzi, 1990–4.
Classen, Peter, *Studium und Gesellschaft im Mittelalter*. Stuttgart: A. Hiersemann, 1983.

Villages

Archéologie du village déserté. 2 vols, Paris: EHESS, 1970.
Bourin, Monique and Durand, Robert, *Vivre au village au Moyen Age. Les solidarités paysannes du XIe au XIIIe siècle*. Rennes: Presses universitaires de Rennes, 2000.
Chapelot, Jean and Fossier, Robert, *Le Village et la maison au Moyen Age*. Paris: Hachette, 1980.
Homans, G. C., *English Villages of the Thirteenth Century*. Cambridge: Harvard University Press, 1941.
Le Village au temps de Charlemagne, catalogue of the exhibition in the Musée des Arts et Traditions populaires. Paris: Réunion des Musées nationaux, 1988.

Violence

Contamine, Philippe and Guyotjeannin, Olivier (eds), *La Guerre et les gens au Moyen Age*. 2 vols,\Paris: Comité des Travaux historiques et scientifiques, 1996.
Gauvard, Claude, *"De grace especial." Crime, État et société en France à la fin du Moyen Age*. 2 vols, Paris: Publications de la Sorbonne, 1991.
Gonthier, Nicole, *Cris de haine et Rites d'unité. La violence dans les villes, XIIe–XIVe siècle*. Turnhout: Brepols, 1992.

Nirenberg, David, *Communities of Violence: Persecution of Minorities in the Middle Ages*. Princeton: Princeton University Press, 1996.

Raynaud, Christiane, *La Violence au Moyen Age, XIIIe–XVe siècle*. Paris: Le Léopard d'Or, 1990.

War

Cardini, Franco, *La Culture de la guerre, Xe–XVIIIe siècle*. Paris: Gallimard, 1982 (translated from Italian).

Contamine, Philippe, *La Guerre au Moyen Age*. Paris: PUF, 1980 (1st edn), 1992 (3rd edn).

Duby, Georges, *Le Dimanche de Bouvines*. Paris: Gallimard, 1973.

Flori, Jean, *La Guerre sainte. La formation de l'idée de croisade dans l'Occident chrétien*. Paris: Aubier, 2001.

Russell, F. H., *The Just War in the Middle Ages*. Cambridge: Cambridge University Press, 1975.

Witchcraft

Bechtel, Guy, *La Sorcière et l'Occident*. Paris: Plon, 1997.

Cardini, Franco, *Magia, stregoneria, superstizioni nell'Occidente medievale*. Florence: La Nuova Italia Editrice, 1979.

Caro Baroja, Julio, *Les Sorcières et leur monde*. Paris: Gallimard, 1992 (translated from Spanish).

Cohn, Norman, *Europe's Inner Demons*. St Albans: Paladin, 1976.

Ginsberg, Carlo, *Le Sabbat des sorcières*. Paris: Gallimard, 1992 (translated from Italian).

Ginsberg, Carlo, *Le Marteau des sorcières* (trans. and introd. Arnaud Danet, 1973), new edn. Grenoble: Jérôme Million, 1990.

Michelet, Jules, *La Sorcière* (introd. Robert Mandrou). Paris: Julliard, 1964.

Muchembled, Robert (ed.), *Magie et sorcellerie en Europe. Du Moyen Age à nos jours*. Paris: Armand Colin, 1994.

Nabert, Nathalie (ed.), *Le Mal et le diable. Leurs figures à la fin du Moyen Age*. Paris: Beauchesne, 1996.

Schmitt, Jean-Claude, "Sorcellerie," in Le Goff-Schmitt, pp. 1084–96.

Women

Borresen, K. E., *Subordination et équivalence. Nature et rôle de la femme d'après Augustin et Thomas d'Aquin*. Oslo–Paris, 1968.

Dinzelbacher, Peter and Bauer, Dieter, *Frauenmystik im Mittelalter*. Ostfildern: Schwabenverlag, 1985.

Dinzelbacher, Peter and Bauer, Dieter (eds), *Religiöse Frauenbewegung und mystische Frömmigkeit*. Cologne: Böhlau Verlag, 1988.

Dronke, Peter, *Women Writers of the Middle Ages*. Cambridge: Cambridge University Press, 1984.

Duby, Georges, *Dames du XIIe siècle*. 3 vols, Paris: Gallimard, 1995–6.

Duby, Georges and Perrot, Michelle, *Histoire des femmes. 2: Le Moyen Age*, ed. Christiane Klapisch-Zuber. Paris: Plon, 1991.

Duggan, Anne (ed.), *Queens and Queenship in Medieval Europe*. Woodbridge: Boydell Press, 1997.

La Femme dans la civilisation des Xe–XIIIe siècles (Poitiers colloquium, Sept. 1976). *Cahiers de civilisation médiévale*, 20 (1977).

Iogna-Prat, Dominique, Palazzo, Eric and Russo, Daniel, *Marie. Le culte de la Vierge dans la société occidentale*. Paris: Beauchesne, 1996.

Klapisch-Zuber, Christiane, "Masculin, féminin," in Le Goff-Schmitt, pp. 655–68.

Le Jan, Régine, *Femmes, pouvoir et société dans le haut Moyen Age*. Paris: Picard, 2001.

Linehan, Peter, *The Ladies of Zamora*. Manchester: Manchester University Press, 1997.

Pancer, Nina, *Sans peur et sans vergogne. De l'honneur et des femmes aux premiers temps mérovingiens*. Paris: Albin Michel, 2001.

Parisse, Michel, *Les Nonnes au Moyen Age*. Le Puy: C. Bonneton, 1983.

Parisse Michel (ed.), *Veuves et veuvages dans le haut Moyen Age*. Paris: Picard, 1993.

Power, Eileen, *Medieval Women*. Cambridge: Cambridge University Press, 1975.

Rouche, Michel and Heuclin, Jean (eds), *La Femme au Moyen Age*. Maubeuge: Publications de la ville de Mauberge, 1990.

Schmitt, Jean-Claude (ed.), *Eve et Pandora. La création de la première femme*. Paris: Gallimard, 2002.

Zapperi, Roberto, *L'Homme enceint. L'homme, la femme et le pouvoir*. Paris: PUF, 1983 (translated from Italian).

Work

Allard, Guy H and Lusingnan, Serge (eds), *Les Arts mécaniques au Moyen Age*. Paris–Montreal: Vrin–Bellarmin, 1982.

Fossier, Robert, *Le Travail au Moyen Age, une approche interdisciplinaire*. Louvain-la-Neuve: Publications de l'Institut d'études médiévales, 1990.

Hamesse, Jacqueline and Muraille, Colette (eds), *Le Travail au Moyen Age*. Paris: PUF, 1965.

Heers, Jacques, *Le Travail au Moyen Age*. Paris: Hachette, 2000.

Lavorare nel medioevo (Todi colloquium, 1980). Perugia, 1983.

Le Goff, Jacques, "Travail," in Le Goff-Schmitt, pp. 1137–49.

Wolff, Philippe and Mauro, Federico (eds), *Histoire du Travail*. II: *L'Age de l'artisanat (Ve–XVIIIe siècle)*. Paris, 1960.

Writing, books

Alexandre-Bidon, Danièle, "La lettre volée: apprendre à lire à l'enfant au Moyen Age," *Annales ESC*, 44, 1989, pp. 953–992.

Avrin, Leila, *Scribes, Script and Books. The Book Arts from Antiquity to the Renaissance*, Chicago-London: American Library Association and the British Library, 1991.

Bataillon, Louis J., *La Production du livre universitaire au Moyen Age. Exemplar et pecia*. Paris: Ed. du CNRS, 1988.

Batany, Jean, "Ecrit/oral," in Le Goff-Schmitt, pp. 309–321.

Baumgartner, Emmanuelle and Marcello-Nizia, Christiane, *Théories et pratiques de l'écriture au Moyen Age*, Paris-X, Nanterre, Centre de recherches du département de français, "Littérales" collection, 1988.

Bourlet, Caroline and Dufour, Annie (eds.), *L'Écrit dans la société médiévale. Divers aspects de sa pratique du XIe au XVe siècle. Textes en hommage à Lucie Fossier.* Paris: Ed. du CNRS, 1991.

Cavallo, Guglielmo, *Libri e lettori nel Medioevo. Guida storica e critica*. Rome-Bari: Laterza, 1989.

Cavallo, Guglielmo and Chartier, Roger (eds), *Histoire de l'édition française. I. Le livre conquérant. Du Moyen Age au milieu du XVIIe siècle.* Paris: Fayard/ Le Cercle de la librairie, 1989.

Cavallo, Guglielmo and Chartier, Roger (eds), *Histoire de la lecture dans le monde occidental* (1995). Paris: Seuil, 1997 (translated from Italian).

Civiltà comunale. Libro, scrittura, documento (proceedings of the Genoa congress, 1988). *Atti della Società ligure di Storia Patria* (Genoa), n.s., XXIX (CIII), fasc. II (1989).

Clanchy, Michael T., *From Memory to Written Record: England, 1066–1307.* Cambridge: Harvard University Press, 1979 (1st edn); Oxford: Blackwell, 1993 (2nd edn).

Ganz, P. F., *The Role of the Book in Medieval Culture*. 2 vols, Turnhout: Brepols, 1986.

Glénisson, Jean (ed.), *Le Livre au Moyen Age*. Paris: CNRS, 1988.

Hamman, Adalbert-Gauthier, *L'Épopée du livre. Du scribe à l'imprimerie*. Paris: Perrin, 1985.

Martin, Henri-Jean and Vezin, Jean (eds), *Mise en page et mise en texte du livre manuscrit*. Paris: Éd. du Cercle de la librairie, Promodis, 1990.

Ornato, Ezio, *La Face cachée du livre médiéval*. Rome: Viella, 1993.

Parkes, M. B., *Pause and Effect: An Introduction to the History of Punctuation in the West*. Aldershot: Scholar Press, 1992.

Parkes, M. B., *Scribes, Scripts and Readers: Studies in the Communication, Presentation and Discrimination of Medieval Texts*. London: Hambledon Press, 1991.

Petrucci, Armando, "Lire au Moyen Age," *Mélanges de l'École française de Rome*, 96 (1984), pp. 604–16.

Petrucci, Armando, *La scrittura, ideologia e rappresentatzione*. Turin: Einaudi, 1986.

Recht und Schrift im Mittelalter (Vorträge und Forschungen 23). Sigmaringen, 1977.

Roberts, C. H. and Skeat, T. C., *The Birth of the Codex*. London: Oxford University Press, 1983.

Saenger, Paul, "The Separation of Words and the Order of Words: The Genesis of Medieval Reading," *Scrittura e civiltà*, 144 (1940), pp. 49–74.

Saenger, Paul, "Silent Reading: Its Impact on Late Medieval Script and Society," *Viator*, 13 (1982), pp. 367–414.

Sirat, Colette, *Du scribe au livre. Les manuscrits hébreux au Moyen Age*. Paris: CNRS, 1994.

Stock, Brian, *The Implications of Literacy: Written Language and Models of Interpretation in the Eleventh and Twelfth Centuries*. Princeton: Princeton University Press, 1983.

Vocabulaire du livre et de l'écriture au Moyen Age, CIVICIMA, Études sur le vocabulaire intellectuel du Moyen Age, II. Turnhout: Brepols, 1989.

Zerdoun Bat-Yehouda, Monique (ed.), *Le Papier au Moyen Age. Histoire et techniques*. Turnhout: Brepols, 1986.

The young

Duby, Georges, "Les 'jeunes' dans la société aristocratique dans la France du Nord-Ouest au XIIe siècle," *Annales ESC*, 19 (1964), pp. 835–46; repr. in *Hommes et structures du Moyen Age*, Paris–The Hague: Mouton, pp. 213–25.

Gauvard, Claude, "Les jeunes à la fin du Moyen Age. Une classe d'âge," *Annales de l'Est*, 1-2 (1982), pp. 2224–44.

Levu, Giovanni and Schmitt, Jean-Claude (eds), *Histoire des jeunes en Occident*. I: *De l'Antiquité à l'époque moderne* (1994). Paris: Seuil, 1996 (translated from Italian).

Index

Persons with the same name have been arranged hierarchically with saints coming before popes, then emperors, royalty, and commoners.